INVASION OF PRIVACY

A Reference Handbook

Other Titles in ABC-CLIO's
**CONTEMPORARY
WORLD ISSUES**
Series

Books in the Contemporary World Issues series address vital issues in today's society such as genetic engineering, pollution, and biodiversity. Written by professional writers, scholars, and nonacademic experts, these books are authoritative, clearly written, up-to-date, and objective. They provide a good starting point for research by high school and college students, scholars, and general readers as well as by legislators, business people, activists, and others.

Each book, carefully organized and easy to use, contains an overview of the subject, a detailed chronology, biographical sketches, facts and data and/or documents and other primary-source material, a directory of organizations and agencies, annotated lists of print and nonprint resources, and an index.

Readers of books in the Contemporary World Issues series will find the information they need in order to have a better understanding of the social, political, environmental, and economic issues facing the world today.

INVASION OF PRIVACY

A Reference Handbook

Kevin M. Keenan

CONTEMPORARY WORLD ISSUES

A B C ☰ C L I O

Santa Barbara, California
Denver, Colorado
Oxford, England

Library of Congress Cataloging-in-Publication Data
Keenan, Kevin M.
    Invasion of privacy : a reference handbook / Kevin M. Keenan.
        p.   cm. — (Contemporary world issues)
    Includes bibliographical references and index.
    ISBN 1-85109-630-2 (hardback : alk. paper) — ISBN 1-85109-635-3
(ebook)   1. Privacy, Right of—United States—Handbooks, manuals,
etc.   I. Title.   II. Series.
JC596.2.U5K44 2005
323.44'8'0973—dc22

                                                                    2005018577

07   06   10 9 8 7 6 5 4 3 2

This book is also available on the World Wide Web as an eBook.
Visit abc-clio.com for details.

Production Team
    Acquisitions Editor: Mim Vasan
    Production Editor: Laura Esterman
    Editorial Assistant: Alisha Martinez
    Editorial Interns: Renee Caputo and Gayle Woidneck
    Production Manager: Don Schmidt
    Manufacturing Coordinator: George Smyser

ABC-CLIO, Inc.
130 Cremona Drive, P.O. Box 1911
Santa Barbara, California 93116-1911

This book is printed on acid-free paper ∞.
Manufactured in the United States of America.

Contents

Preface

At the 2004 Summer Olympics in Athens, Greece—the cradle of democracy—and four other Olympic cities, a surveillance system costing $325 million kept watch. The "C41" system included more than 1,000 cameras, computerized chemical "sniffers," and other surveillance and sensor devices—as well as nine police helicopters, dozens of high-tech vans, and a cutting-edge surveillance blimp that floated above the crowds fifteen hours a day—all of which were networked to command posts for real-time viewing and detection of any problems. In all, 70,000 security personnel protected the Olympics. NATO provided three AWACS surveillance planes, naval ships to conduct maritime surveillance, enhanced intelligence sharing, and specially trained troops. Costing a total of $1.2 billion, the 2004 Summer Olympic games were Europe's longest and largest peacetime security operation (Cambanis 2004).

There were no terrorist attacks during the Olympics, and so, it could be argued, the system proved effective. A post-Olympics poll found that 70 percent of Athenians were pleased with the security measures, and only 21 percent found them excessive (Associated Press 2004). In a world that has suffered catastrophic losses from terrorist attacks—among the worst, approximately 3,000 dead in the United States on September 11, 2001; 191 dead and more than 1,400 wounded in Madrid, Spain, on March 11, 2004; approximately 350 dead, mostly young children, in Beslan, Russia, on September 3, 2004; and approximately 52 dead and 700 injured in bomb explosions during the London rush hour on the morning of July 7, 2005—the Athens surveillance system may be the model for a new reality. This new reality monitors more behavior in more places than ever before; it uses high-tech surveillance devices integrated over electronic networks and connected to private and public security agents in headquarters and on patrol. For privacy—both the relatively young legal right to privacy and the much more deeply rooted social value of privacy—this model raises some of the hardest questions ever posed.

Does greater security requires less privacy? Which do we value more—the feeling of safety from being watched or the feeling of being free from being watched? On one hand, surveillance proponents argue, "If you're not doing anything wrong, you have nothing to fear." On the other hand, civil libertarians and privacy advocates cite Benjamin Franklin's admonition, "Those who would give up essential Liberty, to purchase a little temporary Safety, deserve neither liberty nor safety." The more practical middle ground—which the legal right to privacy by virtue of being defined as qualified and balanced against other interests almost always occupies—asks whether an invasion of privacy is truly necessary to solve the problem; whether all other approaches have been tried first; whether there are checks on the decision makers; and whether the private information collected is returned, destroyed, or protected, as appropriate. As elaborated in the first three chapters, often—and especially after a crisis—governments invade privacy unnecessarily and without satisfying these precautions.

Another question of unprecedented difficulty for privacy posed by the Athens model: When surveillance draws ever closer to being total and complete, does the old notion that one has almost no right to privacy in public spaces require updating? It is presumed that, once we leave the house, we have voluntarily waived the right to be free from surveillance, tracking, and monitoring—at least of the low-tech kind. After all, we are "in public." In a high-tech world, where constant, ubiquitous monitoring is becoming a reality in some places and a feasible possibility everywhere, perhaps this presumption should be shifted. In the same way that expression is broadly and strongly protected in the United States in part out of fear of chilling dialogue, debate, artistic expression, and minority views, it may be time for the right to privacy to protect against constant, total surveillance (even in public) out of fear of chilling freedom of movement, association, and expression essential to democracy.

The Athens model also raises the question of what happens to a surveillance infrastructure once it is constructed. Is it dismantled when the reason for its construction no longer exists? Do the Olympic cameras come down? Will the Greek police return to using less advanced technology? Will the blimp be warehoused?

On one hand, the high cost of maintaining a total surveillance model may lead to its dismantling. In the United States, a study found that security vigilance on the part of corporations seemed to be waning, and approximately half of corporations interviewed did not increase their spending on surveillance after September 11, 2001 (Weiser and Deutsch 2004). On the other hand, surveillance infrastructures are often built up rather than dismantled. Camera surveillance systems, electronic door locks, passports and identification cards with bar codes or computer chips, and the tracking of purchases on the Internet or at the supermarket have all become part of the baseline infrastructure that will be built up and made more powerful as technology improves. Like electrical wires, phone lines, or plumbing, it seems likely that—should the Athens model take hold—the surveillance infrastructure will become part of our permanent, unnoticed, everyday world. If so, we are perhaps in the midst of choosing between a future reality of near constant, total surveillance or a reaffirmation of the value of privacy in our individual and community lives, protected by restraints on surveillance and oversight by independent watchdogs.

Chapter 1 provides a historical overview of the development of privacy rights and the abuses that spurred their growth, as well as some of the arguments for and against the social and psychological worth of privacy. It explains what the legal right to privacy is, laying out five categories of privacy: associational, bodily, communication, data, and spatial. It recounts the history of the right to privacy, starting with some of its ancient roots, such as Hippocrates' ethical oath for practitioners of medicine, which protected confidentiality as early as 400 BCE. It details profound abuses of privacy, such as those by the Nazis in the 1930s and 1940s and by the Soviet Union and the United States during the cold war, that led people and governments to understand better the need for legal protection of privacy. Finally, it lays out support and criticisms of privacy from mostly nonlegal perspectives, such as the view that privacy is essential to creativity and the view that privacy costs more than it is worth.

Chapter 2 examines an array of privacy issues affecting many parts of the world, especially the implications of high-tech surveillance and databasing. From centuries-old national ID card systems to the decades-old international communication-tapping system Echelon, there is nothing new about governments' efforts to track and monitor people and their communications. However, GPS satellites, radio-frequency identity (RFID) communication microchips, powerful and microscopic cameras, high-speed Internet, enormous databasing capacity, and other technological developments have greatly empowered and emboldened governments to move in the direction of near total surveillance, or "total information awareness," as President George W. Bush's administration called one such program.

Chapter 3 focuses on issues of particular concern in the United States, especially those driven by politics and fear in the aftermaths of the September 11 attacks and the Columbine High School shootings. It also examines the state of bodily privacy in light of developments in genetics, such as the historic mapping of the human genome. Finally, it lays out ideas that have been proposed to bolster the protection of privacy for a high-tech age anxious with security concerns.

Chapter 4 summarizes the history of privacy in a chronology that emphasizes both important developments in the right to privacy and significant invasions of privacy. The chronology also details significant historical events that have indirectly impacted privacy, such as terrorist attacks that have made people feel less secure and inspired governments to increase surveillance, stops, searches, or other police measures.

Chapter 5 relates some details of the lives of people who have been important to privacy, including such newsmakers and history makers as former U.S. attorney general John Ashcroft, whose perspective on privacy changed dramatically after September 11, 2001; author George Orwell, who largely created the language and ideas that are most commonly used to discuss privacy and its invasion; and former Federal Bureau of Investigation (FBI) director J. Edgar Hoover, who practiced total information awareness to the degree his power and the technology of the day would permit. But the biographical sketches also treat less well-known figures, thinkers, and activists in the struggle over privacy, such as pioneer academic Alan Westin, lawyer and author Jeffrey Rosen, and electronic-privacy advocate Marc Rottenberg.

Chapter 6 provides excerpts of books, treaties, brochures, and other materials that are sources of privacy law, inspiration, or controversy. These include excerpts of ancient Jewish law, the Bible, the Qur'an, and the Constitution of the Iroquois Nations. It includes the 1933 Reichstag Decree suspending civil liberties in

Germany, as well as the ACLU's "Bust Card," which explains your rights when stopped or searched by the police.

Privacy and technology are quickly evolving topics. Chapter 7 provides places to go to get the latest news on privacy developments, report abuses, join others in advocating for greater privacy protections, or consider another perspective. It lists some of the advocacy organizations, government agencies, and news sources that treat privacy rights or issues.

References

Associated Press. 2004. "Names in the Game." *San Francisco Chronicle*, Sept. 4.

Cambanis, Thanassis. 2004. "Security Didn't Hold the Line Financially." *Boston Globe*, Aug. 31.

Weiser, Benjamin, and Claudia H. Deutsch. 2004. "Many Offices Holding the Line on Post-9/11 Security Outlays." *New York Times*, Aug. 16.

Acknowledgments

A few words of gratitude to friends, family, and colleagues without whom this book would not have been possible. How blessed I am to have such a wonderful partner in Sarah Azaransky, whose patience, support, and intellect made this work—and indeed makes all of my life's work—better. Thanks as well to my kind, intelligent father, who spent many days of his retirement helping me with this project, and to my creative, thoughtful mother, whose quiet social and political engagement has made me a better citizen. Thanks also to Sam Walker for facilitating this significant opportunity, among others. Thanks to Brian Hunt, Barry Steinhardt, and Georges Viallet. Finally, thanks to my editors Mim Vasan and Laura Esterman and the staff of ABC-CLIO for their able, professional assistance. All flaws and faults are my own.

1

Background and History

What Is the Legal Right to Privacy?

In every culture, people learn about the idea of privacy at a very young age. From bathroom privacy to when to keep secrets to signs that warn "Private: Do Not Enter," children gain a sense of what is private or what should be. Some argue that the need for privacy is part of being human. The Bible says that Adam and Eve felt the need to clothe their bodies once they were expelled from the Garden of Eden. Many Muslims believe that the home should be the most private of all places because the Qur'an places a priority on the privacy of family relations, or *al-istitar*. Several of the 110 "Rules of Civil Behavior" that George Washington studied as a child related to privacy of customs, including number 7, "Put not off your clothes in the presence of others, nor go out of your chamber half dressed."

Others argue that privacy—either in the form of individual seclusion or the intimacy of small groups—is a need common to most animals, not just humans. Alan Westin argues, "Even rats need time and space to be alone" or else they suffer physical symptoms that affect their longevity as well as their social and reproductive behaviors. They fight more and are more sexually hostile. A controlled study of rat concentrations found that, given the privacy of dozens of tiny pens, rats could sustain much larger aggregate populations than they could in one big open pen. The constant exposure to a larger crowd—even in a much larger space—caused heart disease, high blood pressure, and circulatory problems (1967, 8–10).

1

Around the world, social, cultural, religious, and scientific views of the need for privacy have helped to shape the legal right to privacy—the subject of this book. The legal right to privacy refers to the various protections of privacy that exist in the laws of a nation or government.

Historical events also influence or change the extent of these protections. For example, following the September 11, 2001, terrorist attacks on the United States, many Americans were willing to sacrifice some degree of privacy rights *if* it would prevent future attacks. By contrast, Adolf Hitler's campaigns against Jews and other minorities during the 1930s and 1940s, including terrible violations of their privacy and dignity, had the opposite effect: they led much of the world to place a greater value on protections of privacy.

The judges and lawmakers who craft the law are not immune to the influences of history, culture, and religion. But the law—in the United States and most other nations—is bound by other norms. These constraints on the law include:

- International treaties
- National constitutions
- Precedents
- Respect for universal human rights

Treaties are formal agreements between two or more states. The European Convention for the Protection of Human Rights and Fundamental Freedoms is a treaty adopted in 1950, which forty-four European countries have agreed to follow. It holds, "Everyone has the right to respect for his private and family life, his home and his correspondence" (Art. 8).

Constitutions are the fundamental laws and principles that establish and define the structure, functions, and limits of governments. The Constitution of the Russian Federation states, "Everyone shall have the right to privacy, to personal and family secrets, and to protection of one's honor and good name" (Art. 23).

Precedents are rulings or interpretations of the law by judges in the context of a particular case. They are used in some systems as standards for subsequent similar cases. In Argentina, the Supreme Court heard the case *Urteaga v. Estado Nacional* (1998) involving a provision in the Argentine Constitution that allows individuals to find out what information the government is keeping about them (Art. 43). The court interpreted the provision to mean that a person could find out information not only about himself but also about his missing brother. This precedent will allow others to find out information about their missing or deceased relatives in the future.

Universal human rights are the basic rights and freedoms to which all humans are entitled no matter where they live, such as the right to be free from genocide. In other words, no government has the legitimate authority to violate a universal human right. Although there is debate as to whether privacy is itself a universal human right, it is clear that privacy can be important to other human rights widely recognized as universal. For example, keeping one's religion, ethnicity, or nationality private may be critical to avoiding discriminatory or genocidal abuse by a government. Enforcing the protection of universal human rights remains a challenge for the world, although the creation of the International Criminal Court in 2002 may promote greater accountability.

In the past 150 years, a legal right to privacy has come into being in most countries either through their own laws or through international law. International treaties, such as the Universal Declaration of Human Rights, recognize the right to privacy. The right to privacy and the idea of privacy have expanded and evolved.

There are different categories of privacy, including the following:

- *Associational privacy:* the ability to have relationships and associate with people without others knowing about it or interfering
- *Bodily privacy:* an individual's power over his or her own body, to decide what goes into it and who can touch it, search it, take things from it, and make decisions affecting it
- *Communication privacy:* the ability to communicate with people without others knowing what was communicated, including communications in person or by mail, telephone, computer, or other means
- *Data privacy:* one's power to determine who can collect and access information about oneself
- *Spatial privacy:* the physical zone—home, hotel room, vehicle—in which a person controls who has access to the zone or who can see, hear, or detect what is happening in the zone

Privacy rights are often different when it is a government that is accused of intruding than when it is a private actor who is accused of intruding on a person's privacy. For example, a person is likely to have more legal rights when a police officer searches inside his or her pockets than when a tabloid newspaper publishes a photo of him or her on the beach, even though millions more people may see the photo than will witness the search.

Origins of the Right to Privacy

Louis Brandeis is often considered the father of the legal right to privacy. As a young American lawyer, Brandeis first coined the term "the right to privacy" in an article he coauthored in 1890. He and coauthor Samuel Warren summarized privacy as "the right to be let alone." Later, as a Supreme Court justice, Brandeis wrote an important dissenting opinion that spurred the development of the legal right to privacy and was the inspiration for the Supreme Court's formal recognition of the right to privacy in cases such as *Griswold v. Connecticut* (1965) and *Katz v. United States* (1967) (discussed later). However, different types of privacy—although called by other names—existed well before

Brandeis's 1890 article. His contribution was to identify a broad concept of privacy that connected them and to popularize that concept.

Among the earliest examples of privacy, ancient Jewish law prohibited gossip and protected private spaces from being viewed by neighbors. One text, the Mishnah, states, "No one may place an entrance . . . opposite the entrance [of another] . . . nor a window opposite [another's] window . . . No one shall open up windows facing a jointly owned courtyard" (Elon 1994, 1859–1860). The Qur'an states, "O you who believe! enter not houses other than your own, until you have asked permission and saluted those in them: that is best for you, in order that you may heed [what is seemly]" (24:27–28). The Bible's book of Samuel, written around 800 BCE, reveals God's anger at Israel's King David for conducting a census of the people, putting himself between God and God's people (2 Sam. 24:1–15).

Other ancient examples contributed to the evolution of privacy. Hippocrates, a physician who lived in ancient Greece sometime between the years 460 and 377 BCE, wrote an oath for doctors that stated in part, "Whatever, in connection with my professional service, or not in connection with it, I see or hear, in the life of men, which ought not to be spoken of abroad, I will not divulge, as reckoning that all such should be kept secret." The oath of Hippocrates was an important contribution to privacy, and the idea that professionals should keep confidential any private, personal information they learn as part of their duty in a professional relationship of trust has continued to expand to this day. Even present-day China, which has very few privacy rights, requires lawyers to protect the confidentiality of their clients' personal secrets.

Centuries later, in England in 1361, King Edward III adopted the Justices of the Peace Act, which prohibited peeping toms and eavesdropping. In seventeenth-century England, a person could sue someone—both private persons and government officers—for various invasions of privacy. These legal claims were expanded through the nineteenth century, especially with the invention of photography, and still exist today. A person could sue someone for trespassing on his property, for using his name without permission to make money, for using his picture without permission to promote a publication that he had nothing to do with, and for unreasonably intruding upon his "solitude or seclusion."

These legal remedies—although not called "privacy rights" at the time—protected privacy in important ways. For example, in 1763, John Wilkes, a member of Parliament and publisher of a caustic newsletter critical of the king, sued the king's sheriffs for breaking into his home, riffling through the papers in his locked desk drawers, and taking his diary and personal letters. The court found the sheriffs liable for trespassing on Wilkes's property and ordered them to pay Wilkes the large sum of 1,000 pounds. English commoners and American colonists celebrated the court's decision for its protection of a person's most intimate thoughts and possessions. A pamphlet supporting Wilkes stated, "A man's writings lying in his closet, not published, are no more than his thoughts, hardly brought forth even in his own account, and, to all the rest of the world, the same as if they yet remained in embryo in his breast" (Rosen 2000b, 29). Member of Parliament William Pitt stated, "The poorest man may in his cottage bid defiance to all the force of the Crown. It may be frail; its roof may shake; the wind may blow through it; the storms may enter; the rain may enter—but the King of England cannot enter; all his forces dare not cross the threshold of the ruined tenement" (Electronic Privacy Information Center and Privacy International 2003, 5).

Wilkes's cause was most popular in the British colonies of America. At the time, American colonists were becoming increasingly occupied with their rights as Englishmen, especially the right to be free from taxation without due representation in Parliament. As the rift over taxation and representation grew, more Americans saw their future as separate and independent from England and became more insistent on their independence. The British government, in turn, stepped up its intrusion into the lives of the colonists, even taking over private homes in order to house British troops. Courts issued general warrants, called *writs of assistance*, that were meant to provide customs officials the assistance of sheriffs and justices of the peace in tracking down smugglers but that in fact permitted almost any authority to search any home, store, or warehouse for any smuggled material at any time. Unlike special warrants, the writs did not specify the place to be searched or the items sought. The practice led a Boston lawyer for the colonial government, James Otis, to quit his job and argue against the writs. In court in 1761, he stated, "[The general warrant] is a power that places the liberty of every man in the hands of every petty officer" (1761). Otis's arguments touched a nerve; John Adams, among others, credited Otis with catalyzing the American movement for independence. Samuel Adams attributed "the Commencement of the Controversy, between Great Britain and America" to the issue of general warrants (Levy 1988, 227–228).

After Americans declared independence in 1776, they enshrined certain protections from government intrusion in their states' constitutions and, in 1789, in the federal Bill of Rights. The first ten amendments to the Constitution included the following rights, which the Supreme Court would later identify as part of the right to privacy:

- *The right to "freedom of speech, or of the press; or the right of the people peaceably to assemble, and to petition the Government for a redress of grievances"* (First Amendment). In other words, the people have a right to think and inquire—and express those thoughts—by themselves or in a group without intrusion by the government. Political and social organizations ordinarily do not have to open their meetings or disclose who their members are. With some exceptions, thought and expression are private matters, not legitimately regulated by government.
- *"No Soldier shall, in time of peace be quartered in any house, without the consent of the Owner, nor in time of war, but in a manner to be prescribed by law"* (Third Amendment). Americans remembered the indignity of British troops invading and taking over their homes and so incorporated strict limits on such behavior.
- *The right to be "secure in their persons, houses, papers, and effects, against unreasonable searches and seizures."* No search shall be conducted without first obtaining a warrant supported by probable cause, and this warrant must describe particularly *"the place to be searched, and the person or things to be seized"* (Fourth Amendment). The government can intrude in people's most private spaces, but only if it satisfies specific criteria. James Otis's arguments against the writs of assistance inspired the Fourth Amendment protection against other similar types of general warrants.
- *No person shall be "compelled in any criminal case to be a witness against himself"* (Fifth Amendment). Although primarily intended to prevent authorities from beating confessions out of people, this amendment also prevents a

person from being forced to yield his private thoughts, words, or possessions for use in a prosecution against himself.

- *Those rights not mentioned in the Constitution shall be retained by the people* (Ninth Amendment). This provision, although little used by the Supreme Court, allows a person to argue that his or her right to be let alone, or other rights not specifically mentioned in the Constitution, should be respected.

Around the same time, across the ocean, privacy rights made further strides in Europe. In 1776, the Swedes adopted a law prohibiting the government from keeping information about its citizens that was not to be used for legitimate purposes. In 1789, French Revolutionaries adopted the Declaration of the Rights of Man and of the Citizen, which defined liberty as "the freedom to do everything that injures no one else" and limited law to "prohibit only such actions as are hurtful to society"— similar to "the right to be let alone" described by Brandeis more than 100 years later.

Privacy in Modern Times

Although elements of the right to privacy existed prior to the modern era, there was neither a complete nor robust "right to privacy" recognized or protected by law anywhere in the world. The right to privacy truly emerged and evolved in the late twentieth century, especially after World War II.

When Adolf Hitler took power in Germany in 1933, he began a campaign to isolate, ostracize, and exterminate Jews and other minorities. Among Hitler's first acts as chancellor of Germany was the persuasion of President Paul von Hindenburg to suspend the rights guaranteed by the Weimar Constitution, including the rights to habeas corpus; to privacy of correspondence, including mail, telegraph, and telephone; and to be free from searches without a warrant (Shirer 1960, 193–195).

In 1933, the Nazis conducted a census in Germany to identify practicing Jews. Jews were forbidden from voting, owning businesses, and serving in professions. In 1939, in an expanded Germany, a census targeted "racial Jews." Later, in Germany and the countries it conquered, the Nazis further stripped away the privacy and dignity of dissidents and minorities, especially Jews, requiring them to register with central authorities, carry specially marked identity papers, and wear symbols indicating their religion or minority category. The Nazis stopped and harassed Jewish people as they went about their daily affairs, invaded their businesses and homes, sterilized them, and conducted harmful medical experiments on them. The registries were used to find Jews and deport them to concentration camps where millions were killed. The Nazis and their accomplices invaded the privacy of their victims' bodies, homes, family lives, properties, papers, and consciences.

The Nazi degradation of human dignity and invasion of privacy operated on many levels, from the macro to the micro. On the macro-, bureaucratic, and mechanical level, the Nazis pioneered the use of electric, mechanized data processing to organize their persecution. Using hole-punched cards that summarized information about an individual or family (the location of the hole corresponded to a classification, category, letter, or number) and high-speed IBM card counters, the Nazis were able to record, analyze, and use information from its 1933 and 1939 censuses of Jews and other minorities to terrifying effect (Black 2001). On the microlevel, the street stops, home invasions, and countless other daily experiences of inconvenience, insecurity, and terror—even leaving aside the animal-like herding and abuse in the concentration camps—combined to destroy individuals' ability to be themselves.

Young Anne Frank, a German Jew who moved with her family to Amsterdam to avoid Nazi repression only to be forced into hiding when the Nazis and Dutch collaborators began their persecution of Jews and other minorities in Holland, may have described it best. In her diary, detailing the tragedy and heroism of daily life cloistered in a tiny apartment with seven others, she wrote:

> If I'm quiet and serious, everyone thinks I'm putting on a new act and I have to save myself with a joke, and then I'm not even talking about my own family, who assume I must be sick, stuff me with aspirins and sedatives, feel my neck and forehead to see if I have a temperature, ask about my bowel movements and berate me for being in a bad mood, until I just can't keep it up

anymore, because when everybody starts hovering over me, I get cross, then sad, and finally end up turning my heart inside out, the bad part on the outside and the good part on the inside, and keep trying to find a way to become what I'd like to be and what I could be if . . . only there were no other people in the world. (1991, 336)

These were the last words she wrote in the diary and, in all likelihood, the last words she ever wrote. After surviving two years and two months in hiding, most of them never once leaving their hidden space, the two families in the secret apartment were reported to the Nazis, found, and forcibly transported to Auschwitz. One of the family members was gassed at Auschwitz. Except for the sole survivor, Anne's father, Otto Frank, the others died of disease. Anne died of typhus one month before the Allied troops liberated the concentration camp where she was held.

When Germany surrendered to the Allies in 1945, the world took stock of the atrocities that had occurred—the persecution of people based on their religion, ethnicity, nationality, and political viewpoint. In response, countries formed the United Nations and adopted the Universal Declaration of Human Rights (1948), a set of principles asserting every person's right to basic human dignity and rights. The declaration was drafted by a committee of eight persons from Australia, Chile, China, France, Lebanon, the Soviet Union, the United Kingdom, and the United States of America. It encompassed those civil and political rights that had evolved from the U.S. Bill of Rights and the French Declaration of the Rights of Man and of the Citizen—freedom of conscience, speech, and religion; rights to life, rule of law, equal treatment of the law, and fair criminal procedures; among many others—as well as a number of economic, social, and cultural rights, such as rights to social security, work, education, and an adequate standard of living.

Article 12 of the declaration protects privacy, stating that persons shall be free from "arbitrary interference with [their] privacy, family, home or correspondence."

The declaration was adopted by the UN General Assembly with 48 member states voting in favor, 8 abstaining, and 2 absent. In 1993, 171 nations affirmed their commitment to the declaration.

The declaration, however, did not provide a way for individuals to enforce these rights against abusive governments, so other regional and international treaties were adopted with enforcement mechanisms.

- In 1950, European countries created the European Convention on Human Rights and a European court to enforce them. As to privacy, the convention states, "Everyone has the right to respect for private and family life, his home and his correspondence." It allows exceptions when necessary for "national security, public safety or the economic well-being of the country, for the prevention of disorder or crime, for the protection of health or morals, or for the protection of the rights and freedoms of others."
- Countries in North America and South America created the Organization of American States and the American Convention on Human Rights in 1969, which protects a broad "right to privacy" and provides some enforcement through the Inter-American Court of Human Rights.
- In 1963, Africans created the Organization of African Unity and, in 1981, adopted the African Charter on Human and Peoples' Rights, which protects "the integrity of the person" and the "right to liberty and to the security of his person"—a narrower conception of privacy than the "private life protection" in the European and American conventions.
- A large number of nations have signed on to the International Covenant on Civil and Political Rights, which also protects privacy. However, fewer nations have signed on to the covenant's enforcement mechanism, and only nations, not individuals, can bring a complaint.

Although the tide of history since World War II has brought greater recognition and protection of human rights, including the right to privacy, it has also brought waves of abuses. Indeed, the right to privacy has had to contend not only with those who disagree that it should exist and those who ignore it when it suits them but also with increasingly powerful technologies that make it easier to invade people's private lives and spaces.

The cold war between the United States and its democratic allies and the Soviet Union and its communist allies resulted in untold breaches of privacy by both sides. In the United States, the Federal Bureau of Investigation (FBI), under director J. Edgar

Hoover, turned methods developed to spy on U.S. enemies into a means to intimidate, disrupt, and punish Americans it suspected of sympathizing with left-wing causes or political parties. In 1976, the catalog of abuses by the FBI, Central Intelligence Agency (CIA), and other U.S. agencies was documented in a series of reports by a committee chaired by U.S. senator Frank Church. These invasions of privacy included the following:

- The FBI collected information on a conservative, Christian organization—the John Birch Society—because it criticized President Eisenhower (1950s).
- The FBI infiltrated and sought to discredit "New Left" students who demonstrated against the war in Vietnam. FBI tactics included publishing obnoxious photos, reporting scandalous behavior to the students' parents, and distributing false notices to students that events had been canceled (1964–1974).
- The FBI led a major campaign against the Reverend Martin Luther King Jr. Claiming that some of King's advisers were communists, the FBI used wiretaps and microphones to obtain information about his efforts to promote civil and human rights. The FBI then disclosed derogatory tidbits to the media and others, and even sought to disrupt the effort to award the Nobel Peace Prize to King (1957–1969).
- Under a program called COINTELPRO, the FBI systematically sought to disrupt left-leaning domestic organizations and smear and discredit their leaders. It went so far as to attempt to provoke a Chicago street gang to attack the Black Panthers by sending the gang false information (1956–1971).
- The CIA opened and photographed nearly 250,000 first-class letters between 1953 and 1973, producing a database of 1.5 million names.
- During Operation Chaos, the CIA collected information on approximately 300,000 individuals and created files on approximately 7,200 Americans and more than 100 domestic groups (1967–1973).
- The FBI spied on popular singer and former Beatles member John Lennon because he opposed the war in Vietnam and protested harsh sentences for possession of marijuana (1971).

- Informants for the intelligence agencies infiltrated the women's rights movement. Their reports revealed nothing illegal (or even scandalous) yet recommended continued investigation.

According to the *Final Report of the Select Committee to Study Governmental Operations with Respect to Intelligence Activities (the Church Committee Report)*, drafted April 26, 1976:

> The Government, operating primarily through secret informants, but also using other intrusive techniques such as wiretaps, microphone "bugs," surreptitious mail opening, and break-ins, has swept in vast amounts of information about the personal lives, views, and associations of American citizens. Investigations of groups deemed potentially dangerous—and even of groups suspected of associating with potentially dangerous organizations—have continued for decades, despite the fact that those groups did not engage in unlawful activity. Groups and individuals have been harassed and disrupted because of their political views and their lifestyles. Investigations have been based upon vague standards whose breadth made excessive collection inevitable. Unsavory and vicious tactics have been employed—including anonymous attempts to break up marriages, disrupt meetings, ostracize persons from their professions, and provoke target groups into rivalries that might result in deaths. Intelligence agencies have served the political and personal objectives of presidents and other high officials. While the agencies often committed excesses in response to pressure from high officials in the Executive branch and Congress, they also occasionally initiated improper activities and then concealed them from officials whom they had a duty to inform. (U.S. Congress 1976, 5)

Meanwhile, in many communist nations, the secret police conducted even more systemic, intrusive, and physically abusive campaigns to suppress dissent within their borders. For many, the names and nicknames of these police forces are inseparable from the abuses they committed—the East German Stasi (1950–

1989), the Czech StB (1948–1989), the Romanian Securitate (1945–1989), the Albanian Sigurimi (1943–1991), and the Polish Sluzba Bezpieczenstwa (1956–1990).

From 1954 until 1991, the Komitet Gosudarstvennoy Bezopasnosti (KGB), or Committee for State Security, was the Soviet Union's internal secret police—or political police—as well as its international spying agency. Although, with the passing of Stalin in 1953, the Soviet Union officially abandoned and denounced the KGB's programs of genocide and mass extermination of dissenters, it retained a sweeping system of surveillance and informants. It also retained, in Article 70 of the Soviet criminal code, severe punishments for anyone who sought to weaken the Soviet state, which included any artists, scientists, or writers who expressed views that did not conform to the approved messages or art forms of the Communist Party. In its own words, the KGB conducted "countermeasures to fight ideological diversions from outside and anti-Soviet manifestations inside the country" (KGB 1967).

In its annual report of 1967, the KGB detailed its activities—and the invasions of privacy they contained or implied—aimed at suppressing dissent. In one year alone:

- The KGB intercepted 114,000 letters and packages "containing anti-Soviet and politically harmful printed materials."
- Any practice of religion was viewed as anti-Soviet, and the KGB reported that it managed "to suppress and disrupt hostile activities by the emissaries of foreign religious centers" and "to unmask and bring to justice for illegal activity a number of active sectarians."
- Conducting activities associated with the cultural or national identity of the local region was thought to be a first step to promoting the breakup of the Soviet Union. Georgia, Ukraine, and Lithuania were all Soviet republics in the Union of Soviet Socialist Republics but had their own histories, cultures, and national identities. The KGB "carried out a number of measures to disrupt attempts to conduct organized nationalist activities in a number of areas of the country (Ukraine, the Baltics, Azerbaijan, Moldavia, Armenia, Kabardino-Balkar, Chechen Ingush, Tatar and Abkhaz Autonomous SSRs)."

- The KGB "established the identity of 1,198 anonymous authors. The majority among them did this because of their political immaturity, and also because of shortcomings in required educational work at the collectives where they work or study. At the same time some select hostile elements chose this way to struggle against Soviet power." This campaign led to 114 convictions for distributing "anti-Soviet" documents.

- "The KGB branches subjected to prophylactic [or preventative] treatment 12,115 persons, most of whom revealed manifestations of an anti-Soviet and politically harmful character without hostile intent." Although the report does not explain it, "prophylactic treatment" began with threats—for example, by mentioning the name of a possible dissenter at a public meeting of the local Communist Party or having a KGB officer visit and interview the dissenter and his family late at night—and escalated to more coercive actions, including putting dissidents in prison with ordinary criminals, arresting dissenters for possessing guns or drugs that were in fact planted on them by the KGB, sending dissenters to work camps supposedly for reeducation, and committing dissenters to mental hospitals. (In 1981, according to another KGB report, 229 authors of anti-Soviet materials were put in mental hospitals.)

The United States and the Soviet Union were not the only governments that violated the privacy of their citizens. Indeed, to this day, governments everywhere conduct surveillance of people in their countries. Most people agree that much of this surveillance is justified, provided it is conducted according to fair laws and subject to proper oversight, for example, by a court. It can serve to detect crime, deter terrorism, and prevent illegal plots of all kinds.

However, as in the cold war examples above, surveillance powers intended for proper use—to protect national security, for example—are often abused. The Church Committee put it this way: "The tendency of intelligence activities to expand beyond their initial scope is a theme which runs through every aspect of our investigative findings. Intelligence collection programs naturally generate ever-increasing demands for new data. And once intelligence has been collected, there are strong pressures to use it against the target" (U.S. Congress 1976, 5).

Formal Recognition of the Right to Privacy in the United States and Development of the Right Worldwide

The protection of privacy often depends on the existence of mechanisms that promote oversight and openness, such as the separation of powers among the branches of U.S. government. It also depends on the inclination and outrage of citizens. For example, the Church Committee may not have made its shocking discoveries if there had not been widespread outrage over the abuses of President Richard Nixon's administration. The Nixon administration created a secret group of spies and thugs that broke into the Democratic Party headquarters to tap the telephones of Nixon's political rivals. The Watergate burglars were caught and linked to the White House. This incident led to other discoveries and ultimately to President Nixon's impeachment and resignation.

To this day, the public's discovery of privacy invasions is dependent on accountability and transparency winning the day. One tool of accountability is freedom of information laws. These laws hold that, unless some legitimately important reason exists, government must turn over any information or materials it produces to members of the public upon request. Throughout this book, you will read about memoranda, videotapes, and other information that were secured through freedom of information laws, including a videotape of police officers raiding a high school hallway with guns drawn and dogs barking to search students for drugs; a memorandum revealing that, despite the FBI's assurances, the FBI captured improper data with its Carnivore e-mail snooping program; and information that, despite congressional action forbidding it, the U.S. Justice Department continued its efforts to build a total information awareness system by diverting the program to several states. Sometimes, information about abuses is exposed by whistle-blowers, as was the case in Watergate when presidential counsel John Dean chose to reveal the White House's role in illegal surveillance and other illegal activity.

It is likely that Watergate also helped spur the creation of the Church Committee and its comprehensive disclosure of more sweeping invasions of privacy by the White House, previous presidents, and the intelligence agencies. Finally, the outrage and sense of personal invasion inspired by these revelations likely generated the broad support for additional protections for privacy in the United States, including the Privacy Act of 1974 and the Family Educational Rights and Privacy Act of 1974.

Historical events, checks and balances, openness, and popular opinion made up one set of factors that affected the development of U.S. privacy rights in the 1970s. These mechanisms operated primarily on the executive and legislative branches of the U.S. government.

The courts—independent though also influenced by developments of the day—were another source of increasing protection of privacy in the United States during the 1960s and 1970s. The U.S. Supreme Court handed down several decisions that recognized and expanded a constitutional right to privacy.

The Supreme Court first acknowledged the existence of an implied right to privacy in the Constitution in 1965. The Court found that, although the word *privacy* never appears in the Constitution, the right to privacy is part of the fundamental *liberty* protected by the Constitution. Prior to that time, the Court never recognized a right to privacy as such.

The landmark decision was *Griswold v. Connecticut* (1965). Griswold was the director of a Planned Parenthood office in the state of Connecticut. Planned Parenthood provides medical services and counseling, including information about contraception, medicines, and devices to prevent a woman from becoming pregnant. At the time, Connecticut and other states forbade contraception as an immoral practice. Griswold was arrested and charged for helping a woman to prevent pregnancy. The Supreme Court reviewed its past decisions and found several precedents that protected privacy in other contexts—for example, the right of a family to teach its children a language other than English, based on respect for familial privacy; the right to associate with an organization privately without the government forcing the organization to disclose its members; the right to security of one's privacy against arbitrary intrusion by the police, and other rulings. The Court found that—like those other cases—the Connecticut law had a destructive impact on an important aspect of privacy, in this case the private relationships between husband and wife. The Court stated, "Would we allow the police to search the sacred precincts of marital bedrooms for telltale signs of the use of contraceptives? The very idea is repulsive to the notions of privacy surrounding the marriage relationship" (485–486). The Court found that a right to privacy existed, that it protected the marriage relationship, and that the Connecticut law was unconstitutional.

In several decisions after *Griswold*, the Supreme Court expanded what the right to privacy protected, but it also limited the right by balancing it against the legitimate interests and needs of government. Some of the Supreme Court's most important privacy decisions include the following:

- In *Katz v. United States* (1967), the Supreme Court held that the government needs a court warrant to spy on its citizens' private conversations with wiretaps.
- In *Loving v. Virginia* (1967), the Supreme Court struck down a Virginia law banning interracial marriages, holding that the government cannot interfere with the right to marry unless it has a very good reason.
- In *Terry v. Ohio* (1968), the Supreme Court created a limited exception to the rule that a police officer must have probable cause and a warrant to search a person. The Court held that an officer can "pat down" the outer clothes of a person to feel for weapons if the officer has a reasonable suspicion that a person suspected of illegal activity is armed.
- In *Roe v. Wade* (1973), the Supreme Court held that the right to privacy protects a woman's decision whether to have an abortion: the decision is entirely hers in the first trimester of pregnancy; the state can intervene during the second and third trimesters only under certain circumstances.
- In *Whalen v. Roe* (1976), the Supreme Court acknowledged the existence of "at least" two kinds of privacy: "the individual interest in avoiding disclosure of personal matters" and "the interest in independence in making certain kinds of important decisions." In this

case, the Court found that a law requiring the disclosure of information on prescriptions issued for certain narcotic medicines did not violate either type of privacy.

- In *Board of Education v. Earls* (2002), the Supreme Court held that the right to privacy did not prevent a school board from requiring all high school students participating in extracurricular activities to be tested for drugs. The Court found that the students had a limited expectation of privacy and that the government's interest in preventing drug use was important.
- In *Lawrence v. Texas* (2003), the Supreme Court overturned a Texas law that made it a crime for two people of the same sex to engage in certain sexual acts. The Court held that "two adults who, with full and mutual consent from each other, engage in sexual practices common to a homosexual lifestyle . . . are entitled to respect for their private lives" (578).

Although a superpower in other respects, the United States has not been the leader of the free world on privacy matters. Since World War II, other nations and international courts have developed stronger protections for privacy, often much earlier than the United States. In 1950, fifteen years before the *Griswold* decision, the European Convention on Human Rights recognized a right to privacy. Two years before, a right to privacy was in the UN Declaration of Human Rights. Other countries have also been ahead of the United States in recognizing the right of gay men and lesbians to privacy protection.

Important privacy decisions outside the United States include the following:

- In *Dudgeon v. United Kingdom* (1981), the European Court of Human Rights (ECHR) held that the right to respect for private life (Art. 8) in the European Convention on Human Rights protected the right to private, consensual sex between same-sex partners. The decision found a Northern Ireland law criminalizing male sodomy to be in violation of the convention.
- In *Huvig v. France* (1990), the ECHR held that French law was not sufficiently clear about how and when authorities could wiretap a person's phone. Because the law did

not give people reasonable guidance on what to expect, it did not provide the minimal protection required of laws and violated Article 8.

- In *Jansen van Vuuren v. Kruger* (1993), the Constitutional Court of South Africa upheld a patient's claim for money damages against his doctor for revealing to others that the patient was HIV positive. Although unintentional, the doctor's lapse was a grave, harmful violation of confidentiality. "Confidentiality is vital to secure public as well as private health, for unless those infected come forward they cannot be counselled and self-treatment does not provide the best care" (850 B–D).
- In *El Al Israel Airlines v. Danilowitz* (1994), the Supreme Court of Israel held that an "employer must employ a neutral attitude regarding the sexual orientation of his employees . . . That is how he will avoid a violation of the employee's privacy." The decision required the airline to provide the same benefits to same-sex domestic partners as to spouses.
- In *Ople v. Torres* (1998), the Philippine Supreme Court held that an administrative order creating a national ID system was unconstitutional. Although the court based its decision not on privacy rights, but on the executive branch's lack of authority to pass such an expansive system without a law passed by Congress, the court also commented that the system would "put our people's privacy in clear and present danger."
- In *Legal Status and Human Rights of the Child* (2002), an advisory opinion to several member states, the Inter-American Court of Human Rights addressed the rights of people under age eighteen in relation to the state and in particular the juvenile court systems of the member countries. Among other guarantees, the court advised that a youth under eighteen who is brought up on charges for violating the penal law has the right "to have his or her privacy fully respected at all stages of the proceedings" (74).

Despite the growth of the right to privacy, the right has never been an absolute one preventing any intrusion into the lives of individuals. To this day, the right to privacy is—by the way it is defined in every constitution and treaty in which it exists—balanced against the legitimate needs of governments.

Many people speculate that the right to privacy may be shrinking or, at least, facing its greatest challenge. They point to the rapid advance of technology that allows for governments and private individuals to intrude in people's privacy by surveillance and by collecting and sharing personal data. They also point to the responses of governments to the spike in international terrorism and the attacks of September 11, 2001. For American teens, the right to privacy is increasingly ethereal as community leaders and school administrators aggressively address the perception—real or imagined—that young people are more dangerous than ever before.

The Value of Privacy

In the present day, when the threat of terrorism, school violence, and other destructive crimes seems so high, it is tempting to use every means available to prevent such horrors, including invasions of privacy. Certainly, protecting a criminal's or terrorist's privacy is not as valuable as saving a potential victim's life. So why not pass laws allowing police to invade the privacy we currently enjoy in order to prevent crimes and terrorism? What would we be giving up? In other words, what makes privacy valuable, and how valuable is it?

Of course, some people disagree that privacy is valuable. They feel privacy is a mere luxury or that it is not a legitimate right. Others feel that it is overvalued in modern cultures and legal systems. (Those views are considered in the next section.) Still others feel that it is irrelevant to argue about the value of privacy, because it is an inalienable right. It comes with being human, so it does not need any further justification. Privacy, according to this view, embodies the "moral fact that a person belongs to himself and not others nor to society as a whole" (Fried 1977, 288–289). Or, according to a slightly different view, "Personhood and fundamental rights in a free political system create a political space, or buffer, around the individual that permits free expression and unencumbered action" (Sobel 2002, 40). Therefore, privacy trumps even some lawbreaking. In *Olmstead v.*

United States (1928), U.S. Supreme Court justice Oliver Wendell Holmes argued that it is "less evil that some criminals should escape than that government should play an ignoble part" (470). Justice Brandeis added, "If government becomes a lawbreaker, it breeds contempt of law" (468). In that case, the majority of the Court disagreed that the government's wiretapping of phones broke the law.

Whichever view one takes, it is worth discussing the value of privacy because the right to privacy often competes with other interests and rights, and a balance must be struck. Moreover, due to its relatively recent vintage, the right to privacy may be less well understood and more vulnerable to limitation or rescission than other rights. If privacy is to take a firmer, more appropriate root in world cultures and legal systems, it is necessary to know why and in what ways privacy is important.

For these purposes, rather than the definition of a *legal* right to privacy, we will use the broader notion of privacy as keeping others from knowing, seeing, hearing, or touching what we wish to keep to ourselves. There are at least five categories that capture the kinds of value privacy has for people:

- Natural and psychological value
- Creative value
- Protective value
- Social value
- Democratic value

Natural and Psychological Benefits

Privacy is thought by many to provide physical, psychological, and spiritual benefits to human beings. Whether alone or in connection with others, having privacy of space and time provides security for us to be fully human. Psychologists debate the precise hierarchy of human needs, but almost all psychologists agree that security and connectedness rank high among those needs. Invasion of one's privacy disrupts one's sense of safety and security. Invasion of the privacy of relationships can destroy one's sense of connectedness and disrupt the fostering of trust.

Having time to one's self, it seems, is psychologically important. Psychologist Esther Buchholz argues that quiet time and solitude give humans a chance to figure things out, to solve life's problems, to consider and make (one hopes better) choices. Like sleeping and eating, it helps the body and mind to recuperate. Even when such solitude feels hard, it may contribute to our ability to take care of ourselves and to realize our own strengths (1999).

Similarly, this view holds, our words and actions are typically improved by private, confidential contemplation with others. With certain trusted friends or loved ones, we express feelings, unformed ideas, or casual impressions that we would not want others to hear. By either unloading them or working through them with a confidant, we typically arrive at a better place and are able to express our better nature. These confidential expressions are themselves the fuel of intimacy, trust, and love, which are psychologically and physiologically important to our well-being (Fried 1968). If they were intruded upon by surveillance or other invasions of privacy, it could impair positive, loving relations among people, just as gossip and revealing secrets contaminate friendships.

Private time also feeds humans' spirituality. For centuries, spiritualists of every religion have recommended time in solitary contemplation, reflection, meditation, prayer, or communion with God or other higher powers as necessary and beneficial. In the sixteenth century, Martin Luther wrote, "I have so much to do [today] that I should spend the first three hours in prayer."

The calming benefits of finding "peace of mind" are not purely mental. In the early 1970s, Dr. Herbert Benson, now president of Harvard Medical School's Mind/Body Institute, and Keith Wallace published research finding that transcendental yoga meditation led to physiological changes, including a reduction in blood pressure, a reduction in blood lactate levels, and better circulation of oxygen in the blood system (Benson 1975). In other words, meaningful alone time feeds our spiritual life and improves our physical well-being.

Of course, being alone is not always good. Many people have too much time alone, which can be psychologically unhealthy. But in a 1998 study of Canadians age fifteen and older, researchers found that one in four people expressed the desire to have more time alone. Highly stressed people and women with young children were most likely to want more time alone (Clark 2002).

The benefits described above derive primarily from solitude, but solitude is not synonymous with privacy. One could achieve solitude and many of its benefits in public or with other people—meditating near others, thinking as you jog through town, or even daydreaming in class. It is possible one could derive the benefits of solitude without having privacy, either while in public or while mistakenly believing you are alone and not being observed. Nonetheless, privacy and solitude are usually connected. If our thoughts could be overheard—or if we knew our journal writing, thinking aloud, or conversations with confidants were not private—we would likely be more anxious and more self-conscious and inhibited in our explorations of our minds, ourselves, and our spirituality. We would be less likely to achieve peace of mind and the physical benefits associated with it.

Creative Benefits

For many, privacy is conducive to creativity. In 1929, author Virginia Woolf published the essay *A Room of One's Own*, in which she described why so few works of fiction had been authored by women. Predominant among the reasons, she argues, is that a woman's time, space, and money are monopolized by the men and children of her family. The creative process, she contends, is difficult enough by itself. For women, it is nearly impossible due to a lack of private space and time. Woolf insists, "A woman must have money and a room of her own if she is to write" (1993, 3).

Anthony Storr documented the relationship between solitude and creativity in the lives of some of the most notable artists, scientists, and other creative scholars. He draws on psychologist Abraham Maslow to suggest that "creative attitude and the ability to have peak experiences depends upon being free of other people; free, especially, from neurotic involvements, from 'historical hangovers from childhood,' but also free of obligations, duties, fears, and hopes" (1988, 201).

Protective Benefits

Privacy's value is, for many, most starkly revealed by its flagrant violation, particularly physical invasions of people's sense of being safe and secure. It is no wonder then that the legal right to privacy has among its origins the protection of the home from burglary—the most obvious physical intrusion into a zone of traditional safety and security. In the English legal system, protection of the home from burglary was extended to protect against unwarranted invasions of the home by government actors. Then—in both the English and the American systems—this protection was further extended to invasion of a person's privacy outside the home and, to a limited degree, to snooping and intrusions by the media and other profiteers of sensational information. In *Semayne v. Gresham* (1604), relying on an analogy to burglary, the court held that a person could resist the forced entry of the king's sheriff into his home if the sheriff failed to provide prior notice and was merely delivering a civil subpoena. Lord Coke also coined the expression (in this case and a later book) that a person's home is his castle:

> The house of everyone is to him his castle and fortress, as well as his defense against injury and violence, as for his repose; and although the life of a man is a thing precious and favoured in the law so that, although a man kills another in his defense, or kills one per infortunium without any intent, yet it is a felony, and in such case he shall forfeit his goods and chattels for the great regard the law has to a man's life, but if thieves come to a man's house to rob him, or murder, and the owner or his servants kill any of the thieves in defense of himself and his house it is not a felony, and he shall lose nothing.

But our sense of security resides not only in the home but also in our persons. Joan W., the victim of a strip search by Chicago police in 1978, told authors Ellen Alderman and Caroline Kennedy, "I felt like an animal. I felt like I had no control. I felt like I was going through some—some kind of deportation or kind of a—a—I felt like what I thought people I had seen in films of Nazis. I felt like one of those people." For years afterward, the violation of her bodily privacy led Joan to undress in a closet. Joan, who had been arrested for a traffic violation and generated no suspicion of possessing a weapon, was searched under the department's blanket policy of strip searching in the most invasive fashion all women who were arrested, no matter what the charge or level of suspicion. The federal circuit court ruled the policy unconstitutional in 1985, seven years after Joan's upsetting experience (1995, 5–6).

Such physical violations of privacy may be the most dramatic way to illustrate the protective value of privacy. But the disruption of people's sense of security results from less tangible invasions as well, such as watching, listening to, or recording private spaces, moments, or behaviors.

In Brandeis and Warren's 1890 article, the authors track the evolution of the law's protections against invasions and thefts of physical property to its protection of intangible property. They argue that the trajectory of the law protects, or should protect, against the publication of intercepted private images or papers. "Instantaneous photographs and newspaper enterprise have invaded the sacred precincts of private and domestic life; and numerous mechanical devices threaten to make good the prediction that 'what is whispered in the closet shall be proclaimed from the house-tops'" (195). Around this time, legal remedies for taking and selling photographs of another without permission (and other "privacy torts") were developing.

Privacy, at its best, protects us from the unfair use of scraps of information about us. As Jeffrey Rosen notes, people tend to latch on to a lurid detail and make judgments about others without knowing the full story of a person or putting that detail in proper perspective. In an age of information overload and short attention spans, privacy protects us against the human tendency to misjudge a person (2000b, 11–12). It may also protect us from an employer making a decision about a person based on his last visit to the doctor or other forms of discrimination society may find repugnant.

Sometimes, merely being persistently observed and followed in public feels like an invasion of privacy. Recognizing the damaging effects of being followed and watched, most U.S. states adopted laws forbidding stalking in the 1990s. But otherwise the law offers no protection to those who are stalked. For example, it is not a privacy violation for the police to follow you everywhere you go in public every time you leave your house. Rather—as U.S. law formulates it—in the absence of a specific law or constitutional amendment, you are afforded privacy protection against the government only when a court has deemed it reasonable for you to expect such privacy in a given situation (*Katz v. United States* 1967, 360). So U.S. courts have held that it is unreasonable for you not to expect someone to take photographs of you through an open window to your apartment, to riffle through your trash can on the curb, or to follow you in your car. This view does not comport with the ancient view that accorded far more menacing powers to being watched. Ancient Jewish law held, "Even the smallest intrusion into private space by the unwanted gaze causes damage, because the damage caused by the gaze has no measure" (Rosen 2000b, 19). As discussed next, this traditional view still holds some influence today in notions of social norms, propriety, and shame.

Social Benefits

As evidenced by the ancient Bible story of Adam and Eve being expelled from Eden, humans have long experienced the powerful force of modesty, social mores, self-consciousness, and shame. These social rules usually revolve around the body, its exposure and uses: how much skin is it okay to show, where can one urinate, and what practices of personal hygiene are odd or inappropriate? But they also measure what types of relationships, pastimes, or expressions of intimacy are respectable or within the mainstream at a given point in time.

Laws exist, and always have existed, to enforce many of these mores, while public shame or ridicule has enforced the rest. It is unreasonable to suggest that society could or should abandon all social mores. For example, as a young boy, George Washington copied the rules of civility of the day, including, "When in company, put not your hands to any part of the body not usually discovered." Even today, most people would not want to see others scratching "private parts" of their bodies.

Of course, what precisely society's standards should be is a more difficult question—one that people of different ages, regions, cultures, and religions would disagree over. Also, some social standards can be oppressive and, in retrospect, reprehensible. Historically, women have been subject to a vastly disproportionate share of social mores than men. To make matters worse, society's disapproval can take a harsh or violent form. For most of U.S. history, social standards have forbidden African American men from having intimate relationships with white women; violations of this social rule—whether true or merely alleged— often resulted in extreme physical violence against black men. Debate over what society's standards should be is essential to making progress and correcting society's unjust judgments. Often, this debate is fueled by the increased practice of supposed transgressions in private or the controversy surrounding private behaviors that are brought into the public light.

Significantly, many of society's mores apply to what is done in public (or "when in company"). Therefore, they presume or imply there is a private space where it *is* permissible to disregard those rules. Why is it permissible in private but not in public? Perhaps because it is simply no one else's business. Perhaps these impermissible things—such as scratching an itchy part— need to happen somewhere at some time. Perhaps it is easier or more comfortable to live up to a lower standard, such as walking around in underwear in the privacy of one's own home. Or perhaps, in society's most generous moments, we accept that the diversity and variety of human interests, passions, and expression are valuable or, at least, that they should not be filtered through the social standards that apply to public behavior. At some level, perhaps we recognize that society's judgments have often been unfair and unjust and that there needs to be a place for nonpublic or alternative habits, behaviors, and modes of being to exist. Whichever the answer, these private spaces are the necessary flip side of social mores. Privacy is as necessary to a functioning society, therefore, as social standards themselves. In these private spaces, we can relax in the knowledge that no one is watching, recording, or judging us. It makes it easier to live up to social expectations when we walk outside the next day. (By contrast, many people argue that a separation of the public and private spheres exists only as an unnecessary social construction to preserve a status quo that benefits those who already hold power, especially male power that is harmful to women; this view is discussed in the next section.)

This inevitable division of public standards and private spaces is partly responsible for the distasteful feeling that arises when social judgment is passed on acts that we otherwise expect to be private. For example, when, in the course of investigating U.S. president Bill Clinton's lying under oath to a grand jury about his extramarital affair with White House intern Monica Lewinsky, independent prosecutor Kenneth Starr's office secured and disclosed the contents of letters and e-mails Lewinsky drafted but never sent. Was it necessary to publish her unsent love letters? (Rosen 2000a). Likewise, when U.S. Circuit Court judge Robert Bork was being considered for a seat on the U.S.

Supreme Court, a Washington, D.C., newspaper published a list of the movies he had rented from a video store. The incident led to passage of the Video Privacy Protection Act of 1988, which protects the privacy of video rentals.

Even when the exposure reveals lawbreaking behavior, the privacy violation can feel unseemly. In 1995, Senator Bob Packwood resigned from the Senate after the Senate's Ethics Committee found him guilty of a long history of sexual harassment, accepting and soliciting bribes, and altering his private diary to obstruct the committee's inquiries. In the course of its investigation, the committee released 10,000 pages of Packwood's personal diaries. Many of these pages dealt with legitimate subjects of inquiry, such as his financial deals with corporations. But the vast majority dealt with his self-recorded sexual bravado and private thoughts. The media—followed by the late-night television talk shows—picked up on comments he recorded about the grooming of his hair, which made Packwood seem like a buffoon. The public was able to laugh at Packwood while also being upset about his egregious behavior toward women and his abuse of the public trust. At least three different plays based almost entirely on his diaries were produced and staged around the country. "We use all the juicy entries," said a *Village Voice* reporter who cowrote *The Packwood Diaries* (*International Herald Tribune* 1996). After Packwood's resignation, the U.S. Justice Department decided not to prosecute him for altering his diaries.

The implications of the subpoena and release of Packwood's diary were far reaching. When asked by news anchor Jim Lehrer, "Are you keeping a diary? Are you keeping good notes on what's happening?" then first lady Hillary Clinton replied, "'Heavens no! It would get subpoenaed. I can't write anything down" (Miller and Gao 2001).

As Jeffrey Rosen points out, acting appropriately in different social settings requires a person to wear different masks. Rosen argues these differences do not make the actor inauthentic; rather, they reveal different parts of a person. Citing sociologist and dramaturge Erving Goffman, Rosen writes, "Individuals, like actors in a theater, need backstage areas where they can let down their public masks, tell dirty jokes, collect themselves and relieve the tensions that are an inevitable part of public performance" (2000b, 12).

Democratic Benefits

Privacy is often cited as being essential to autonomy or liberty and therefore beneficial to democracy. Democratic government, at its core, is rule by the governed. A healthy, sustainable democracy requires informed, independent citizens able to know and act on their individual interests and the collective interests of the democracy. This independence and authority (which together constitute autonomy) are made possible, at least in part, by the existence of private spheres (the home, the doctor's office, the voting booth) in which it is presumed the citizen will be free to explore and actualize his or her interests (Samar 1991, 99). In this way, privacy affirmatively contributes to democracy.

Alternatively—in the more libertarian conception of democratic government—privacy *is* liberty, "the right to be let alone," as Brandeis and Warren called it. Or as the president of the libertarian Cato Institute put it, "We live in a free society and our first right is a certain level of privacy. We shouldn't be forced to show our papers wherever we go" (Gribbin 2001, A4).

The Czech novelist Milan Kundera lived through totalitarian communism in Czechoslovakia and considers the threat of constant surveillance and snitching fundamental to repression. In his novel *The Unbearable Lightness of Being,* Kundera has the police destroy a leader of the Prague Spring uprising by publishing his private phone conversations with a good friend, in which he jokes irreverently about serious topics and figures of the day. The revelation discredits the leader with much of the public (Rosen 2000b).

Arguments against the Value of Privacy

Privacy has its detractors. Or, at least, there are many who worry about placing too high a value on privacy. They have different reasons for their concern:

- Privacy is so enormous and amorphous a topic that it is either meaningless or all-consuming.
- Privacy laws infringe other important rights, including freedom of expression.

- Privacy restrictions pose too great a cost on convenience and on the marketplace.
- Privacy serves to protect and benefit male dominance over women.

Privacy Is Too Amorphous

Privacy is readily vulnerable to criticism. First, there is the fact that it is difficult to define. Privacy "is an unusually slippery concept," writes Professor James Q. Whitman (2004, 1153). The definition problem stems not only from the range of situations that privacy may cover (associational, bodily, data, communication, spatial, and so on) but also from the varying sensibilities among different people and societies about what ought to be kept private. Like *liberty, democracy,* or *justice,* it means too many things to too many people to be useful. Without a clear definition of what privacy is, some critics argue, there is the potential to invoke privacy restrictions whenever it is convenient. Or, worse, the looseness of privacy creates the opportunity for those with power—such as judges—to impose their views of what should be private in an arbitrary fashion.

In the United States, the legitimacy of the right to privacy is further attacked for its lack of pedigree. Critics, such as Robert Bork, cite the fact that the word *privacy* does not appear in the Constitution or any amendments. The only privacy rights are limited ones, such as the right against unreasonable search and seizure without due process. Rather, the argument goes, the right to privacy was invented by judges who wished to impose their particular views on social issues (1990).

Similarly, privacy is mocked by the arguably unartful language used in the decisions recognizing the right: it was said to exist in the "penumbras and emanations" of other rights. Professor Amitai Etzioni, writing after the September 11, 2001, terrorist attacks, taunts: "We must recall that privacy is a right fashioned (in the U.S. by the *Griswold* decision) as recently as 1965! If we can create a whole new right out of the penumbra of the Constitution, we surely can refashion it some, not because we have just experienced the most devastating attack on our homeland ever, but because we face the prospect of more and worse" (2003, xi).

Privacy Laws' Infringement of Other Rights

As is true of all rights, privacy at times comes into conflict with other rights. For example, the right to freedom of expression may conflict with the right to privacy when a newspaper wants to report that a player on a popular sports team has twice cheated on his wife. Eugene Volokh claims, "I love privacy! Privacy—what a great word." He asks, "Who can be against privacy?" But his answer reveals some of his critique of privacy laws: "Well all of us are, sometimes. The privacy of my home sounds great until it turns out I might be hiding a dead body in my basement. A witness's privacy is nice until you need the witness's testimony to prove the justice of your case. Privacy of people's personal information is good until the government starts censoring what newspapers write, or letting people bankrupt us for gossiping about them with friends" (2000a).

Some argue that privacy rights inhibit homeland security and law enforcement, thus leading to loss of life and infringement of humans' inalienable right to life and liberty. Etzioni has argued that privacy rights should give way to other concerns of public security and public health as well. He supports not only public disclosure of private information about sex offenders (referred to as "Megan's laws" in the United States) but also putting these people in guarded villages and forcing them to stay there (1999, 73–74). He supports ensuring that law enforcement has the power to decode online encryption technology (102) and the testing and treating of newborn babies without their mothers' consent (42). In each instance, he argues, privacy rights should be restricted if there is a true threat to community welfare and other methods that do not violate privacy have been tried (1999).

Volokh is concerned about laws to control how nongovernmental actors (including businesses, the media, and neighbors) use information about people, often called by the attractive term *fair information practices*. They include disclosure torts, laws that allow a person to sue another for money damages for disseminating highly personal, nonnewsworthy information about him or her; laws that restrict how companies can gather and share information about your purchases or Web site visits; and restrictions on sharing information that might allow others to commit crimes, such as social security numbers or the names of jurors or witnesses (2000b, 1055–1057). He fears these laws often violate the right to freedom of expression, give courts the power to decide what people can hear and think, and, worst of all, lay the framework for further restrictions of freedom of expression. "If the legal system accepts the propriety of laws mandating 'fair information practices,'" Volokh writes, "[p]eople may become more sympathetic to legal mandates of, for instance, fair news reporting practices or fair political debate practices" (1053).

Privacy Restrictions Cost Too Much

The classic economic view of privacy holds that the most efficient balance of privacy protection and unrestricted information flow will be achieved by the forces of supply and demand. Consumers will seek out more privacy-friendly competitors if they want more privacy, and the market will adjust accordingly. If, instead, consumers are more concerned about convenience or low cost, that too will be reflected in what suppliers provide. Of course, if only a niche group is interested in paying for privacy-friendly services, then just enough service to meet that need (and remain profitable) will exist. This market equilibrium can be achieved only in the absence of artificial barriers, such as government laws dictating choices and amounts of privacy (Posner 1978, 1981).

According to more strident free-market enthusiasts, privacy is fine so long as it does not pose costs for the private sector. They argue that the right to privacy is a right against government intrusion, not against the behavior of nongovernmental actors.

The promarketers argue that restricting the free flow of information has significant economic costs, especially in the present "information age." The financial services firm Ernst and Young reported:

> [The] ability of [financial service companies] to appropriately use information produces annual savings of $195 per year for an average customer household, or $17 billion per year. It also saves an average customer household four hours per year, or 320 million hours per year. Ernst and Young determined that restrictions on how information is used could squelch customer cost

savings, resulting in what amounts to a three percent excise tax. (Glassman 2000)

Another view holds that privacy has economic benefits, namely, that consumers desire privacy, but this desire is outweighed by their desire for convenience and cost savings, "with which the protection of privacy often interferes" (Cate 2001, 9). The free flow of personal information about consumers—the "lifeblood of the twenty-first century economy"—is critical to meeting consumer needs, enhancing service and convenience, and tailoring to their particular interests the product information consumers receive. In consumer credit, such information allows loan decisions to be based on real, individualized information, rather than assumed generalized information about the individual's demographic group (xiii).

Privacy May Serve to Protect the Status Quo of Male Dominance

A much different critique of privacy is that it creates a lawless zone that helps the more powerful and hurts the less powerful, particularly women. For women, privacy has been problematic over the course of history. In recent years—since the 1965 *Griswold* decision in the United States, for example—privacy has been the basis for allowing women greater control over their behaviors and bodies. However, privacy has also been used to protect husbands from being held accountable for beating their wives.

Through the latter half of the 1800s, the common law of England and the United States recognized a prerogative of husbands to chastise or correct their wives with physical abuse so long as it did not lead to permanent or serious injury. Courts began to discard these laws during the nineteenth century—at the same time that slavery and corporal punishment of children, sailors, and prisoners came into question—and, by the 1870s, repudiated the prerogative of chastisement. However, rather than outlaw the tradition altogether, some courts allowed it to continue by preventing women from taking action. They cited as justification their concern for the privacy of the marital relationship. For example, in the 1852 case of *State v. Hussey*, the North Carolina Supreme Court held that wives could not testify against husbands in cases of assault and battery unless serious bodily harm resulted. The court wrote:

> We know that a slap on the cheek, let it be as light as it may, indeed any touching of the person of another in a rude or angry manner—is in law an assault and battery. In the nature of things it cannot apply to persons in the marriage state, it would break down the great principle of mutual confidence and dependence; throw open the bedroom to the gaze of the public; and spread discord and misery, contention and strife, where peace and concord ought to reign.

In a similar case sixteen years later, the same court wrote:

> The courts have been loth to take cognizance of trivial complaints arising out of the domestic relations—such as master and apprentice, teacher and pupil, parent and child, husband and wife. Not because those relations are not subject to law, but because the evil of publicity would be greater than the evil involved in the trifles complained of; and because they ought to be left to family government. (*State v. Rhodes*)

Over the years and to this day, male violence against women, including spousal abuse, has remained a major problem. Advocates have pointed to the apparent reticence of police, courts, and legislatures to take effective action. In the 1970s and 1980s, feminist theorists identified part of the problem as the division of space and action into a public and private sphere. This way of imagining and constructing the world protects long-established male power and reinforces women's role as subjects of that power: In the public sphere, women are held to a higher standard than men, judging women harshly and contradictorily on their propriety and their sensuality or attractiveness. In the private sphere, women can be mistreated and others are meant to look away (Pollitt 1996). As Catharine MacKinnon describes it, "When the law of privacy restricts intrusions into intimacy, it bars change in control over that intimacy. The existing distribution of powers and resources within the private sphere will be precisely what the law of privacy expects to protect... [A]bstract privacy protects abstract autonomy, without inquiring into whose freedom of action is being sanctioned, at whose expense" (1987, 101).

In the 1990s, there was a renewed effort by U.S. federal and local governments to tackle the problem with new laws, support services, and policing strategies. Perhaps because of progress in addressing the problem of spousal abuse, some feminists have argued for reclaiming privacy and the public-private distinction. Some argue that privacy's virtue could be salvaged if it was divorced of its uses to mask exploitation and abuse. Anita Allen argues that women should not withdraw from the public sphere but rather should exercise the increasing opportunities to control their participation in both public and private spheres, for example, by getting an education, delaying marriage, timing childbearing, and working part time (1999). Linda McClain calls for a notion of privacy that does not merely say what others cannot do, see, or hear but also creates conditions for people to have meaningful choices about their private spaces and autonomy (1999).

The following chapters provide the facts with which to assess the state of privacy around the world and in the United States. They lay out the threats to privacy as well as the legitimate concerns of those who feel the need to infringe on privacy. Finally, the book gives you, the reader, ideas on how to learn more and, if you choose, take action.

References

Alderman, Ellen, and Caroline Kennedy. 1995. *The Right to Privacy*. New York: Alfred A. Knopf.

Allen, Anita L. 1999. "Coercing Privacy." *William and Mary Law Review* Vol. 40, 723–757.

Benson, Herbert. 1975. *The Relaxation Response*. New York: Harper Collins.

Black, Edwin. 2001. *IBM and the Holocaust: The Strategic Alliance between Nazi Germany and America's Most Powerful Corporation*. New York: Crown.

Bork, Robert. 1990. *The Tempting of America: The Political Seduction of the Law*. New York: Simon and Schuster.

Buchholz, Ester Schaler. 1999. *The Call of Solitude: Alonetime in a World of Attachment*. New York: Simon and Schuster.

Cate, Fred H. 2001. *Privacy in Perspective*. Washington, DC: AEI Press.

Clark, Warren. 2002. "Time Alone." *Canadian Social Trends* Catalogue No. 11-008, 2-6, No. 66.

Dudgeon v. United Kingdom, 45 European Court of Human Rights 52 (1981).

El Al Israel Airlines v. Danilowitz, Supreme Court of Israel sitting as the High Court of Justice, HCJ 721/94 (Nov. 30, 1994). http://www.tau.ac.il/law/aeyalgross/Danilowitz.htm.

Electronic Privacy Information Center and Privacy International. 2003. *Privacy and Human Rights: An International Survey of Privacy Laws and Developments.* Washington: Electronic Privacy Information Center and Privacy International.

Elon, Menachem. 1994. *Jewish Law: History, Sources, Principles: Ha-Mishpat Ha-Ivri.* Philadelphia: Jewish Publication Society.

Etzioni, Amitai. 1999. *The Limits of Privacy.* New York: Basic Books.

———. 2003. "Introduction: Rights and Responsibilities, Post 9/11." In *Rights vs. Public Safety after 9/11: America in the Age of Terrorism,* edited by Amitai Etzioni and Jason H. Marsh. New York: Rowman and Littlefield.

Frank, Anne. 1991. *Diary of a Young Girl: The Definitive Edition.* Otto H. Frank and Mirjam Pressler (eds.). Susan Massotty (trans.). New York: Doubleday.

Fried, Charles. 1968. "Privacy: A Rational Context." *Yale Law Journal* 77: 475–493.

———. 1977. "Correspondence." *Philosophy and Public Affairs* 6: 288–289.

Gerhart, Ann, and Annie Groer. 1996. "The Reliable Source." *Washington Post,* Sept. 26.

Glassman, Cynthia. 2000. Ernst and Young Financial Services Roundtable. Customer Benefits from Current Information Sharing by Financial Services Companies, http://www.privacyalliance.org/resources/glassman.pdf.

Gribbin, August. 2001. "Public May Favor a National ID Card." *Washington Times,* Sept. 27.

Griswold v. Connecticut, 381 U.S. 479 (1965).

Huvig v. France, 12 European Court of Human Rights 528 (1990).

International Herald Tribune. 1996. "People." *International Herald Tribune,* Sept. 28, Lexis.

Jansen van Vuuren v. Kruger, Constitutional Court of South Africa, 1993(3) SA 842(A).

Johnson, Marvin. 2002. *The Dangers of Domestic Spying by Federal Law Enforcement: A Case Study of FBI Spying on Dr. Martin Luther King.* Washington, DC: American Civil Liberties Union Washington National Office.

Katz v. United States, 389 U.S. 347 (1967).

KGB. 1967. *Annual Report to the General Secretary of CC CPSU.* http://www. cnn.com/SPECIALS/cold.war/episodes/21/documents/kgb.report.

Lawrence v. Texas, 539 U.S. 558 (2003).

Legal Status and Human Rights of the Child, Advisory Opinion OC-17/2002, Inter-American Court of Human Rights (August 28, 2002). http://www.corteidh.or.cr/serieapdf_ing/seriea_17_ing.pdf.

Levy, Leonard. 1988. *Original Intent and the Framers' Constitution.* New York: Macmillan.

MacKinnon, Catharine. 1984. "*Roe v. Wade:* A Study in Male Ideology." In *Abortion: Moral and Legal Perspectives,* edited by Jay L. Garfield and Patricia Hennessey, 45–54. Amherst: University of Massachusetts Press.

———. 1987. *Feminism Unmodified.* Cambridge, MA: Harvard University Press.

McClain, Linda C. 1999. "Reconstructive Tasks for a Liberal Feminist Conception of Privacy." *William and Mary Law Review.* Vol. 40, 759–792.

Miller, James D., and Lixin Gao. 2001. "Creating a Subpoena-Proof Diary: A Technological Solution to a Legal Problem." *Journal of Information Law and Technology* 2001, no. 3 (Nov. 7). http://elj.warwick.ac.uk/jilt/01-3/miller.html.

Olmstead v. United States, 277 U.S. 438 (1928).

Ople v. Torres [Decision of the National ID System], Philippine Supreme Court, G.R. 127685 (July 23, 1998). http://www.supremecourt.gov.ph/jurisprudence/1998/jul1998/127685.htm.

Otis, James. 1761. "Against Writs of Assistance." In *National Humanities Institute, Center for Constitutional Studies, Source Documents.* http://www.nhinet.org/ccs/docs/writs.htm.

Pollitt, Katha. 1996. "Of Toes and Men." *Nation* (Sept. 23).

Posner, Richard A. 1978. "An Economic Theory of Privacy." *Regulation* (May-June), 19–26.

———. 1981. "The Economics of Privacy." *American Economic Review* 71, no. 2: 405–409.

Prosser, William L. 1960. "Privacy." *California Law Review* Vol. 48, 383–423.

Rosen, Jeffrey. 2000a. "The Eroded Self." *New York Times Magazine,* Apr. 30. www.nytimes.com/library/magazine/home/20000430mag-internetprivacy.html.

———. 2000b. *The Unwanted Gaze: The Destruction of Privacy in America.* New York: Vintage Books USA.

Samar, Vincent J. 1991. *The Right to Privacy: Gays, Lesbians, and the Constitution.* Philadelphia: Temple University Press.

Scoglio, Stefano. 1998. *Transforming Privacy: A Transpersonal Philosophy of Rights.* Westport, CT: Praeger.

Semayne v. Gresham, 5 Co. Rep. 91a, 93a, 77 Eng. Rep. 194, 198 (K.B. 1604).

Shirer, William L. 1960. *The Rise and Fall of the Third Reich.* New York: Simon and Schuster.

Sobel, Richard. 2002. "The Degradation of Political Identity under a National Identification System." *Boston University Journal of Science and Technology Law,* Vol. 8, 37–74 (Winter).

State v. Hussey, 44 N.C. (Busb.) 123, 126–127 (1852).

State v. Rhodes, 61 N.C. (Phil. Law) 453 (1868).

Storr, Anthony. 1988. *Solitude: A Return to the Self.* New York: Random House.

Strum, Philippa. 1998. *Privacy: The Debate in the United States since 1945.* New York: Harcourt Brace College Publishers.

Thornburgh v. American College of Obstetricians and Gynecologists, 476 U.S. 747 (1986).

U.S. Congress. Senate. Select Committee to Study Governmental Operations with Respect to Intelligence Activities (Church Committee). 1976. Final Report—Book III, Supplementary Detailed Staff Reports on Intelligence Activities and the Rights of Americans. April 23, 1976. 94th Cong., 2d sess. S. Rep. 94-755, Washington, DC: GPO.

U.S. Department of State. 2003. *Country Reports on Human Rights Practices, 2002.* Washington, DC. http://www.state.gov/g/drl/rls/hrrpt/2002/18132.htm.

Volokh, Eugene. 2000a. "The Book Club: *The Unwanted Gaze.*" Review of *The Unwanted Gaze: The Destruction of Privacy in America,* by Jeffrey Rosen. *Slate* (June 6). http://slate.msn.com/toolbar.aspx?action=print&id=2000174.

———. 2000b. "Freedom of Speech and Information Privacy: The Troubling Implications of a Right to Stop People from Speaking about You." 52 *Stanford Law Review* Vol. 52, 1049–1124 (May).

Warren, Samuel, and Louis Brandeis. 1890, "The Right to Privacy." *Harvard Law Review,* 4: 193–220.

Westin, Alan. 1967. *Privacy and Freedom.* New York: Atheneum.

Whitman, James Q. 2004. "Two Western Cultures of Privacy: Dignity versus Liberty." *Yale Law Journal,* 113, 1151–1221 (April).

Woolf, Virginia. 1929. *A Room of One's Own* and *Three Guineas.* Michèlle Barrett, ed. New York: Penguin Books, 1993.

2

Surveillance and
Databasing around the World

A round the world, an individual's right to privacy is protected by the laws and constitution of the country in which
he or she resides, the treaties the country has signed, and
universal human rights that are meant to apply across national
borders regardless of a country's laws or treaties. However, in reality, many governments do not offer strong protections for privacy, many governments violate their countries' laws and
treaties, and it is usually difficult for individuals to vindicate
their universal human rights. Indeed, when it comes to two of
the most intrusive means of privacy invasion in high-tech society—namely, surveillance and databasing—the average person
often does not know it is happening.

High-Tech Surveillance
Echelon and the Interception
of International Communications

Echelon is the code name for a surveillance system that secretly
listens into a vast quantity of communications—cellular, fiber
optic, satellite, and microwave—from around the world and tries
to match it to key words, word patterns, voices, and other criteria
of suspiciousness. It is run cooperatively in complete secrecy by

Australia, Canada, New Zealand, the United Kingdom, and the United States.

Echelon was first revealed to the world in 1988. Margaret Newsham, a former computer programmer for Lockheed Martin, worked on the expansion of Echelon and, in the process, saw some things she did not like—for instance, eavesdropping on the conversations of a U.S. senator unsuspected of any wrongdoing. She reported the news to the U.S. House Select Committee on Intelligence and then leaked it to a journalist with the British magazine *New Statesman,* which published the first article on Echelon. The intelligence community made no comment on the article, and it failed to spark public interest. Eight years later, Nicky Hagar finished a book about New Zealand intelligence, *Secret Power,* that provided much greater detail about Echelon. Again the intelligence community ignored it, and, after an initial splash, it seemed it would have little effect. However, in 1997, the European Parliament's Civil Liberties Commission authored a report titled *An Appraisal of Technologies of Political Control,* which used Hagar's research on Echelon. Apparently, the official stamp of the European Parliament gave the story credibility, and media coverage was intense. The story suddenly produced a great stir. What proved shocking about Echelon was the amount of communications it intercepted, the sharing of this information among many nations, and the fact that few public officials knew of its existence. It also gained notoriety for its enormous potential for abuse and allegations of actual abuse (Hagar 2000).

According to a 2001 European Parliament report, Echelon possesses two unusual features:

> The first . . . is the capacity to carry out quasi-total surveillance. Satellite receiver stations and spy satellites in particular are alleged to give it the ability to intercept any telephone, fax, Internet or e-mail message sent by any individual and thus to inspect its contents.
>
> The second . . . [is that] the states participating in ECHELON . . . can place their interception systems at each other's disposal, share the cost and make joint use of the resulting information. (European Parliament 2001, 23)

This international cooperation also allows these nations to circumvent rules about spying on their own citizens. With Echelon, a nation can claim "it wasn't me who did the spying." Ordinarily, these nations' laws prevent them from spying on their own citizens without first obtaining a warrant. A warrant requires the government to show probable cause that the target of the surveillance has committed a crime. But, for example, if Country A conducts surveillance in Country B, then Country B has not broken its own laws on surveillance. (Country A may be guilty of international espionage, but only if Country B wants to do anything about it.) With Echelon, Country B can get the information that Country A collected and pretend it was not responsible for the surveillance. Of course, in reality, Country B has conspired to invade privacy and colluded in the violation of its own laws—and that is the problem with Echelon, according to privacy advocates.

Another problem is the potential use of Echelon for purposes other than national security. It is suspected that the United States uses Echelon to gain an advantage for U.S. businesses bidding on international contracts. On one occasion, the United States scuttled a contract between the European airplane company Airbus and Saudi Arabia by spying on the contracting parties and revealing that European officials were bribing Saudi officials. According to an MSNBC investigation, the United States "has admitted that it regularly tracks bribery attempts . . . and uses that information to help U.S. companies win . . . contracts" (Windrem 2000). Other documents reveal that the United States tracks not only bribery but also other actions it considers aggressive. On another occasion, the United States allegedly gave information acquired through Echelon to a U.S. company, Raytheon, helping it to gain an advantage in negotiations and scoop a billion-dollar contract with Brazil from the hands of the French company Thomson-CSF.

The Echelon nations are not the only ones using high-tech interception of communications. Many nations conduct this type of spying, and many have crossed the line between spying for national security and spying for commercial advantage. The Russians are in the process of updating their worldwide network, called *Dozor*, left over from the Soviet Union's communist alliances. Dozor includes a large interception station in Lourdes, Cuba, which the Russians rent from the Cubans for a large fee. Located just south of the United States, Lourdes can capture important security and commercial communications. A CIA executive once told a number of U.S. journalists, "Everyone of you in this room has his or her phone calls monitored out of Lourdes" (Windrem 2003). However, the Russian network is out of date, and other single-nation systems do not have the same power and breadth of the multinational Echelon network.

Echelon can be a powerful force for law enforcement. In March 2003, unnamed American authorities reported that Echelon was used to monitor the cell phone calls of several persons suspected of being key al Qaeda leaders who planned and supported the September 11 attacks. The surveillance helped lead to the capture of two leaders, Khalid Shaikh Mohammed and Mustafa al-Hisawai, by Pakistani intelligence agents.

Privacy advocates worry that Echelon is not bound by any legal guidelines to limit its use to appropriate purposes. With no independent oversight of Echelon's activities, history suggests, the power of Echelon is likely to be abused. Although not enough is known about Echelon to determine if this abuse occurs (except for the examples of industrial espionage conducted by the United States mentioned earlier), there is ample evidence that governments abuse other forms of surveillance.

Government Wiretapping

Wiretaps have been around almost as long as telephones. Originally, *wiretap* referred to a wire connection to a telephone line that allowed someone to listen secretly to a phone conversation between other people. Today, wiretapping is conducted through computers that the government attaches to the phone companies' networks of switchers and routers. These computers can listen to, record, and store calls to and from selected lines, as well as send the conversations to investigators at remote locations. Today, the term *wiretapping* is often used to refer to many forms of communications surveillance.

In several countries, high-tech eavesdropping has been used illegally to promote a political figure or thwart opponents. The best known wiretapping scandal is the 1973 break in and wiretapping of the Democratic National Committee headquarters in the Watergate apartment complex in Washington, D.C. President Richard Nixon resigned in 1974 after impeachment proceedings were initiated against him due to his administration's involvement in the tapping and in subsequent efforts to cover it up. Despite the lessons of the Watergate wiretapping, this form of abuse persists around the world, spurred in part by advances in surveillance technologies.

In 2002, police in Serbia arrested army general Nebojsa Pavkovic when it was revealed that he was involved in wiretapping the phones of the president's communications department. In 1995, the president of Estonia resigned when his involvement in wiretapping of political opponents was discovered. Since 1990, Chile, France, Georgia, Greece, Norway, Peru, and numerous other countries have also experienced high-profile scandals involving illegal political wiretapping, leading in some cases to the defeat or impeachment of those leaders thought to be responsible. Most recently, in Russia, the police opened an investigation when the media shared transcripts of the private phone conversations of a leader of an opposition political party, Boris Nemtsov.

Some governments have used this same type of political interference at the international level, spying on international diplomats to try to influence the outcome of political debates at the United Nations. In March 2003, the UN launched a high-level inquiry into evidence that the United States was spying on UN Security Council members to find out their positions and negotiating strategies in the debate over authorizing military intervention in Iraq. A memo from a U.S. intelligence agency directed the interception of telephone and e-mail communications from delegates of Angola, Cameroon, Chile, Mexico, Guinea, and Pakistan at the UN headquarters in New York. These six nations held "swing" votes, which those in favor of attacking Iraq wanted to secure. The Vienna Convention on Diplomatic Relations forbids such spying, stating, "The receiving state shall permit and protect free communication on the part of the mission for all official purposes . . . The official correspondence of the mission shall be inviolable."

Most government wiretapping is legal, that is, legally authorized by a court. Wiretaps are a principal tool of law enforcement. They are used to investigate people suspected of committing crimes or conspiring to commit crimes. (The act of conspiring is itself a crime.) Typically, at least in democratic countries, law enforcement officials can use wiretaps for serious crimes only, and they must seek approval from a judge or magistrate. Statistics show that judges almost never reject these requests. For example, of 2,164 requests during a one-year period, 2001–2002, judges in Australia said no to only 7 requests for warrants. Of 1,360 requests during 2002, U.S. judges rejected only 1.

But laws regulating wiretapping have been broadened in recent years, and advances in technology have given governments the power to conduct more of it. With these changes, societies must ask how much privacy they wish to sacrifice to law enforcement efforts to investigate and prevent crime.

Australians are the most tapped English-speaking people in the world. They are twenty times more likely to be wiretapped than Americans, Canadians, or Britons. A 2002 report revealed that there were 2,157 wiretap warrants issued in Australia between 2000 and 2001, and police looked at the phone records of 733,000 people.

In France, 4,654 wiretaps were approved in 2002, and law enforcement sought to identify mobile telephone numbers at a rate between 8,000 and 25,000 times per month. The commission responsible for overseeing wiretaps estimated that private nongovernmental parties conducted more than 100,000 illegal wiretaps in 1996. Many of these taps were done at the request of government agencies.

In South Korea, it is estimated that more than 10,000 wiretaps were placed in 1998. South Korea has since passed a law limiting wiretaps. In 2000, there were 2,380 telephone wiretaps placed. There were 160,485 instances of law enforcement seeking basic phone records.

In the United States, ordinary wiretapping increased 47 percent between 1992 and 2002, from 919 wiretaps in a year to 1,359. (These figures do not include the 1,228 secret orders issued in 2002, which are discussed in Chapter 3.) Of these requests, 77 percent listed drug offenses as the most serious crimes being targeted. The average wiretap was active for 92 days and intercepted 1,702 communications. Of these communications, an average of 403 (or 24 percent) contained incriminating information.

Identification and Tracking Technologies

The rapid improvement in technology allows governments and companies not only to listen into private communications but also to track you by your electronic transactions and—more and more—by your movements. Often, the purpose is benevolent, but the need is debatable and the risk of abuse is significant.

Table 2.1
Law Enforcement versus Privacy Debating Points

Pro Privacy Protection	Anti Privacy Invasion
Privacy is a cherished value and a human right; law enforcement must find ways to do its job with as little invasion of privacy as possible.	Privacy limitations on law enforcement discourage aggressive action and thereby promote crime.
The right to privacy is not absolute, and police already have the tools they need to combat crime, including the power to invade privacy reasonably and with some court oversight. It is reasonable to expect police to follow rules, secure a warrant, and be accountable for their actions.	Too many rules tie the hands of the police. Police need to be able to act on their sense of a situation or a person in light of their experience and the circumstances.
A free society does not regulate people's thoughts, only their actions. Preventive policing must be careful not to cross the line into thought policing.	Surveillance is necessary to *prevent* crimes from happening instead of reacting to them after they happen. As crimes have become more heinous, the need for preventive surveillance has become more urgent.
New technology has created the prospect of recapturing the opportunity for true privacy that people used to enjoy before the growth of the surveillance state. Police should not be allowed to tip the balance once again in favor of instantaneous, total access.	In this high-tech age, it is easier to plan and even commit crimes in total secrecy using technology such as the Internet and encryption. Police need high-tech powers to combat high-tech crime.
The high-tech tools being given to law enforcement agents give them far greater access than they have ever had before. They are not narrowly targeted at suspected wrongdoers, and they are not subject to oversight by a neutral body in order to prevent abuse.	If you have done nothing wrong, you have nothing to fear.
In some instances, law enforcement must respect privacy even if it means some crimes go undetected. It is "less evil that some criminals should escape than that government should play an ignoble part" (Justice Oliver Wendell Holmes in *Olmstead v. United States* [1928]).	Freedom does not include the freedom to commit crimes.
"The confirmed criminal is as much entitled to redress as his most virtuous fellow citizen; no record of crime, however long, makes one an outlaw" (Id.).	

High-Tech National ID Cards

Government-issued identity cards are going high tech. Many countries are considering putting electronic identifiers, such as readable microchips that hold data about the cardholder, into the cards. The advantage is that the cards could provide more information, greater security, and swifter checking. The disadvantages are that the information could be misused or stolen and that people may not wish to disclose so much information about themselves.

Most nations issue ID cards or require its citizens to use ID cards for different reasons. In the United States, there is no national ID card; instead, most people use their driver's license for identification. Although as a practical matter the driver's license is difficult to live without, U.S. law does not require people to have a driver's license as a form of identification unless they are driving. People can use other forms of picture identification when necessary.

So-called smart ID cards contain personal information that can be read by electronic readers, much as the label on a can of tomatoes can be read by a supermarket scanner. Several nations have already experimented with smart ID cards. For example, in 2001, Malaysia began requiring its citizens to carry "MyKad" smart cards with a microchip containing an electronic version of the cardholder's fingerprints, facial-feature measurements, identity number, passport information, driver's license information, and health information. The card also serves as the holder's bank card and allows access to government services on the Internet. Speaking in the days after September 11, 2001, a Malaysian official speculated, "A lot of governments will be looking at better identification systems to monitor the movement of people within their countries after last week's terror attacks" (*Canberra Times* 2001).

However, on May 11, 2005, President George W. Bush signed the Real I.D. Act, which lays the foundation for a nationally uniform identity card.

Indeed, these cards will allow governments to track the movements of their citizens by their electronic transactions. When combined with radio frequency identity (RFID) chips, which transmit a short radio signal that can be detected by receivers, or global positioning system (GPS) chips with cellular communication capacity that can transmit a person's precise geographical location, the cards will allow a person to be tracked without him or her ever using the card. To take advantage of these existing and potential tracking abilities, China, which exercises significant control over the political and associational activities of its citizens, began issuing smart ID cards in 2004.

Privacy and human rights activists fear the types of abuse that can result from the information included in national ID cards. ID cards have played a role in some of the worst moments in history. In 1938, the Nazi government in Germany marked the ID cards of Jews with a *J* stamp and used the cards to target Jews for abuse and torture. More recently, in 1994, the Hutu massacre of Tutsis was facilitated by the "Tutsi" designation on Rwandan national ID cards. One scholar argues, "No other factor was more significant in facilitating the speed and magnitude of the 100 days of mass killing in Rwanda" (Fussell 2001).

More than twenty nations still include a line specifying the holder's ethnic, racial, or religious affiliation. Many others require a special card for certain groups, such as immigrants. Syria requires a special card for Jews, Iran for Christians, and Saudi Arabia for non-Muslim foreigners. Ethiopia, Kenya, and Vietnam are among the nations that specify ethnicity. Israel lists nationality. In the United States, the illegal police practice of racial profiling—singling out people for stops and searches based on their (nonwhite) skin color—could be made easier by national ID cards that included an electronic image or physical description of the cardholder.

But national ID cards pose other significant risks as well, particularly the risk of identity theft. Placing comprehensive information about a person on one card and asking everyone to rely on this one card may make it easier to steal that person's identity, get access to her money and possessions, and ruin her good credit.

Due to these risks and based on the right to privacy, the supreme courts in the Philippines and Hungary have found their national ID systems to be unconstitutional, and the Portuguese Constitution forbids an "all purpose national identity number." In other countries, including Australia, South Korea, and Taiwan, large-scale protests led to the abandonment of national ID systems.

Other technologies pioneered by private companies or government-sponsored companies are starting to track people as well.

Did you know that almost every color photocopy is marked for tracking? Virtually all color copiers, and some color printers, put a unique identification number on the copies it makes. The coded number is hidden by breaking it into pieces throughout the image. It can be decoded only with sophisticated software that knows the numbering algorithm. The copy companies in charge of the code will not decode the number without a court order or the request of certain government agencies.

The system is meant to help law enforcement identify copiers used to make counterfeit money. But does it feel weird to you that hidden in your color copy is a number that could be used to track where you have been?

Swipe Cards and Black Boxes

Some tracking technologies are fairly low-tech. Indeed, they were never intended to track people, but police and others have discovered this additional hidden value.

In 1999, Marco Valencia was charged with robbing a supermarket in New York City and assaulting the manager. He claimed he was in Staten Island at the time, but the police examined his subway fare card, which had been swiped through a turnstile in Manhattan. The electronic reader—created merely to replace subway tokens—not only reduced the balance on his card by the fare price but also recorded its unique serial number on the subway system's computers, showing that he passed through a turnstile near the crime scene. The police used this evidence to persuade Valencia to confess.

Data recorders are being installed regularly in new vehicles to track their speed and system performance. These "black boxes" were originally intended to help in the triggering of airbag deployment. But now they are being used by police in accident investigations. Many consumers are not aware their vehicles' every move is being tracked, because automobile companies have kept quiet about the system to avoid controversy over customers' privacy.

These examples show how the privacy implications of even benign, simple technologies must be considered at the outset, because any potential for tracking is likely to be exploited.

GPS

To this day, sailors are trained in the ancient tradition of determining their approximate location by reference to stars in the sky. The GPS serves a similar purpose, but it relies on man-made "stars," and it is far more precise. The most advanced GPS devices can pinpoint locations to within a centimeter.

Originally created in 1978 by the U.S. military to guide missiles to their targets and locate soldiers, GPS is now available for public and commercial uses throughout the world. The system consists of twenty-four satellites orbiting the earth that send signals that can be received and bounced back by GPS receivers. If four satellites can connect with a receiver, they can quadrangulate the precise location of the receiver. The receivers are so small, they can be contained in hand-size devices, such as cell phones. Access to the system, as well as its maintenance, is still controlled by the U.S. military.

In 2003, police outside of Washington, D.C., made use of the onboard motorist-assistance system in a luxury car—which includes both a GPS navigator and a cell phone connection that transmit location data and connect the driver to an operator—to rescue two carjacked children. The carjacker ejected the mother and drove off in her Mercedes sports utility vehicle with the two small children still inside. The motorist-assistance operator was notified, and the police were able—through the operator—to track the vehicle and listen to the carjacker's mumblings. They caught him at a roadblock in Maryland.

However, these same onboard systems could be used against the owner of a vehicle, either by law enforcement or possibly by hackers, to listen in on his or her calls or other behavior. Automobiles have long been associated with a feeling of freedom and privacy. "You can talk to yourself in your car, you can scream at yourself in your car, you can go there to be alone, you can ponder the heavens, you can think deep thoughts all alone, you can sing," says Beth Givens of the Privacy Rights Clearing-house. "Now, the car is Big Brother" (Schwartz 2003, C1).

Trucking companies were among the first to use GPS to track their goods as well as their employees' behavior. Many employees did not like the constant monitoring. The sense of invasion and, some say, harassment by employers that came with GPS led the largest truckers' union in the United States to negotiate a term in its contract to prevent GPS tracking information from being used for employee discipline.

At a local television station in Washington, D.C., news reporters and camera crews were allowed to take company vehicles home so they could quickly get to the scene of a story. Since the station installed GPS devices in the vehicles, however, managers have been tracking employees to nag them about their driving habits, unscheduled stops, and use of their vehicles on days off. According to one cameraman, "You have managers who call you and say, 'Why have you stopped here, why did you stop there?' You're like, 'I had to go to the bathroom,' or 'I had to get something to eat'" (James 2003, 1).

Rental car companies have installed GPS in many cars as a convenience for their customers, to help them navigate or be located at their request in an emergency. But some have used it to catch their customers at speeding. Acme Rent-a-Car in New Haven, Connecticut, fined customers $150 each time they exceeded seventy-nine miles per hour for more than two minutes. They fined twenty-six customers and withdrew $450 from the checking account of one customer before being ordered to stop by the state for duping and overcharging customers.

Governments are getting in on the surveillance potential of GPS locators. British authorities are exploring the use of ankle bracelets with GPS devices to keep track of asylum seekers. Australian authorities are considering using GPS to keep track of prisoners released on probation—a practice that is already widespread in the United States.

Police in Olympia, Washington, installed a GPS locator with a cellular transmitter underneath the car of a suspected killer. The car led them to the body of the nine-year-old victim and proof that the suspect was in fact the killer. Although the police first secured a warrant from a neutral magistrate, the defendant appealed the validity of the warrant. The defendant argued that there was not enough evidence to constitute "probable cause" that he was involved in wrongdoing, that the police had nothing more than a hunch. The police argued that they did not even need a warrant, that using the device was the same as following someone on public roadways. The American Civil Liberties Union (ACLU) disagreed, arguing a warrant is required: "It is more the equivalent of placing an invisible police officer in the back seat of your vehicle" (Associated Press 2003). The Washington Supreme Court agreed that a warrant is necessary but also found that the police warrant in this case was valid. The court stated, "In this age, vehicles are used to take people to a vast number of places that can reveal preferences, alignments, associations, personal ails and foibles. . . . We perceive a difference between the kind of uninterrupted, 24-hour-a-day surveillance possible through use of a GPS device . . . and an officer's use of binoculars or a flashlight to augment . . . senses" (*State v. Jackson* 2003, 262).

Radio Frequency Identity Tags

Radio frequency identity, or RFID, tags are tiny microchips that emit a shortwave radio signal. They have been used for many years in all sorts of devices. For example, the antitheft tags that are attached to clothes or expensive items in a shop and make a loud sound when they pass by the detectors at the exit contain RFID chips. The electronic passes that allow drivers to zoom through toll booths are RFID technology. So too are building security passes that open gates or unlock doors. The technology behind these chips has improved, allowing the chips to get smaller and cheaper, to power themselves, and to emit their signals farther distances.

One company is selling implantable RFID chips, which are the size of a grain of rice and can be inserted under a human's skin. The chip emits a unique number, which links to a person's electronic file of information. The company is pitching the chip as a way to share medical information in case of an emergency; to provide secure access to buildings, rooms, or computers; or to identify abducted children. In 2004, the attorney general of Mexico and more than 160 of his employees had these chips inserted under their skin. The chip will serve as a security pass to a new top-secret crime database and have the additional value, according to the attorney general, of allowing him to be "found wherever I am" (Tuckman 2004). In Japan and Denmark, a few schools are requiring chips to be attached to clothing or backpacks in order to regulate who enters the school and to track students' movements (Best 2004).

Critics worry about the time coming when "getting chipped" is no longer voluntary, but required by an employer or the state. New Zealand police and transport officials have proposed putting a chip in every vehicle to automatically detect and punish speeding, illegal parking, and expired vehicle registrations.

In 2003, a group of private U.S. companies combined two technologies—known by their acronyms RFID and EPC—that, together, promise to become as common as canned food and possibly as invasive as the hidden camera. These enhanced RFID chips are being used in electronic product codes, or EPCs. EPCs are the replacement for bar codes. Bar codes are the series of lines that, when scanned by a computer scanner usually at a cash register, translate into a number. The number then brings up a registered company ID, the product code of a food or clothes item, the destination of a letter, or a person's number on his or her identity card, to name a few examples. EPCs would hold and transmit many more numbers than bar codes and, consequently, much more information about the tagged item than bar codes convey. EPCs can tell a scanner the exact serial number of the can or item being scanned, the date of expiration, where the item was produced, and much more.

A Giant Leap and a Risk for Privacy: Moving from Bar Codes to Electronic Product Codes

Bar Codes

When passed over a scanner, bar codes identify an item, company, or person. How? The scanner has a light emitter and a reader. When the scanner emits light over the bar code, the black bars absorb the light, and the white space in between the bars reflects the light into the reader. The width of each bar and white space has been matched to a number. For example, counting the thinnest width as a unit of 1, the sequence of bar widths 1-4-1-1 could be matched to the number 3. All the bars together create a long number that has been matched to a certain product, company, animal, or person listed in a database. The database contains information about the item or being, which then appears on the computer or register of the person who scanned the item. So, for example, the supermarket register determines that the bar code scanned is the number for a six-pack of Coca Cola and that number is associated with the price $2.49.

Although the idea dates back to 1949, the first item to be scanned was a ten-pack of Wrigley's chewing gum at a supermarket in Troy, Ohio, in June 1974. Today, approximately 5 billion items are scanned every day. By contacting the Uniform Code Council and European Article Numbering, International, companies may register a six-digit "manufacturer identification number" for themselves and unique numbers for their different products; these numbers will be recognized in more than ninety-nine countries.

EPC Tags

Like a bar code, an EPC tag links the being or thing that is tagged with information contained in a database. But the technology is very different from that of a bar code. With RFID, a tiny microchip contains data, including a long identifying number *unique* to the specific being or thing tagged. (In 2004, EPC chips held 94 bits of information, but technology experts anticipate further increases.) This chip is imbedded in a small tag or label that can be put on an item, person, or animal. Some chips have their own tiny batteries and are transmitting constantly, whereas others are inactive until they come into the magnetic field of a reader. A reader hooked up to a power source and containing an antenna emits a magnetic field that, within a certain range, gives power to EPC tags. The EPC microchip sends the identity number out over radio waves from a tiny, coiled antenna. When the reader's antenna receives the radio waves containing the encoded number, the reader checks it against an enormous database and retrieves the information associated with that number. So an EPC reader in a mall could activate the EPC chip on a bottle of Coke in a person's hand as he or she walked by and—even if there were a *trillion* bottles of Coca Cola in the world—know which specific bottle it is, where it was produced, when it was bottled, where it was bought, when it was bought, who the cashier was at the time, who bought it (provided the person used a discount card, credit card, or bank card), and what else that person has bought.

When combined with RFID tags, EPCs provide an easy way to identify what products are in the vicinity of a reading device. A supermarket worker can stand in an aisle, point a reading gun toward a shelf of canned vegetables, and collect precise inventory information about every item in range, without scanning each item. This same worker could walk down an aisle with his detector and discover which products have passed their expiration dates or locate items that have been recalled for health or safety reasons.

These two aspects of EPC—its ability to identify and track literally *one in a trillion* items and the ease of picking up the tag's signal—promise certain convenience for companies. But these same aspects frighten privacy advocates. EPCs raise the specter of private companies, governments, or thieves being able to find out myriad details about a person by simply setting up a receiver in a hallway, next to a sidewalk, or alongside a highway. This idea of all-knowing marketers and government who track people's every movement was captured in the movie *Minority Report* (2002), in which electronic advertisements accost Tom Cruise's character by name while he is trying to walk through a shopping mall without being noticed. There are efforts under way to address these concerns about RFID chips and debate over how to do it, including encrypting the emitted signals, "killing" the chip at the moment of purchase, creating signal blockers, and passing laws regulating their use. But these protections may be vulnerable to abuse, for example, by hackers. Or, they may be abandoned over time by companies in order to increase profits or by governments in the name of state security or law enforcement.

Cameras

When in Singapore, be careful where you throw your candy wrapper. Singapore police use video cameras to catch litterbugs and enforce traffic laws.

Private companies were the first to make regular, widespread use of camera surveillance systems for security purposes. Now, more and more, governments around the world are covering their public spaces with these paternal eyeballs to catch criminals and scare would-be wrongdoers. The use of surveillance cameras by towns and cities is becoming so common, they have been called the "fifth utility" (after water, gas, electricity, and telephones). As described in the preface, cameras are becoming part of the social and physical infrastructure—so common that they are unnoticed.

Over ten years, the United Kingdom has installed approximately 4,285,000 surveillance cameras. Many of these cameras are equipped with night vision and infrared powers. The average Londoner is taped more than 300 times a day, according to one sociologist's estimate. The London Underground is set to increase its number of platform cameras from 6,000 to 9,000 by 2005 and to start installing cameras on subway cars. France already has 2,000 cameras on city buses.

The United States has 2 million camera surveillance systems, according to an industry estimate. In downtown Chicago, there are an average of 3 cameras per block. In New York City, the average person is recorded 73 to 75 times a day, according to another industry estimate from 2000. To catch illegal immigrants along one part of the U.S.-Mexico border, the United States is installing 60-foot poles at every mile with four high-tech cameras on each pole, at a price of $300,000 per pole.

More and more, these recorded images do not go away. According to the CEO of a leading camera manufacturer, "People want images stored in a huge storage file so that if anything is discovered later they can go back and see what happened" (Murphy 2002, 1).

Proponents argue that the cameras deter crime and terrorism. But critics contend that the cameras are a public relations gimmick. They cite the fact that, even in the most optimistic studies, cameras merely move crime to areas just outside of view. Some studies have even found an increase in crime in monitored areas. Others show that better lighting is more effective in reducing crime than surveillance cameras.

At the cutting edge, these cameras are tiny, wireless, digital, and connected to other computers over the Internet. The cameras can record images and send them through the air to a Web site or computer terminal. The images can then be viewed and stored.

Some new systems detect unusual or suspect patterns of movement or stillness. For example, underwater cameras at a pool in France detected a drowning swimmer and alerted lifeguards who saved his life. In London, software being tested in the London Underground automatically alerts police when someone in the camera's eye has been lingering in one area "too long."

Although convenient and, in many cases, quite helpful, these latest camera technologies pose greater risks to privacy. They increase the chances that people will abuse the cameras, for example, to peep on people undressing in a locker room. In December 2003, at Sutherland High School in upstate New York, school officials discovered a hidden camera in the women's bathroom; the school's chief custodian was charged with taping at least twelve students and staff members.

These camera technologies also increase the chances of unauthorized people intercepting the images. Moreover, digital storage increases the odds of images falling into the wrong hands. Companies and individuals often replace computers without erasing the information on them, and it is notoriously difficult to completely erase everything on a computer.

Critics also worry about the tendency for cameras installed for one purpose to be used for another. In particular, civil libertarians worry that the rights to free speech and assembly will be undermined by video surveillance.

Indeed, there is evidence that the sorts of political surveillance that Senator Church decried in 1976 may be starting anew in the United States. In 2002, U.S. attorney general John Ashcroft relaxed rules limiting the FBI's surveillance of domestic political activities, allowing agents to conduct surveillance at rallies, religious services, and other public events. In 2003, Ashcroft took "the final step in tearing down the legal wall that had separated criminal and intelligence investigations since the spying scandals of the 1970s," according to the *Washington Post* (Eggen 2003, A1).

In November 2003, the *New York Times* revealed a secret FBI memo sent to 15,000 local police departments advising them to monitor "indicators of protest activity" and report "any potentially illegal" activity to joint counterterrorism squads. The memo was sent just before major protests of the U.S. war in Iraq. In San Francisco, undercover police dressed as protesters marched in demonstrations and videotaped antiwar paraders. Following earlier protests against the war in Iraq, the New York Police Department questioned antiwar protesters it had arrested about their political activities and affiliations. And at the University of Massachusetts, a campus security guard was recruited by the FBI to work part time for its Anti-Terrorism Task Force, following FBI questioning of an Iraqi-American professor and a Sri Lankan student and union organizer at the school. The ACLU's executive director worries, "What the F.B.I. regards as 'potential terrorism' strikes me as civil disobedience" (Lichtblau 2003, 1).

Great Britain experienced the challenge of fighting terrorism "at home" in Northern Ireland, using covert intelligence operations while trying to respect the rule of law. In 2003, it was revealed that long-held suspicions that an elite British antiterrorism unit operating in complete secrecy helped murder people it was meant to be monitoring were true.

Case in Point: The Risk of Secret, Domestic Antiterrorism Operations

Members of the British Army's Force Services Unit and the local police department's Special Branch "were allowed to operate without effective control and to participate in terrorist crimes," according to a fourteen-year investigation by London police commissioner Sir John Stevens released in 2003. The British units were established to monitor and disrupt terrorist groups that want the province of Northern Ireland to be free from Great Britain and part of the Republic of Ireland. Instead, these intelligence units illegally passed the names of the people they were tracking to their enemies, knowing the rival groups would target them for murder. Indeed, some were murdered, and the British units took no action to prevent the murders. Some of the victims, including defense attorney Patrick Finucane, were innocent of any involvement in terrorist activities.

> The Northern Ireland murders are an extreme example of how things can go wrong when the lines among intelligence operations, military operations, and domestic law enforcement become unclear or are erased. Both spying and warmaking are based on complete secrecy, extreme force, and few rules. Law enforcement in a democratic state subject to the rule of law is not.

In the United States, the rules separating intelligence operations from law enforcement have been all but erased. But the 125-year-old rule restricting the U.S. military still stands, for the time being. The Posse Comitatus Act of 1878 prohibits the use of the U.S. Army for domestic law enforcement (that is, deputizing the army as a posse) except as specifically authorized by Congress or the Constitution (18 U.S.C. § 1385). Other branches of the military are similarly prohibited (10 U.S.C. § 375).

That may change. In 2004, for the first time, unmanned military robot planes were deployed to patrol the Arizona border between the United States and Mexico. The Israeli-made Hermes 450 aerial drones can detect movement fifteen miles away and carry high-tech cameras that can transmit live video even in the dark of night (Reuters 2004). A U.S. senator from Virginia has proposed using unmanned aircraft with cameras—currently used only by the military—for domestic law enforcement. And when John Allen Muhammad, age forty-one, and John Lee Malvo, seventeen, terrorized the Washington, D.C., area in 2002, killing twelve people and wounding several more with a sniper rifle over a seven-week period, the Pentagon loaned military spy planes and pilots to the search efforts of the FBI and local law enforcement. The RC-7 military spy plane uses high-powered cameras, infrared cameras, and voice recorders. With its slow speed and high altitude, the plane can do the work of several police helicopters. If focused on the correct area, the thermal cameras can even detect the flash of a muzzle. The direct involvement of the military in this domestic law enforcement operation was unprecedented.

More recently, New York's *Newsday* reported, "The horizon someday may be lined with giant floating orbs guarding people below from the enemy." High-altitude blimps are under development as an alternative to unmanned spy planes and satellites. They would be far cheaper and easier to repair than satellites and could be used for equally good surveillance (Minor 2004). The *Washington Post* reported that the U.S. Army is testing a high-tech surveillance blimp over Maryland and the District of Columbia. If the new onboard surveillance technology works well, the Department of Homeland Security may employ the blimp to monitor the U.S. border. A spokesperson for the company American Blimp said a study found that "universally, blimps give people a big warm fuzzy. People just like blimps" (Morello 2004, B1). Civil liberties advocates worry that warm, fuzzy feeling may be exploited to further erode the Posse Comitatus Act or create a regular aerial surveillance system.

Traffic Cameras

Cameras that monitor traffic—some for the convenience of commuters, some to enforce traffic laws for the police—watch over an increasing number of roads and intersections around the world.

In the United States, at the end of 2003, cameras sat atop traffic lights photographing violators in more than eighty cities. Typically, the cameras activate when vehicles pass over an underground sensor while the light is red. The camera captures the license plate number, and a bureaucrat sends a ticket in the mail to the vehicle's registered owner.

In France, the minister of transportation, Gilles de Robien, and the minister of the interior, Nicolas Sarkozy, were caught in their own speed trap. France installed automatic radar detectors that measure a vehicle's speed and photograph offenders going a certain amount above the limit. In late 2003, the ministers were driving—each in his own car—to the grand unveiling of the new system when they were photographed going well above the speed limit.

Britain and Germany are planning to use cameras with the ability to recognize letters and numerals on its roadways. The cameras will scan license plates of passing vehicles and check the numbers against a database of wanted criminals and "suspicious" people.

Proponents of the cameras argue that they save lives and eliminate any unfair subjectivity in traffic enforcement. Critics do not like the idea of being watched so extensively. They also worry about the temptation for governments and companies to raise money by putting cameras everywhere. Whether intentionally or by malfunction, there is also the risk that minor changes in the timing and calibration of the detectors could haul in a large number of additional fines from people who would otherwise not be committing traffic violations.

Facial-Recognition Cameras

Facial-recognition cameras are meant to pick people out of a crowd—people whom law enforcement officials have put in a database or on a watch list. The software takes the camera-captured image of a face and matches the geometry of its features to the face of the suspect in an image database. These systems have the potential to detect persons in disguises, since—unless a person has cosmetic surgery—certain facial features are unlikely to change. For instance, the software might measure the distance between a person's pupils and the width of his or her chin. For the time being, these cameras are facing technical hurdles.

In the United States, these technical problems have limited the adoption of facial-recognition systems. Three sites tried recognition systems and abandoned them, because of their unreliability. Boston's Logan Airport loaded the faces of volunteers into its system to see how well the cameras could pick them out of a crowd: the cameras succeeded 153 times but failed 96 times. A 2002 U.S. Department of Defense study found success rates as low as 20 percent.

Another problem has been the lack of facial measurements in the database. In other words, there is not yet enough "biometric data" on criminals and suspicious people against which to check passersby. To address this problem, governments have started using three-dimensional cameras or collecting high-quality photographs of citizens and criminals. The state of West Virginia is taking biometric data when drivers get their licenses.

Nonetheless, technology is constantly advancing, and, soon, unreliability may not be an argument against the systems' widespread adoption. The U.S. military's Biometrics Management Office is working with hundreds of companies to improve facial recognition. According to a Ph.D. candidate in engineering who is working on new software, society will be better served "if we are technically capable of insuring no one can get through a security gate unless the person has plastic surgery" (Newswise 2003). But these cameras are not only being used at secure perimeter gates. In Virginia Beach, they are being used to monitor and find people walking down the street or boardwalk.

Ultimately, the public must answer the following questions:

1. Does this method of law enforcement provide enough value to compensate for the erosion of the comfort and enjoyment of walking anonymously down a street?
2. Are there accountability mechanisms in place to prevent and correct abuse of recognition systems and *mission creep*? For example, are police putting minor offenders— one-time pot smokers or a person wanted for too many parking tickets—on the watch list? Can the system quickly correct for people who are wrongly identified or wrongly put on the watch list?

Thermal-Imaging Cameras (Infrared)

Thermal-imaging cameras detect energy waves below the visible light spectrum—what humans cannot see but experience as degrees of heat. Human eyes can see only when there is a light source, but any object that has a temperature greater than zero degrees Kelvin gives off energy waves. Thermal-imaging cameras receive these waves and convert them to a visible image. In other words, these cameras let you see the heat given off by an object or person.

Thermal cameras allow police officers to find human bodies in pitch-black darkness. They allow firefighters to see a baby through impenetrable, billowing smoke. In Sacramento, California, officers flying above the city in a police helicopter were testing a new forward-looking infrared camera when they spotted a bank robbery in progress. Police on the ground caught the robber. That department has since acquired the ability to broadcast the camera images—regular and infrared—to screens in squad cars on the ground.

Presently, thermal imagers cannot see *through* walls or other hard or thick objects, but they can detect the amount of heat they carry. So, for instance, when antinarcotics agents wanted to determine whether Danny Kyllo was growing marijuana using special heat lamps in his home in Oregon, they focused a thermal imager on parts of his house. They found that the garage roof and side wall of his house were hotter than the rest of the house and hotter than the neighbors' houses. Based on this information, as well as informant tips and electricity bills, federal agents secured a search warrant and found heat lamps. Kyllo appealed his conviction, arguing that the use of the thermal imagers was illegal. In an important victory for privacy rights, the U.S. Supreme Court held that the agents' use of the thermal imager constituted a search and therefore required a warrant. The Court's decision in *Kyllo v. United States* (2001) is likely to apply not only to thermal imaging but also to other technologies that can invade private spaces—for instance, high-tech microphones that can hear through walls and through-wall motion detectors.

Justice Scalia signaled the far reach of its decision, stating, "It would be foolish to contend that the degree of privacy secured to citizens by the Fourth Amendment has been entirely unaffected by the advance of technology. For example, . . . the technology enabling human flight has exposed to public view (and hence, we have said, to official observation) uncovered portions of the house and its curtilage that once were private . . . The question we confront today is what limits there are upon this power of technology to shrink the realm of guaranteed privacy" (33–34).

Although Justice Scalia's opinion constituted an important victory for privacy rights, especially the right to protection of the home from technological intrusions, the decision also contained an important exception. "We think that obtaining by sense-enhancing technology any information regarding the interior of the home that could not otherwise have been obtained without physical 'intrusion into a constitutionally protected area,' . . . constitutes a search—at least where (as here) the technology in question is not in general public use" (34).

Should peoples' privacy in their home depend on whether a particular technology is "in general public use"? If everyone gets thermal imaging cameras, does that make it okay to use them to "look" into the homes of others? How is this formulation different than other Supreme Court opinions that protect privacy rights only when there is a reasonable expectation of privacy?

The dissent in *Kyllo* raised similar questions. Scalia responds that the Court is bound by precedent that says, for instance, it is unreasonable to expect one's backyard not to be observed from the air when private and commercial flight is routine. Nonetheless, Scalia's opinion introduces a reformulation of the "reasonable expectation" test that is likely to be important in future cases of privacy-invading technologies.

X-Ray and Through-the-Wall Technologies

Other technologies, some still in their infancy, allow officials to "see" through walls or people's clothing. Like radar technology from World War II, some of these devices send out radio waves that bounce off an object and come back, providing information about distance and change in position to the viewer. Others rely on x-ray scanning technology based on that used by doctors since 1885.

Many airports are abandoning metal detectors in favor of a new generation of scanners that electronically undress travelers, revealing metal, wood, and plastic objects under their clothes. Some of these scanners—such as the Secure 1000 by Rapiscan—run a narrow, low-energy x-ray beam over a person and then detect the different kinds of scattered waves that are reflected back. A computer program assembles these signals into recognizable images. Although the amount of exposure is set low so as to not go beneath the skin, travelers may be reluctant to expose themselves to x-rays, which damage cells and, in large amounts, cause cancer. Other systems use millimeter waves—which are not as damaging—to produce similarly revealing images. Both devices produce a close-to-nude image of the person being scanned. Naturally, many people are not happy about exposing their naked selves to whomever is behind the security monitor. Companies are working on software that will blur out private body parts.

Similar technology is being used to see through trucks, shipping containers, and walls. Billboard-size gamma-ray scanners take x-ray pictures of trucks on the border between Mexico and Guatemala, revealing undocumented immigrants, drugs, and weapons. Passive millimeter-wave imagers scan passing containers in the Channel Tunnel between Great Britain and France.

Soldiers and law enforcement officers now have the ability to detect movement—even the slightest twitches—on the other

Table 2.2
Camera Surveillance Debating Points

Pro Camera Surveillance	Anti Camera Surveillance
Cameras promote public safety and protect people's right to life, liberty, and security.	Being watched and recorded is disquieting in and of itself; the implicit threat of police action if you step out of line makes it difficult to enjoy one's liberty.
Any sense a person may have that his privacy is being violated by cameras should be outweighed by the sense of security he receives from knowing the cameras help protect his physical safety.	The growth of camera surveillance systems promotes a surveillance state with totalitarian characteristics. A free society entrusts its citizens with freedom of movement, choice, and self-reliance. A surveillance state impinges this freedom and reduces the autonomy and self-reliance of its citizens.
Once a person leaves her house, she volunteers to be in public and be seen. She has given up her privacy, so watching or recording her on camera is not a violation of privacy.	Camera surveillance systems give police and citizens a false sense of security. They have not been proven to deter crime, and they discourage vigilance and assistance by fellow citizens.
Cameras serve as deterrents. Even when the camera is not being monitored or is not recording, it looks like it is and therefore will deter wrongdoers.	Camera surveillance in the public square coerces people to choose between losing their privacy and staying in their homes.
Camera recordings can help police prosecute crimes that might not otherwise be solved or even detected.	Camera systems can be abused by authorities or by hackers, subjecting victims to worse invasions of privacy.
Camera systems can catch officials, including police, abusing their authority and thereby promote accountability.	Ever "smarter" camera systems are more invasive than cameras that merely watch or record. They connect to databases of information about a person—compounding the invasion of privacy and risk of abuse.

side of concrete walls. Two through-the-wall cameras—handheld SoldierVision and briefcase-size RadarVision—send out millimeter waves accompanied by simultaneously dispatched marking waves. These precisely "labeled" pulses pass through walls and bounce back when they hit objects on the other side. When a second pulse shows a change in position of the mass on the other side, the viewer reveals the movement on a viewing screen. The image appears as a somewhat undefined blob of light, but it is enough to give an accurate idea of the size and movement of the object or person. RadarVision is available to law enforcement agencies for $29,000 per machine. It can detect through-wall motion at distances up to thirty feet.

Although we do not yet have the ability to see clear images through walls, such technology seems likely to arrive, and with it the unprecedented capacity to look into private spaces—for good or bad.

Collecting Personal Data

Since the first censuses in ancient Rome and Israel, governments have collected personal information about their people. Today, more information than ever is being collected by both governments and private industry. Increasingly, those sources of information are aggregated or linked to one another so that users can have quick access to more complete information. This trend is likely to bring increased efficiency. But without protections, it is certain to bring invasions of privacy. The first risk is that other people will know more information about you than you prefer or permit. The second risk is that this information will be used against you.

DNA Databases

John Athan received a letter from a law firm saying he was eligible for a monetary award in a lawsuit over improper parking tickets. He filled out the form, put it in the return envelope, licked the envelope, and dropped it in the mail. Soon after, he was arrested for the murder of a thirteen-year-old girl. There was no law firm or lawsuit over parking tickets; the letter had been a ruse by police detectives who suspected him of the murder but needed a sample of his DNA to check against evidence at the scene of the crime. The suspect's mere licking of the envelope provided the police with what they needed. Tiny beads of saliva left "genetic material" on the envelope that forensic experts were able to collect and test.

DNA has helped identify guilty criminals, the wrongly convicted, the Vietnam War casualty in the Tomb of the Unknown

Soldier, a president of the United States caught in a lie, and the descendants of Thomas Jefferson and his slave and likely mistress, Sally Hemmings.

DNA (deoxyribonucleic acid) is the set of molecules that make up the genes of living things. The pattern of DNA in a gene determines many characteristics in living things and, consequently, can be used to identify a species, biologically related family member, or individual. In humans, the vast majority of DNA is the same from human to human, but a tiny amount (some say as little as 0.1 percent) is unique to each individual.

Developed in the United Kingdom in the mid-1980s, DNA profiling takes genetic material found at a crime scene (blood, saliva, semen, hairs, sweat, or skin cells) and tries to match its DNA code with that of known suspects or a database of individuals' genetic codes. If there is a match, it is strong evidence that the person was at the crime scene. Of course, being at the scene is not *by itself* proof that a person committed the crime. As one crime scene analyst explains, "You have to be able to place the suspect at the scene, place the victim at the scene and place the suspect and victim in contact. If you can't make the triangle fit, you'll have a hard time explaining the crime" (Langbein 2002, 1A). The accuracy of DNA matching has increased significantly since the 1980s, and it has become possible to use smaller and smaller bits of genetic material, including drops of saliva on the back of a postage stamp or the root of a hair. For these reasons, "genetic fingerprinting" is rapidly replacing its predecessors—fingerprinting, blood-typing, and hair analysis—that are more difficult to find and match and are less unique identifiers.

The United Kingdom has the largest database of DNA files of any country, and police are asking for more. In 2003, the British police proposed the establishment of a database containing the DNA of every resident in the country, not just convicts and arrestees.

The international police agency Interpol found that forty-one countries had DNA databases in 2002. The number of countries is growing rapidly, and the uses and size of databases in these countries are expanding. For example, the fifty U.S. states first adopted laws to collect DNA samples from convicted sex offenders only. By 2003, twenty-eight states expanded their collection of DNA to other types of convicted felons, Louisiana passed a law to collect DNA from people once they are arrested, and Utah began collecting DNA from persons found to have immigration violations. In China, it is expected that national ID cards will contain DNA identifiers. Having a larger database of DNA will allow law enforcement agencies to match more crime suspects.

There is no doubt DNA profiling is a powerful tool for law enforcement. However, DNA reveals more than identity. It also reveals one's genetic disposition for inherited diseases and abnormalities. It reveals how an individual is likely to respond to drug therapies or environmental agents, including bacteria, viruses, and chemicals. For example, in 2003, scientists discovered an abnormal DNA pattern in a gene that makes people twice as likely to develop depression after a traumatic incident. Many people (57 percent) who had the abnormal gene did not develop depression, and some people (17 percent) with a normal gene did develop depression under similar stress. The study shows both the power of DNA analysis and its ability to lead to unfair presumptions. If you were on the board of a multinational company, would you hire a CEO who had the normal gene over one who had the abnormal gene? The genetic test might incline you to favor a candidate who is not "predisposed" to depression in the face of stress, even though it is likely the candidate with the abnormal gene might never have such a problem. What if DNA analysis can one day reveal information related to some measure of intelligence? Will parents, schools, and employers change their treatment of a child based on this shorthand "predisposition," rather than looking at environmental factors that also affect intelligence or a child's actual performance, passion, diligence, drive, and creativity? Will elite universities select students based on genetic test scores rather than academic ones?

DNA research is allowing scientists not only to identify but soon, it is expected, to prevent, treat, and cure certain diseases and problems as well. For this reason, and despite the risks of abuse, several nations have begun to collect massive nationwide DNA databases and share them with private companies. Iceland has a database with DNA from approximately 90 percent of its citizens. It gave access to the database to a private company for medical research and drug development in exchange for free services resulting from the research. Estonia has a similarly broad database. The United Kingdom and Sweden have smaller ones.

Privacy advocates fear the growth of DNA databases for several reasons:

- Genetic material can be collected without consent. Even if a person is not suspected, arrested, or convicted of a crime, it would be possible for a government or a company to collect DNA information from individuals without their consent through the saliva used to lick the back of an envelope, hairs left behind, or myriad other ways.
- Genetic material can be stored indefinitely and tested repeatedly, so it is not entirely reassuring that presently such material is kept by law enforcement labs or even that the present owners observe certain privacy practices.
- Deeply personal information about a person may be revealed that he or she does not want to know or does not want others to know. For instance, if your father carries a gene for an incurable disease, you may not want to know that you too might be predisposed to the disease.
- The deeply personal information in these databases might be abused by law enforcement or lab employees.
- New laws might be enacted to permit law enforcement to make broader use of DNA. For instance, if a national database allows the police to locate a family member of someone suspected of criminal activity based on DNA evidence, the police might investigate, monitor, and harass the family member as leverage against the suspect. (For years and as recently as 2004, Nigerian police have placed relatives and friends of suspects in detention to persuade the suspects to turn themselves in.) Even without official mission creep, the protections limiting access to these databases might malfunction or be infiltrated.
- Unauthorized individuals or companies might get access to valuable genetic information and use it to make decisions that harm or discriminate against the owner. For instance, health or life insurance companies might charge a person more based on their genetic predispositions. Employers might discriminate against applicants based on their DNA.

Chapter 3 discusses other aspects of the privacy implications of DNA identification and gene research and therapy.

Carnivore

In July 2000, the *Wall Street Journal* revealed that the FBI was using a high-powered program to monitor e-mail (King and Bridis 2000, A3). The FBI named the system Carnivore. Carnivore is installed by the FBI in the offices of an Internet service provider (ISP)—the companies that provide connections to the Internet, e-mail accounts, and other online services. Carnivore reads the headings of all of the e-mail messages being sent and received by users of that ISP. It then captures the contents of e-mails that fit the FBI's search criteria, as well as the addresses of all the Web sites that those users visit. The U.S. example has been followed by other countries, including China, India, Norway, and South Korea. China is expected to use the system to monitor and suppress dissent.

The FBI promises that the search criteria are tailored to capture only information of suspected criminals as authorized by a court order. In other words, according to the FBI, Carnivore sifts through everyone's information, but spits out only the information that the FBI is authorized to see.

However, there is some evidence that the FBI has not been able to keep its promise. An internal FBI memo written in 2000 revealed a major blunder by its Carnivore team. While tracking "targets" suspected of helping the terrorist group al Qaeda, the FBI accidentally misprogrammed the Carnivore system at one ISP and captured the e-mails of innocent civilians. An FBI technician then overreacted, throwing out all of the intercepted communications, including those of the al Qaeda suspects. The memo stated the incident was not an isolated one but one example in a "pattern" showing "an inability on the part of the FBI to manage" its surveillance (FBI 2000, 1).

It is impossible for citizens and the public to know how widespread the abuse of Carnivore is—and whether it is intentional or accidental—because the FBI will not say. The FBI has denied requests to reveal what searches have been conducted because, it states, they involve national security. It is uncontested that Carnivore technology gives the FBI the power to search and capture much more than what is authorized. With such a powerful tool—and knowing that, historically, power that goes unchecked tends to be abused—privacy advocates are reluctant to trust the FBI's promises by themselves. These advocates want the Carnivore system to be abandoned or, at the least, to create some independent oversight of the FBI's surveillance activities.

"Total Information": Government Data Merging for Efficiency, Prediction, ... and Control?

In the first years of the 2000 millennium, many government offices—even those in technologically advanced countries—remained surprisingly low tech. Certainly, most offices had computers, a network, and a connection to the Internet. But many still had old database programs and no way to integrate data with, say, the neighboring agency or city. Following the September 2001 attacks, efforts to upgrade and integrate technologies took on new urgency, whether in response to actual or imaginary needs for increased surveillance and security.

By 2004, local police departments throughout the United States were finally unveiling upgraded systems that could communicate with crime databases in a greater number of jurisdictions. Sifting software was being employed to make sense of the ever increasing amount of data. In Boston, for example, the police adopted software that scanned existing criminal records to look for connections between people or incidents—such as a specific firearm, residence, or financial agent—that might merit investigation. Localities began experimenting with ways to give police officers in the field wireless access to information networks, eliminating the need for someone at headquarters to access the information and relay it. And agencies with seemingly unrelated mandates—health departments and tax collection agencies, law enforcement and work-training offices—were making information about individuals available to one another.

Although upgrades and integration were long overdue in certain sectors, such as among law enforcement databases, other initiatives seemed to be based on weak, unexamined premises, namely:

1. There is a lot of information being collected about individuals.
2. New technology makes it possible to store and share all of this information.
3. It is better to have more information than less.

In their enthusiasm for data merging, governments ignored an old warning. As the U.S. Privacy Protection Study Commission put it in 1977, the gradual erosion of individual liberties is likely to come "through the automation, integration and interconnection of many small, separate record-keeping systems, each of which alone may seem innocuous, even benevolent, and wholly justifiable" (App. 4, 108).

In 2002, the U.S. government revealed the most ambitious and controversial program yet to collect and merge data on individuals. The ominous-sounding "Total Information Awareness" office planned to merge data from government sources with data from private companies and then sift these data to ferret out supposed indicators of terrorism. According to Director John Poindexter, the project's hypothesis was that terrorists "make transactions in support of their plans and activities, and those transactions leave a signature in the information space . . . The only way to detect [terrorist sleeper cells imbedded in free societies] is by looking for patterns of specific activities that have proven in the past or estimated for the future to be indicative of terrorist planning" (2003). But as Marc Rottenberg of the Electronic Privacy Information Center (EPIC) put it, "It is easy to construct a device that can determine whether a person is carrying a gun before he boards an airplane. It is much more difficult to construct a device that can probe his thoughts and determine his intent to commit a crime" (2003, 6).

More than any prior governmental initiative in decades, Total Information Awareness spurred a quick, popular backlash and raised the specter of government as "Big Brother"—a government that seeks to control its citizens by knowing every detail about their lives and actions, purporting to watch out for their best interests by constantly watching them. Despite the Bush administration changing the name of the project to Terrorism Information Awareness, Congress suspended funding for the effort. But the administration moved the office's projects to other agencies and supported state-based efforts to replicate the total information approach. With funding from the U.S. Department of Homeland Security, eight U.S. states began testing the total information Multistate Anti-Terrorism Information Exchange (MATRIX). The federal funding has some strings attached; in its contract with the program's manufacturer, the department included a provision saying it "would maintain managerial oversight and control" of the program (ACLU 2004).

The system's manufacturer argues, "It is a powerful system. Not scary, not frightening, but much more efficient . . . This stuff we have is nothing more than what law enforcement has had access to for decades" (Oliveri 2003). For some, however, there is in fact something frightening about such comprehensive efficiency. Taken to the extreme, it could be argued that anything anyone has ever said or done that reaches outside the shuttered privacy of one's abode is in some sense public, but who would like each of those statements or actions collected in one place for another to examine? Total information databases are not so far-reaching as that, but they are the greatest technological step in that direction in history. The prospect of law enforcement using such data to predict who will commit criminal or terrorist acts also frightens privacy advocates. The fear is that data of innocent behavior will be aggregated and characterized as suspicious, resulting in aggressive police interference in people's private lives.

Meanwhile, the United States pursued large-scale data-mining projects on people in other countries as well. In 2003, it was revealed that the United States purchased access to a private company's database containing information on 65 million Mexicans and citizens of nine other Latin American countries. However, when Mexico complained that the information might have been attained illegally from Mexico's electronic voting files, the private company shut down the list.

In June 1995, it was revealed that the U.S. Department of Denfense is working with a private company to collect data on all sixteen- to eighteen-year-olds and college students to help bolster the military's recruiting efforts. The data includes social security numbers, e-mail addresses, class subjects, grade-point averages, and ethnicity. Under the 2002 No Child Left Behind Act, schools could lose federal funding if they do not provide the federal government with student data.

"Audience Targeting": Merging for Marketing, Convenience, and Electioneering

In part, governments were merely following the lead of the private sector, which had become prodigious collectors of information about customers in the late 1990s and early years of the millennium. An information collection industry had sprung up—calling itself Customer Relations Management (CRM)—that integrated and centralized far-flung pieces of information about a person. CRM companies aggregate personal information from Internet purchases, credit card purchases, supermarket savings card purchases, credit reports, census records, product registration information, driving records, property records, survey information, sweepstakes entries, magazine subscriptions, and more. CRM companies sell these data to other companies who wish to target advertising to segments of the population or to study consumer behavior. Some companies sell these data to individual purchasers over the Internet.

In 2000, Internet advertising company DoubleClick raised the ire of Web surfers. DoubleClick provides targeted advertising on the Internet by tracking the sites that Internet users visit. The premise of this profiling is that, for example, if a person visited a camping Web site, an online canoe store, and a mapping Web site, he or she would be more receptive to an advertisement for tents than for curling irons. Online advertisers can track where a person has been by the cookies (tiny files) that Web sites drop into the user's computer; the user can limit or delete cookies from the computer. Web sites and advertisers can also track a user by collecting the electronic footprints left by the computer's unique Internet protocol address when the user accesses the site; a user cannot detect or control this type of tracking. Without users knowing, Double-Click collected profiles on 100 million users based on their Internet travels. For many years, advertisers like DoubleClick rebutted privacy concerns by saying that the profiles, although unique to individuals, were not connected with any personally identifiable information, such as name, address, phone number, income level, survey answers, and other *offline* data. In other words, it could detect the online movements of some individual, but it did not know who that individual was. However, in 2000, DoubleClick purchased a huge offline profiling company and revealed plans to merge the online and offline data, such that it would be able to track the online journey of any Jane Q. Smith and also know what she bought at the grocery store that week. Web users were furious, and the storm of (mostly online) protest led government officials to investigate and other companies to back away from DoubleClick. The company soon abandoned its planned merger of online and offline data and eventually scrapped the profile building of its so-called intelligent targeting service. In addition to the privacy concerns, DoubleClick found that the service was not cost effective. According to one advertising analyst, "The lift you get from that kind of profiling just isn't enough to pay all that extra data storage and process costs" (Olsen 2002).

Yet the temptation to be all-knowing is powerful, and, in 2004, DoubleClick and other companies sought to reenter the data-merging business on a more limited scale. Rather than building profiles on users traveling anywhere on the Internet where a DoubleClick ad appears, the new plan limits the use of merged online and offline profiles to the Web sites of a particular company and its affiliates. One of the companies, Weather.com, is affiliated to many sites that use its weather forecasts in a corner of the site; visits to these sites will be tracked as well. Other companies will limit the type of offline information that is used to name, age, sex, address, and magazine subscriptions. Nonetheless, this foot-in-the-door merging may be a precursor to more expansive merging and tracking.

During the first six months of 2005, it is estimated that 50 million electronic accounts were breached. In July, a hacker broke into the security system of CardSystems Solutions, gaining access to as many as 40 million credit card accounts. That same month, Citigroup lost computer tapes containing data on 3.9 million customers. Meanwhile, numerous other corporations have moved large amounts of deeply personal or sensitive information onto Internet-accessible databases, from health insurance companies and banks to schools and credit agencies. Protected by little more than a user name and password, these data mines make countless users vulnerable to identity theft or other privacy violations by errant employees, technological malfunctions, or other nefarious actors. This trend toward putting everything online poses a threat not only to the security of individuals' personal and financial information but also to national financial security. In 2004, the U.S. Federal Reserve began transferring the nation's largest financial transactions among the Reserve, other agencies, banks, and financial institutions over the Internet, rather than a stand-alone network it used previously. Security experts worry that, despite the extreme security precautions taken by the Reserve, the nation's financial system is at greater risk to hacking or terrorism (Kramer 2004).

In the United States, political-campaign machines have adopted the practices—and purchased the data—of advertising companies. The two major political parties have each developed their own databasing and profiling systems and fed it with CRM data. Both parties insist they do not keep consumer behavior data, because brand preferences do not reveal much about politics (Farhi 2004). Rather, these databases track political preferences, feelings on various issues, and other "psychographic" data, including hints about a person's sexual orientation (Benson 2003).

Winning first place for scariest name, the Democratic National Committee (DNC) calls one of its two programs Demzilla, which is described by its programmer as an "Internet based database of voters and donors with state-of-the-art marketing and analysis capabilities." Demzilla and its larger counterpart Data Mart contain files on 166 million Americans. The Republicans' Voter Vault contains files on 165 million Americans. The DNC chair praised Demzilla's "far-reaching, aggressive technology that will allow Democrats to get out the message and the vote in 2004, sending us to victory" (Plus Three 2003). But others worry, not only about the intrusiveness of such information but also about its effect on the political process. "Democracy suffers when you tailor your message 12 different ways depending on who you want to reach out to," said Beth Givens, director of the Privacy Rights Clearinghouse (Benson 2003). Moreover, it may be unrealistic to expect elected representatives to protect your privacy from government or corporate intrusion when they owe their election to a form of total information databasing.

Presently, in the United States, voter registration lists are available to the public and can be resold by private companies. Only twenty-two states restrict who may purchase the lists and how they may be used, and it appears these laws are not enforced by either governments or resellers. A reporter for *Wired News* purchased information about 1,700 California and 900 South Carolina voters using the aliases Condoleezza Rice and Britney Spears; with his unverified purchase, he received mislabeled regulations concerning California's restrictions. One South Carolina voter said, "If I knew this, I would never have registered. This is very disappointing, and I'm very disappointed in the system" (Zetter 2003).

Airline Travel and Databasing

International air travel grew from fewer than 100 million passengers worldwide in 1970 to more than 600 million passengers in 2000. Within the United States, another 638 million passengers flew. During this time, airline travelers have been targets of terrorist hijackings, and, consequently, airline passengers have been the subject of screenings and searches by airline and government employees. Following the most devastating hijackings ever on September 11, 2001, governments around the world sought to increase the thoroughness of passenger screening.

The United States, in particular, took severe measures to enhance security, even pressuring luggage and lock manufacturers to sell baggage locks that air transportation officials could routinely open without busting the lock or bag.

The United States is testing backscatter x-ray machines, which produce a near naked image of the person scanned, including an image of any hard metal or plastic objects being carried under clothing, as replacements for metal detectors. "It does basically make you look fat and naked, but you see all this stuff," said an official with the Transportation Security Administration (TSA) (Miller 2003).

The United States also started a controversial program called U.S. Visitor and Immigrant Status Indicator Technology (VISIT), which takes the photograph and digital fingerprint of every foreigner arriving in the United States with a visa. The program's intent is to check fingerprints against FBI databases of dangerous and wanted people, but the referenced databases consist primarily of illegal aliens and conventional criminals. The VISIT program also aims to build a massive database of fingerprints of foreigners and to habituate travelers to having their fingerprints checked for authenticity. Along with biometric passports, the United States hopes digital fingerprinting will become part of international practice. The effort has perturbed many foreigners. In 2004, the Brazilian government retaliated by requiring the same screening for U.S. travelers arriving in Brazil. Critics contend that the referenced database does not contain terrorists' fingerprints and, therefore, serves only to alienate tourists and distract from more effective terrorism-fighting strategies.

Computer Assisted Passenger Pre-Screening System (CAPPS) II, based on the data merging and profiling of Total Information Awareness, was set for release in 2004. The program analyzes information from law enforcement and private databases to come up with a potential threat level for each passenger. Passengers with higher threat levels would be subject to more intensive scrutiny. However, in September 2003, passengers were upset when they learned that airline JetBlue shared information about 5 million passenger itineraries with a government contractor, which merged the data with income levels, social security numbers, and other information to test CAPPS II. Congress suspended funding for the program until a report could be issued that satisfactorily addressed erroneous threat identifications, due-process procedures, and safeguards against abuse. When the report came out in 2004, it was apparent that CAPPS II presented too many insurmountable problems. In July 2004, the Bush administration announced that it was scuttling the program. However, subsequent statements reveal that a similar program is being pursued in its place, and government contractor Lockheed Martin continues to work with the U.S. Transportation Security Administration under a $12.8 billion contract for CAPPS II. The new program focuses more on checking all passengers against an expanded watch list (or "no-fly list") of terrorism suspects (Matthews 2004).

The European Union, ordinarily quite strong on data privacy, succumbed to pressure from the United States to share data on airline passengers. Around Christmas 2003, several flights were aborted based on possible security threats stemming from shared data. These threats did not materialize, and no one was arrested. The *Los Angeles Times* reported, "Despite the application of the most advanced technology, experts warn that would-be terrorists could likely foil the security system protecting air travel in the United States. Meanwhile, tens of thousands of innocent passengers would be flagged by such a system and subjected to searches while the commercial and government records of millions of passengers would be combed for suspicious activity" (Piller and Alonso-Zaldivar 2003, A1).

No-Fly Lists

No-fly lists have proved nearly as problematic and controversial as the CAPPS II system. In November 2002, the United States confirmed that it was requiring airlines to use "no-fly" and "strict-scrutiny" blacklists to screen passengers. At the time, the no-fly list contained names of approximately 1,000 people, and another list contained an undisclosed number of people who were to be subjected to rigorous searching and examination (Lindorff 2002). The lists had been adopted after the September 11, 2001, attacks but quickly proved controversial when they picked up the wrong people (in cases of mistaken identity) and people whose only reason for suspicion was their political beliefs.

For instance, staff of the left-leaning Center for Constitutional Rights, a human rights organization, discovered they were on the strict-scrutiny list. The assistant legal director of the organization was carefully searched and even ordered to pull her pants down while still within view of other passengers. According to the TSA, the "list is composed of names that are provided to us by various government organizations like the FBI, CIA and INS . . . We don't ask how they decide who to list. Each agency decides on its own who is a 'threat to aviation'" (Ibid.). The list also netted a Milwaukee nun and fellow peace activists on their way to Washington to lobby their elected representatives about U.S. aid to Colombia, as well as dozens of people whose names were the same or similar to people on the list. In April 2004, the ACLU sued the federal government on behalf of seven plaintiffs, including a priest, an ACLU staff attorney, and an army sergeant, who had been given extra scrutiny and subject to delays due to their names appearing on the list. The suit challenged both the names appearing on the list and the near impossibility of getting one's name off the list. Indeed, even after several plaintiffs showed airport security letters provided by TSA explaining that their names were on the list by mistake, they were nonetheless stopped and searched repeatedly.

With all the negative publicity concerning the no-fly lists and the inscrutable or nonexistent system for clearing one's name, it might seem unlikely that a highly recognizable person of great political influence would endure the same problems. But in August 2004, Senator Edward Kennedy of Massachusetts, brother of the late president John F. Kennedy and attorney general Robert F. Kennedy, revealed that he had been subject to five airport searches in a five-week period due to his name resembling an alias ("T. Kennedy") on the no-fly list. On one trip, ticket agents refused to give him a ticket or let him board and would not tell him why. Airport supervisors overruled the ticket agents and let Kennedy fly, but the problem recurred. After the third ex-

Table 2.3
Databasing Debating Points

Pro Databasing	Anti Databasing
Data collection and information sharing allow markets to function more efficiently by reducing the cost of identifying and delivering the right product to the right consumer at the right time.	Data collection almost never comes with a guarantee that the information will be returned or destroyed. Therefore, it is likely to remain part of your record far beyond the stated need for collecting it and far beyond it being an accurate representation of who you are now.
Supermarkets' tracking purchases through customer loyalty cards allows them to stock items the customer is more likely to want.	Amassing data profiles increases the risk that important personal and financial information could fall into unauthorized hands, including employees with internal access who will misuse the information, external hackers, identity thieves, or terrorists.
For companies that sell expensive items such as cars and computers, detailed tracking and sharing of credit card transactions permit them to make more accurate instantaneous decisions about a customer's credit-worthiness, which allows customers to purchase a car or computer with a loan.	Databasing provides an opportunity for the government to outsource work, such as data collection, to private companies that do not have to follow any of the rules or respect people's rights the way that government must.
By including more information—both good and bad—about your credit, rather than just negative reports (as is done in countries with stronger data-protection laws), companies can better assesss credit risks and offer, overall, lower interest rates.	
In most countries, laws already exist to protect the privacy of data., including, in the United States, laws targeting health care, financial information, and other specific areas, as well as contract law and privacy torts.	
Restrictions on data collection are likely to muzzle social accountability mechanisms like the press, public trials, and gossip and to reduce free speech more generally.	

Source: McCullagh, Declan. 2004. "Database Nation: The Upside of 'Zero Privacy.'" *Reason*, June.

perience, Kennedy's office contacted TSA, which promised to take care of it. But Kennedy was again stopped and nearly barred from flying on two occasions. Finally, Homeland Security secretary Tom Ridge intervened and called Kennedy to apologize, and there were no further incidents (Savage 2004). The story illustrates the troubles ordinary people who have little political influence can have under the no-fly lists.

Public-Private Cooperation in Privacy Invasion: The Specter of a Surveillance-Industrial Complex

Another way to get around privacy rights, one that is being pioneered in particular by the United States, is for governments to acquire the extensive personal data about individuals that are collected by private corporations and associations. In many countries, these private groups are not held to the same legal limitations on data collection that governments are, nor are they subject to oversight by legislative committees or freedom of information laws. As a practical matter, governments can extend their large but still limited reach by, in effect, deputizing large corporations to build databases for them. The governments also benefits from the good reputations and trust that corporations develop with their customers, who are unlikely to suspect their data are ending up in government hands. In the United States, the ACLU pejoratively describes this growing public-private data partnership as the "Surveillance-Industrial Complex" (Stanley 2004).

The ACLU describes three ways the U.S. government is cooperating with the private sector to acquire data and build dossiers on individuals, a trend that is likely to become international:

- *By purchase:* The U.S. government is purchasing data about individuals from private data collection companies. For example, the U.S. Department of Justice has an $8 million contract with the largest U.S. data company, Choicepoint, to access its stores of information on individuals. Seisint, another behemoth of individualized information collection, received $9.2 million from the Department of Justice to provide data to the MATRIX program (Ibid., 26). LocatePlus, a data company that claims to have 6 billion records covering 98 percent of the U.S. population, is providing data directly to handheld wireless computers carried by officers with fifty law enforcement agencies (Associated Press 2004).

- *By broad court order or national security letters:* The U.S. government has increased its power to require corporations to share records containing personal information. The Patriot Act expanded these powers by allowing the government to get a court order demanding records from businesses, libraries, and other institutions with only a general statement of the information to be produced. The Patriot Act also dramatically lowered the standard for the FBI's unilaterally issuing of national security letters demanding information about a company's customers. Now the information sought must only be relevant to an investigation of terrorism or espionage, rather than sought on the basis of particular, articulable suspicion about the person (Stanley 2004, 13).

- *By simply asking for it:* The U.S. government has received large amounts of personal information by merely asking companies for it. American, JetBlue, Northwest, and United Airlines are among the companies that have admitted handing over large amounts of customer information to the FBI, not because of any particular suspicion or investigation but merely because the FBI asked for it. This information was attached to other personal information purchased by the FBI from data aggregators and used to research supposedly suspicious patterns of behavior. Also, universities and travel companies have voluntarily provided extensive data on individuals (Ibid., 10–11).

The U.S. government also provides data to the private sector—in the form of watch lists (discussed at greater length in Chapter 3). In some cases, the government requires corporations to discriminate against people on these watch lists, which contain the names of people suspected of terrorist activities and other crimes. The ACLU learned about this requirement the hard way when it discovered that its agreement to participate in a program that collects and coordinates donations from federal government employees, called the Combined Federal Campaign, meant that the organization also had to agree to actively check its employees against three government watch lists, including one created by the Patriot Act. After some hesitation, the ACLU withdrew from the Combined Federal Campaign, suffering a loss of approximately $500,000 per year. Indeed, this requirement, which was put into effect in October 2003, applies to more than 10,000 nonprofits that benefit from the $250 million per year fund-raising program. They must each certify that they do not knowingly employ any of the people listed on the watch lists and that they do not give funds to any of the groups on the list (Wolverton 2004).

In other cases—such as American citizen Hossam Algabri who received an inexplicable notice from Fleet Bank stating his bank account was canceled due to unelaborated "suspicious activity"—companies are voluntarily taking action against people listed on government-provided watch lists. Blue Cross, a medical insurance company, voluntarily combed its 6 million members' files and found 6,000 people whose names matched those on government watch lists but who were not the people the government was seeking (Stanley 2004, 19). Some credit-screening companies now offer as part of their standard services a check of a government terrorist watch list that is on the Internet and that, in July 2003, included approximately 300 names. Landlords and car dealers are among the users of the new service. Given the unlikelihood that one of the top 300 terrorists in the world would use his real name or known alias, this check is more likely to cause trouble for people with similar names who are entirely innocent (Hanks 2003).

The final way in which the U.S. surveillance-industrial complex is emerging, according to the ACLU, is the one most similar to what President Eisenhower warned of in his speech describing the military-industrial complex. There is money to be gained by all sides—whether through campaign contributions or job creation in their home districts, this booming data market is good for U.S. politicians. Meanwhile, with the help of aggressive lobbying, the data companies stand to gain millions or even billions of dollars from the public treasury (Stanley 2004, 27–29).

References

American Civil Liberties Union (ACLU). 2004. "ACLU Unveils Disturbing New Revelations About MATRIX Surveillance Program." May 20. http://www.aclu.org/news/newsprint.cfm?ID=15834&c=130.

Associated Press. 2003. "Cops Challenged on GPS Use." *Wired News,* May 21. http://www.wired.com/news/privacy/0,1848,58948,00.html.

————. 2004. "Cop on the Beat Now a Walking Database." *Boston Herald,* June 24. http://business.bostonherald.com/technologyNews/view.bg?articleid=33216.

Becker, Elizabeth. 2001. "As Ex-Theorist on Young 'Superpredators,' Bush Aide Has Regrets." *New York Times,* Feb. 9.

Benson, Miles. 2003. "'Demzilla' and 'Voter Vault' Are Watching You." *Newhouse News Service,* June 9. http://www.newhousenews.com/archive/benson061003.html.

Best, Jo. 2004. "Japan: Schoolkids to Be Tagged with RFID Chips." *C | Net Asia,* July 12.

Canberra Times. 2001. "Malaysia's Smart Card Touted as Weapon against Terrorism." *Canberra Times,* Sept. 21. http://canberra.yourguide.com.au/detail.asp?class=news&subclass= %20international&category=general%20news&story_id=90624&y=2001&m=9.

Eggen, Dan. 2003. "FBI Applies New Rules to Surveillance." *Washington Post.* Dec. 13.

European Parliament. Temporary Committee on the ECHELON Interception System. 2001. Report on the existence of a global system for the interception of private and commercial communications (ECHELON interception system). 2001/2098(INI). Final, A5-0264/2001. Gerhard Schmid, Rapporteur. July 11. http://www2.europarl.eu.int/omk/OM-Europarl?PROG=REPORT&L=EN&PUBREF=-//EP//TEXT+REPORT+A5-2001-0264+0+NOT+SGML+V0//EN.

Farhi, Paul. 2004. "Parties Square Off in a Database Duel." *New York Times,* July 20.

FBI. 2000. Memorandum from undisclosed author to Spike (Marion) Bowman re: undisclosed subject. April 5. http://www.epic.org/privacy/carnivore/fisa.html.

Fussell, Jim. 2001. "Group Classification on National ID Cards as a Factor in Genocide and Ethnic Cleansing." Paper presented to the Yale Genocide Studies Program's Seminar Series, Nov. 15. http://www.preventgenocide.org/prevent/removing-facilitating-factors/IDcards.

Hagar, Nicky. 2000. "Echelon—a Story about How Information Spreads (or Doesn't)." *Telepolis,* Feb. 8.

Hanks, Douglas, III. 2003. "Credit Bureaus Screening for Terrorists." *Miami Herald,* July 6.

Holmes, Stephen A. 2000. "Census Blamed in Internment of Japanese." *New York Times,* Mar. 17.

James, Frank. 2003. "GPS Grows as Tool to Spy on Spouses, Employees." *Chicago Tribune,* Feb. 11.

King, Neil, Jr., and Ted Bridis. 2000. "FBI's System to Covertly Search E-mail Raises Privacy, Legal Issues." *Wall Street Journal,* July 11.

Kramer, Hilary. 2004. "Cyber Fears on Fed's Web Plan." *New York Post,* Aug. 15.

Kyllo v. United States, 533 U.S. 27 (2001).

Langbein, Sarah. 2002. "CSI: Fort Collins." *Fort Collins Coloradoan,* Dec. 3.

Lichtblau, Eric. 2003. "F.B.I. Scrutinizes Antiwar Rallies." *New York Times,* Nov. 23.

Lindorff, David. 2002. "Grounded." *Salon,* Nov. 15. http://www.archive.salon.com/news/feature/2002/11/15/no_fly/index_np.html.

Matthews, William. 2004. "TSA's New Passenger-Screening System Aims for Tighter Focus." *Federal Times,* Aug. 11.

McCullagh, Declan. 2004. "Database Nation: The Upside of 'Zero Privacy.'" *Reason,* June.

Miller, Leslie. 2003. "Feds Want See-Through Security." *Associated Press/Wired News,* June 26. http://www.wired.com/news/print/0,1294,59401,00.html.

Minor, Elliott. 2004. "Interest Growing in 'Security' Blimps." *Associated Press,* Apr. 27.

Morello, Carol. 2004. "Army Floats a Trial Balloon: Equipped Blimp Hovers above Area in Test of Technology." *Washington Post,* Sept. 25.

Murphy, Dean. 2002. "As Security Cameras Sprout, Someone's Always Watching." *New York Times,* Sept. 29.

National Institute of Justice. n.d. "Understanding DNA Evidence: A Guide for Victim Service Providers." http://www.ojp.usdoj.gov/nij/dna_evbro/index.html.

Newswise. 2003. "Doctoral Student Developing New Facial-Recognition System." *Newswise,* July 16. http://www.newswise.com/articles/view/500150/.

Oliveri, Frank. 2003. "Police Database Called Intrusive by Rights Group." Gannett News Service, Dec. 31. Lexis.

Olsen, Stephanie. 2002. "DoubleClick Turns Away from Ad Profiles." *C|Net News,* Jan. 8. http://news.com.com/2100-1023-803593.html.

Piller, Charles, and Ricardo Alonso-Zaldivar. 2003. "A Suspect Computer Program." *Los Angeles Times,* Oct. 2.

Plus Three. 2003. "Plus Three Builds Democrat National Committee's 2004 Weapon." Press Release, Mar. 4. http://www.plusthree.com/newsdesk/announcements/20030304.html.

Poindexter, John. 2003. Letter to Dr. Anthony Tether, Director, Defense Advanced Research Projects Agency. Aug. 12. http://www.epic.org/privacy/profiling/tia/poindexterletter.pdf.

Porter, Ira. 2004. "Police Get New Way to Match DNA." *Philadelphia Inquirer,* Sept. 17.

Privacy Protection Study Committee. 1977. *Personal Privacy in an Information Age.* Washington, DC: U.S. Government Printing Office.

Reuters. 2004. "Aerial Drones Assigned to Arizona Border Patrol." *My Way News,* June 25. http://news.myway.com/top/article/id/411558%7Ctop%7C06-25-2004::22:46%7Creuters.html.

Rosen, Jeffrey. 2000. *The Unwanted Gaze: The Destruction of Privacy in America.* New York: Vintage Books.

Rottenberg, Marc. 2003. Statement to the National Commission on Terrorist Attacks on the United States. Dec. 8.

Savage, Charlie. 2004. "No-Fly List Almost Grounded Kennedy, He Tells Hearing." *Boston Globe,* Aug. 20.

Schwartz, John. 2003. "This Car Can Talk: What It Says May Cause Concern." *New York Times,* Dec. 29.

Stanley, Jay. 2004. "The Surveillance-Industrial Complex. How the American Government Is Conscripting Businesses and Individuals in the Construction of a Surveillance Society." Washington, DC: American Civil Liberties Union. Aug. http://www.aclu.org/SafeandFree/SafeandFree.cfm?ID=16226&c=282.

State v. Jackson, 150 Wash.2d 251 (2003).

Tuckman, Jo. 2004. "Put a Chip in Your Arm to Outfox Kidnappers." *Guardian,* July 14. http://www.guardian.co.uk/print/0,3858,4970385-103681,00.html.

Windrem, Robert. 2000. "U.S. Steps Up Commercial Spying." *MSNBC,* May 7. http://www.msnbc.com/news/403435.asp?cp1=1.

———. 2003. "At Lourdes, Air Is Filled with Secrets." *MSNBC,* Oct. 19. http://www.msnbc.com/news/502361.asp.

Wolverton, Brad. 2004. "Federal Campaign Flap." *Chronicle of Philanthropy,* Aug. 19.

Zetter, Kim. 2003. "For Sale: The American Voter." *Wired News,* Dec. 11. http://www.wired.com/news/evote/0,2645,61543,00.html.

3

Privacy in Post-9/11, Post-Columbine, Gene-Mapped America

The United States faces many, if not all, of the same privacy issues that other countries do. However, it is unique in some ways. The United States, like any nation, has a unique history, mix of cultures and religions, social problems (such as gun violence in schools), and other influences that have shaped its right to privacy. With one of the world's largest and most advanced militaries, secret intelligence services, and private technology industries, the United States often experiences privacy controversies before the rest of the world. The country has been, at different times, a world leader both in the creation of privacy rights and in the violation of privacy.

Three events from the turn of the millennium continue to have a significant impact on privacy in the United States. The attacks of September 11, 2001, and the government's response to them have forced Americans to think about personal privacy and homeland security: how much they are worth, how they relate to one another, and how Americans wish to preserve each. For young Americans, the shootings at Columbine High School in Colorado on April 20, 1999—along with the perception that young people are more violent and dangerous than ever—have accelerated a diminution in their privacy. It may be a trend that follows them into the future. Finally, the mapping of the human genome, celebrated in June 2000, is emblematic of the significant role that genes now play in science, medicine, law enforcement, and other aspects of society, with serious implications for privacy and equality. These privacy problems are not uniquely American, but this chapter considers them in their uniquely American context.

Privacy in the Wake of September 11

September 11, 2001

On the morning of Tuesday, September 11, 2001, nineteen men boarded four flights at airports on the East Coast of the United States. Sometime after takeoff, they hijacked the planes and took over the controls. The hijackers flew two airplanes into the twin towers of the World Trade Center in New York City and one into the U.S. Department of Defense headquarters in the Pentagon building in Washington, D.C. The fourth plane, which was in all likelihood bound for Washington as well, crashed in a rural field in Pennsylvania. The crash may have been due to an onboard rebellion by passengers who learned of their probable fate from cell phone calls to loved ones. With the world watching live on television, the towers of the World Trade Center collapsed. More than 3,000 people died as a direct result of the attacks.

It was determined that the hijackers were connected to al Qaeda. Al Qaeda, which means "the base" in Arabic, is a terrorist network that aims to eliminate the allegedly profane influence of the West from Arab and Muslim parts of the world and install fundamentalist Islamic regimes. Fifteen of the hijackers were from Saudi Arabia, two from the United Arab Emirates, one from Egypt, and one from Lebanon. Fifteen entered on business or tourist visas. One entered with a visa to attend a vocational school. Several of them were from middle-class backgrounds, were well educated, spoke English and other languages well, and were familiar with Western culture.

The four principal hijacker pilots arrived in the United States by June 2000. The remaining hijackers were in the country by June 2001. During their time in the United States, the terrorists maintained a low profile and lived fairly ordinary lives. At different times, some of them joined gyms, opened bank accounts, received wire transfers, purchased tickets online, sent instant messages, sent letters, went to bars, and withdrew cash from bank machines. However, at the same time, they were preparing for their eventual mission. Six attended flight schools in the United States to learn how to fly airplanes, improve their skills, and, in some cases, obtain commercial flying licenses. The leaders circulated in and out of the country frequently.

The U.S. Response to September 11

The terrorist attacks of September 11, 2001, murdered 3,000 innocent people, broke apart families, and traumatized people throughout the world who watched the attacks and aftermath as they transpired. The attacks demanded a response by the United States and other nations, requiring new and different tactics and policies to prevent terrorist activity and reduce its causes, as well as more aggressive and efficient intelligence, border security, and law enforcement. But one of the most difficult questions still being asked in the United States and elsewhere is whether the September 11 attacks demanded a reduction in the core rights valued by democratic societies—the right to be free from discrimination on the basis of race, ethnicity, and nationality; the right to due process; the right to freedom of expression; and the right to privacy.

In the wake of September 11, the U.S. government acted quickly and forcefully to pursue the organizers of the attacks, prevent any further attacks, and expand the powers of government to spy, catch, and prosecute suspected terrorists. Many think the United States acted too quickly and too forcefully, at the cost of important democratic values and, in many cases, with little value for the fight against terrorism. Others think the United States needs to do more, including giving intelligence operatives more discretion to invade privacy if they think it is necessary.

A mere six weeks after the attacks, Congress passed the massive USA PATRIOT Act of 2001. On October 26, 2001, the president signed it. (The acronym stands for Uniting and Strengthening America by Providing Appropriate Tools Required to Intercept and Obstruct Terrorism.) Executive Department and congressional staff were able to come up with hundreds of pages of technical provisions in such a relatively short period of time because many of the provisions had been written before September 11. According to ACLU attorney Ann Beeson, "The Patriot Act is a law enforcement wish list of new powers rejected by

Congress as too broad on several prior occasions" (Leone and Anrig 2003, 297). The Patriot Act expanded the government's power to spy, search, and seize and reduced the oversight of the courts. It also increased penalties for terrorist crimes, increased requirements for drivers of hazardous materials, gave government more power to prevent money laundering, and many other things. Many provisions merely modernized old laws to conform with new technologies—for instance, giving the FBI the power to use "roving wiretaps" in intelligence investigations, which it already had in criminal investigations. More controversial are the ways in which the act reduces the roles of the courts in overseeing intrusive actions by executive agencies. Also, many of the provisions did not respond to issues related to September 11. Some provisions expanded law enforcement powers that had no relation to terrorism. Civil libertarians and privacy advocates have objected to many but not the majority of the act's provisions. Certain provisions were given a four-year sunset—meaning they would have to be renewed by act of Congress or else expire. But, only some of the act's most controversial provisions are tagged to sunset.

Specifically, the Patriot Act's more controversial measures:

- Expanded the government's authority to get a court order to enter homes, search them, and take property without notifying the owner until weeks or months later. The act allowed these "sneak and peek" warrants in cases having nothing to do with terrorism, and it created a low standard for when they are allowed (§ 213).
- Expanded the government's power to get a court order to search or seize a person's records from third-party record holders, including library, bookstore, medical, educational, and other records. The act does not require the FBI to name whose records it is seeking or offer any facts linking the person to spying or terrorism. It also allows the FBI to obtain entire databases, which are likely to include records of people not suspected of anything (§ 215).
- Eliminated the requirement to have individualized suspicion when the head of the FBI (or his designees) issues a "national security letter" instructing banks, telephone companies, and credit agencies to release information about a person. The request must still be part of an in-

vestigation to protect against terrorism or clandestine intelligence activities, but now an agent has to show only that the information is relevant, a very low standard—and the FBI director is the final decision maker (§ 505).

- Made it a crime for providers of records to reveal that the FBI has searched or seized records. For example, a librarian could be arrested for revealing that the FBI conducted a search of library records (§§ 215 and 505).
- Allowed network operators (ISPs, universities, and so on) to invite the government in to spy on "computer trespassers" without any court authorization, supervision, or other accountability (§ 217).

And more measures are controversial. (See the summary of privacy concerns and proposed fixes in Chapter 6.)

Since adoption of the Patriot Act, the U.S. government has expanded surveillance and law enforcement powers in other ways. It has vastly increased its collection of information on foreign visitors and interfered significantly with the liberty that Arabs and Muslims in the United States previously enjoyed.

In December 2003, the United States further expanded the Patriot Act by extending the definition of third-party institutions from which the FBI may require disclosure of personal information using national security letters. Previously, FBI agents could demand such information only from traditional "financial institutions," such as banks and credit unions. Under the expanded definition, however, they are able to demand information from car dealers, casinos, real estate agents, post offices, pawnbrokers, travel companies, and other businesses—again (without court oversight) by the FBI director's determination that the information sought is relevant to an investigation into terrorism or espionage.

Soon after September 11, the United States deported more than 600 Arabs and Muslims who supposedly had immigration violations. It is believed the United States arrested more than 1,000 noncitizens, but the exact numbers are not known, because the government refuses to disclose any further information, including their names. The ACLU has referred to these persons secretly arrested as America's "disappeared." Immigration attorneys noted that many legal immigrants have become "out of status" due to the government taking months or years to process their applications to become legal. In other words, the United

States caused some of these violations of law and then deported those immigrants for them. Starting in the fall of 2002, the United States required approximately 82,000 male immigrants and visitors from twenty-five predominantly Muslim countries to report and register at immigration offices. Their information and photographs were taken and stored to be checked against existing and future data collected by the government. And they were subject to cumbersome check-in requirements upon departure and reentry. Those who did not report and register are subject to immigration violations and possible deportation. In June 2003, government sources told the *New York Times* that more than 13,000 of those who registered might be deported, even though only 11 had any links to terrorism. Another system was established to track the 1 million foreign students studying in the United States. Many Arabs and Muslims chose to leave the United States in the face of the arbitrariness and uncertainty of their legal status and the increased tracking.

In a 2004 University of Michigan survey, 15 percent of Arab Americans in the Detroit area reported experiencing harassment or intimidation by other individuals since September 11, 2001. The abuse ranged from derogatory comments and jokes to, in 3 percent of cases, serious harassment, such as being threatened with physical violence or a firearm or actually being beaten. According to the study, many Americans hold a general bias against Arab American citizens: 49 percent of the general population would support increased surveillance of Arab Americans; 41 percent would support "preventative detentions," that is, detentions even when insufficient evidence exists to prosecute, of Arab Americans; and 23 percent would support increased police powers to stop and search Arab Americans (Slevin 2004, A5).

In October 2001, Attorney General John Ashcroft allowed federal prison officials to monitor confidential communications between lawyers and their detained clients—citizen or immigrant, convicted or not—without a court order. The regulation requires only the low standard of reasonable suspicion and limits the use of confidential information in prosecutions.

In January 2002, the White House proposed a pilot project called Operation TIPS (Terrorist Information and Prevention System) that would recruit 1 million citizen volunteers in ten cities to report "suspicious" activities. The volunteers would include people whose jobs allow them access to others' homes, such as package couriers, phone repair workers, garbage collectors, and utility workers. In August 2002, due to widespread outrage against the proposal, the administration scaled back the plan, and, by the end of the year, Congress passed a law forbidding implementation of it. Critics compared the plan to the forty-year practice in communist East Germany by which citizen informants were encouraged to spy on and report their neighbors to the secret Stasi police. The ACLU said, "This program epitomized the government's insatiable appetite for the surveillance of law-abiding citizens" (Scheeres 2002).

In May 2002, the attorney general changed department rules to allow FBI agents to conduct surveillance at public meetings and events of domestic groups and organizations, including churches, mosques, and synagogues, without providing any rationale for spying on the group and with little guidance on what information could be recorded and how long it could be kept.

In the buildup to the 2004 Republican National Convention in New York, the FBI began questioning political protesters, stopping by their homes and, in a few cases, even subpoenaing them. The FBI urged its field offices to follow up on a list of people it believed may know about plans to use violence. Six agents visited one young woman working with a peace group in Denver. Secret Service agents visited a man reported by a feuding neighbor to have made threats against the president, and they asked questions about his political activities. Three young men who intended to protest at the 2004 Democratic Convention in Boston were followed by federal agents and then subpoenaed just prior to their intended departure, forcing them to cancel their plans. Prosecutors say they are suspects in a domestic terrorism investigation but will not disclose the reasons for that suspicion. Their lawyer stated, "What's so disturbing about all this is the preemptive nature—stopping them from participating in a protest before anything even happened" (Lichtblau 2004, A1). Also in 2002, the attorney general opened the door to unfettered data mining of commercial databases by agents. And Ashcroft reduced the supervision of agents by expanding the definition and length of so-called preliminary inquiries that do not require any proof of a criminal or terrorist connection.

In 2003, the United States scaled back but did not eliminate efforts to build "total information" data systems for profiling possible terrorists based on either a mix of criminal and noncriminal information or a mix of purely innocent transactions and data that might be typical of a would-be terrorist. Congress restricted the federal government's direct work on the system, but the Department of Justice funded similar projects (referred to by the acronym MATRIX) in the states. And a May 2004 report by the Government Accounting Office revealed 199 federal government databases that use data mining, 54 of which use personal data acquired from private data companies. (The study did not include databases from the CIA or the National Security Agency [NSA].) The federal government uses many of these databases for valuable statistical analysis, but others seek to assess a person's risk to homeland security based on data profiles. Four data programs in particular raised concern among civil libertarians:

- The Defense Intelligence Agency's Verity K2 Enterprise, which aggregates data "to identify foreign terrorists or U.S. citizens connected to foreign terrorism activities"
- The Defense Intelligence Agency's Pathfinder, which "can compare and search multiple large databases quickly" and "analyze government and private sector databases"
- The Department of Homeland Security's Analyst Notebook 12, which "correlates events and people to specific information"
- The Department of Homeland Security's Case Management Data Mart, which uses private sector data to "assist . . . in managing law enforcement cases" (ACLU 2004)

At the end of 2003, the U.S. Department of Homeland Security requested and received data on the geographical concentration of people who identified themselves as being of Arab ancestry on the 2000 U.S. Census. One tabulation provided by the U.S. Census Bureau shows the concentration of responses by city, whereas another breaks down responses for specific ZIP-code areas by Arab national ancestry (Egyptian descent, Moroccan descent, and so on). Under existing law, such data sharing is legal so long as it does not provide identifying information about individuals. The department said its reason for requesting the data was to determine at what airports Arab language signs regarding customs rules were needed, but it did not explain why it needed the data only on Arabs and not other ethnic groups. The revelation stirred a public controversy in part due to the long history of suspicion toward and abuses of censuses. The Census Bureau slightly modified its policy, requiring that a senior member of the department approve such specific analyses in the future (Hudson 2004).

Mistrust of censuses has ancient roots. According to the Bible, God punished King David and Israel with seven years of famine after David interjected himself between God and God's people by taking a census (2 Sam. 24:1–15). In 1939, the Nazi government of Germany ordered a census of the greater Reich that tracked people's Jewish ancestry by all four grandparents, categorized them by supposed degrees of Jewishness, and identified them by address. This information was provided to the secret police who later rounded up Jews to various ends, including moving millions to concentration camps and executing them. The Nazis used IBM technology first developed for the 1890 U.S. Census—punch cards and punch card counters—to count the Reich's population and target Jews and other minorities rapidly and precisely (Black 2001). Two years after the 1939 Nazi census, the U.S. Census Bureau provided data to the U.S. War Department on concentrations of people of Japanese ancestry on the Pacific Coast by city block, which directly aided the War Department in rounding up and interning 117,000 Japanese and Japanese Americans in U.S. concentration camps (Holmes 2000). This historical backdrop fueled resistance by religious groups, especially Jewish groups, newspaper editorial boards, and the ACLU, when, in 1956, the U.S. government proposed adding a question asking people's religion on the 1960 census. The Census Bureau withdrew the proposal (Westin 1967, 303). If it had not, it is likely that, in 2003, the Department of Homeland Security would have sought data on concentrations of Muslim Americans in addition to people of Arab ancestry.

By 2004, the United States was implementing numerous programs that sought to gain more information about international and national travelers (see discussion in Chapter 2). First, the United States took over the job of screening passengers from the airlines and required that every screener be a U.S. citizen (even though no such requirement exists to be part of the U.S. military). These programs included the U.S. VISIT program, which photographs and fingerprints every foreigner arriving in the United States with a visa, as well as the CAPPS II total information screening system, which—if implemented—would have assigned a threat level to every traveler when he or she checked in for a flight. These travel screening programs also included high-tech scanning machines that produce a near nude image and a requirement that every piece of luggage be scanned. It even included efforts to have luggage manufacturers make luggage locks that could be opened by the government with a special key.

In 2005, the U.S. State Department planned to add a 64k radio frequency identification (RFID) microchip to every new or renewed passport it issues to U.S. citizens.

Under the government's proposal, the chip will contain a high-resolution digital image of a photograph of the passport holder's face as well as other information. When a passport holder goes through a passport control station or is stopped by authorities, the digital image can be compared by computers with facial-recognition software to a new photo taken on the spot and to a database of wanted and suspected persons. The State Department chose digital photos—rather than, say, taking fingerprints and conducting digital fingerprint scans, which is vastly more accurate with current technologies and which it uses for foreigners visiting the United States—because Americans would consider it less intrusive to allow their picture to be taken than to be fingerprinted. Applicants for a passport under the new system will still be responsible for purchasing and submitting their own photos; the State Department will then scan the provided photos. Commercial passport photographers will be asked to ensure better lighting. Presently, fingerprint-checking systems that check two fingerprints have demonstrated 99.6 percent accuracy, whereas facial-recognition systems that use the best possible photographs demonstrate 90 percent accuracy (Krim 2004).

The chip will be read by a machine that emits an electromagnetic field. When the passport is passed within 10 centimeters of the machine, the electromagnetic field activates the chip and the chip transmits data to the machine. It is possible to encrypt the data signal so that only a machine with the proper decrypting code can read it. In fact, the companies that are providing this technology to the State Department tout encryption in their promotional materials. However, the State Department did not purchase this feature. The passport chips will not use encryption, heightening concern among privacy advocates about the potential for identity theft by thieves with reading machines of their own. Government and corporate officials felt encryption would make it more difficult for many countries to use the same reading technology. They also argue that the close distance required to read the chips and the state of current technology make identity theft close to impossible. However, technology is constantly improving, and data skimming of wireless information and networks is already a problem. The United States could have promoted a computer chip that requires contact with the reading machine and avoided the risk that comes with chip signals that can be activated at a distance. But contact would take slightly longer than contactless reading. Security expert Bruce Schneier appreciates the government's desire to enhance screening at the airport gate; "I just worry that they are building a technology that the bad guys can surreptitiously access" (Leach 2004).

The new passports are an example of how protecting privacy is often a lower priority than cost and convenience when systems are being designed. It is also a good example of how protecting privacy enhances rather than reduces security. Unfortunately, this lesson may not be learned until a terrorist exploits the unencrypted, contactless passport chip to gain access to a country and cause harm.

Public Resistance to the Erosion of Privacy

Affirming the continuing importance of privacy in U.S. society, large numbers of American people—both liberal and conservative—reacted strongly against some of the administration's actions that they perceived went too far.

As of March 2005, 371 city and county governments and 4 state legislatures (up from a combined 236 in January 2004 and 22 in 2002) had adopted resolutions urging the federal government to narrow the reach of the Patriot Act. Some measures instructed local law enforcement not to participate in racial profiling, not to collect information on the political views or religious affiliations of individuals or groups, and not to enforce federal immigration laws (Blum 2004).

Conservative former Speaker of the House Newt Gingrich wrote, "I strongly believe Congress must act now to rein in the Patriot Act, limit its use to national security concerns and prevent it from developing 'mission creep' into areas outside of national security" (Gingrich 2003, A17). Other conservatives who prefer small and local government have opposed the act and other post-9/11 measures, because they give too much power to government generally or to the federal government in particular.

Librarians played a key role in resistance to the Patriot Act. The American Libraries Association opposes the provisions giving agents access to library records. Individual libraries across the country changed their computer systems to purge lending records as soon as a book is returned. Many posted signs warning that the act may require them to disclose patrons' reading habits and subject the librarians to criminal prosecution for revealing a search has taken place. "What people read is their own business, and as professional librarians we don't feel it's appropriate to share that information," said one librarian (Cambanis 2004, B1).

Many of the act's controversial provisions are being challenged in court. In January 2004, a lower federal court found a provision of the Patriot Act unconstitutional. The court ruled that the expansion of the definition of terrorist activity to include those giving "expert advice or assistance" to known terrorist groups was too vague. The court reasoned that people who wanted to engage in constitutionally protected free expression would not know whether they risked being arrested for it (*Humanitarian Law Project v. U.S. Department of Justice*).

In 2005, politically diverse organizations formed a coalition called Patriots for Checks and Balances to seek the repeal or retirement of the more extreme provisions of the Patriot Act. Chaired by Republican former congressman from Georgia Bob Barr, the group includes the American Conservative Union, the ACLU, Americans for Tax Reform, the Second Amendment Foundation, American Association of Physicians and Surgeons, and others.

Although Congress passed the Patriot Act with little consideration or debate, it resisted certain other post-9/11 efforts by the White House. Congress defunded John Poindexter's efforts in the Department of Defense advanced research office, including the Total Information Awareness project. It prohibited implementation of the TIPS program, and it required a study of CAPPS II prior to its implementation. A provision to defund "sneak and peek" searches passed the House but was eliminated in the final version of the bill.

The inspector general of the Department of Justice, whose office is part of the department, issued reports exposing and criticizing certain actions by the department, including its mistreatment of Arab and Muslim detainees. The inspector general also found that none of the complaints his office received alleging discriminatory use of the Patriot Act were valid, although the complaints turned up other types of unlawful discrimination.

Rationales for Post-9/11 Reductions in Privacy

Two rationales—both contested by rights advocates—underlie the U.S. government's justification for expanding its powers and reducing privacy rights following September 11. The first is that the attacks of September 11 revealed the inadequacies of the government's powers and the harmful restrictiveness of privacy protections. In other words, if the government's hands had not been tied by privacy rights, it might have prevented the September 11 attacks. The second rationale is that, regardless of the role of privacy in the attacks on September 11, the government needs sweeping powers, including new powers to intrude on privacy, to prevent future devious attempts to harm large numbers of people.

The first rationale is a factual allegation that might be resolved by looking at the events leading up to September 11 to determine what degree privacy, versus other issues, contributed to the failure to prevent the attacks. The second rationale is largely speculative; it can be debated but not proven. It is impossible to know whether a ghastly attack of horrific proportions will come about due to the relative degree of freedom enjoyed in the United States, due to human or system failures, or due to some other reason. Moreover, this debate does not answer the important question of how much Americans are willing to wager for security—how much time and money, and how much freedom and privacy?

Under either rationale, the public is justified in asking whether the government is first pursuing every avenue to increase security in ways that do not erode core liberties. Or, as the 9/11 Commission put it when discussing post-9/11 security powers, such as those in the Patriot Act, "The burden of proof for retaining a particular government power should be on the executive, to explain (a) that the power actually materially enhances security and (b) that there is adequate supervision of the executive's use of the powers to ensure protection of civil liberties. If the power is granted, there must be adequate guidelines and oversight to properly confine its use" (National Commission 2004a, 394–395).

The Privacy Wall between Criminal and Intelligence Investigations

After September 11, some people blamed the *privacy wall* between criminal and intelligence investigations for hampering efforts that might have prevented the attacks. Attorney general John Ashcroft testified before the 9/11 Commission, "The single greatest structural cause for the Sept. 11 problem was the wall that segregated or separated criminal investigators and intelligence agents" (Von Drehle 2004). The 9/11 Commissions's final report contradicts Ashcroft's assertion, stating, "It is now clear that everyone involved was confused about the rules governing the sharing and use of information gathered in intelligence channels" (*9/11 Commission Report* 2003, ch. 8).

The privacy wall is the nickname for a variety of rules and laws—primarily the Foreign Intelligence Surveillance Act (FISA) passed in 1978—that try to maintain some boundary between law enforcement and espionage when each takes place within the United States. Traditionally, law enforcement is domestic and thus bound by more rules, restrictions, and rights, such as when a person suspected of a crime may be stopped and searched or when evidence of a crime may be used in court. Espionage, intelligence, and counterintelligence operations are bound by fewer rules, in part because the aim is rarely to prosecute a person in a court of law but more likely to disrupt an operation or deport a person. Traditionally, these operations are conducted in foreign lands.

However, when agents of foreign powers enter the United States—such as spies, terrorists, or, it was once argued, communists—the line between traditional law enforcement and intelligence can get blurry. The FBI or CIA must decide whether to observe them to learn more or to investigate them for arrest and prosecution in a court of law. They may want to switch strategies, or they may want to prosecute one individual but monitor his accomplice. In these cases, the question arises whether they should be allowed to use the looser standards of international espionage or have to satisfy the stronger protections of the laws and Constitution of the United States, particularly Fourth Amendment requirements of due process, warrants, and reasonable searches and seizures. The different standards lead to different results at three different stages: how the surveillance is conducted, how the information is kept, and how it may be used. Under the law enforcement standard, the government must take reasonable steps to protect individuals' privacy at each stage. Under the intelligence standard, reasonableness requirements are vastly reduced.

If given a choice, the government would choose to use the easier standard as much as possible. During the McCarthy era, under the FBI administration of J. Edgar Hoover, and in the Nixon White House, surveillance powers were abused to harass political opponents and suppress lawful dissent. In 1976, the Church Committee concluded, "Unless new and tighter controls are established by legislation, domestic intelligence activities threaten to undermine our democratic society and fundamentally alter its nature" (U.S. Congress 1976). Although the Supreme Court has not yet ruled on the question directly, a 1972 decision left open the possibility that intelligence investigations on domestic soil against foreign powers or their agents might not have to meet the same standard as criminal investigations (*United States v. United States District Court*, Plamondon et al.). These developments laid the foundation for the Foreign Intelligence Surveillance Act and the privacy wall.

The privacy wall was established to make clearer the line between the two approaches, set rules for when information can cross over, and thereby protect constitutional rights while giving latitude to intelligence operations on domestic soil. On the criminal side of the wall, searches must be reasonable and require a warrant. Warrants require probable cause that a crime has occurred or is occurring. Typically, the target of the search must ultimately be informed that a search was conducted. And, there must be a showing that the place to be searched or tapped has been or will be used in furtherance of a crime. On the intelligence side of the wall, surveillance warrants can be obtained from the very secretive Foreign Intelligence Surveillance Court. An order approving electronic surveillance will be approved to "obtain foreign intelligence information" if "there is probable cause to believe that . . . the target of the electronic surveillance is a foreign power or an agent of a foreign power" and "each of the facilities or places at which the surveillance is directed is being used, or is about to be used, by a foreign power or an agent of a foreign power" (FISA § 1805[a][3]).

The court is composed of eleven federal circuit judges appointed by the chief justice of the Supreme Court. It meets in secret, and its opinions are not available to the public. The targets of FISA warrants are never notified of searches or surveillance unless they are prosecuted. Even then, FISA information often may not be obtained by the targets. Decisions on FISA warrants may be appealed to a second secret review court, but only by the government and therefore only if a request for a warrant is denied.

FISA has been amended several times since 1978 to give the government broader powers of surveillance, such as the 1994 addition of power to conduct physical (not just electronic) searches. Indeed, most of the Patriot Act's provisions amend provisions of FISA. Most significantly, the Patriot Act eliminated the requirement that gathering foreign intelligence information be the "primary purpose" of a FISA warrant, that instead it need only be "a significant purpose."

Although it was never written in FISA, the "primary purpose" requirement guided courts in dealing with the overlap problem before and after FISA. Courts found some solace in the fact that government agents had to demonstrate they were not using the lower intelligence standard for warrants merely to sneak around the Fourth Amendment's requirements. If intelligence investigations turned up information that was then used in a criminal case, it was usually viewed by the courts as incidental to the primary purpose behind the intelligence warrant. Therefore, excluding the information from evidence would not serve to promote respect for the Fourth Amendment and the evidence would be admitted even though it was obtained through the back door of a FISA warrant.

However, when foreign-intelligence gathering needs to be merely "a significant purpose," it is more likely that the government will be able to use the lower standard to end-run the privacy protections of the Constitution. Although the government still must show that an investigation has an intelligence component to it, that component can be equal in weight to the goals of the criminal investigation into the same person or matter. Or, the intelligence component can be much less important than the criminal investigation component so long as it is "significant."

The increased use of FISA warrants since 2001 bears out the theory that governments will tend to use the easiest procedure regardless of the privacy interests at stake. In 2000, there were 1,003 FISA warrants sought and issued. In 2004, there were 1,754—an increase of 75 percent. Also, in 2002, for the first time,

FISA warrants outnumbered traditional federal search warrants, which have to meet the higher standard.

Significantly, in its entire history, the FISA court has never denied a FISA warrant request. Between 1979 and 2001, the court approved 14,031 applications. In five cases, the court asked the application be modified and approved the modified requested.

In 2002, perhaps concerned about the "significant purpose" change, the Foreign Intelligence Surveillance Court took two unprecedented steps: it denied part of a government request and it published its opinion. The Department of Justice requested a FISA warrant to conduct surveillance on a U.S. citizen or permanent resident whom it suspected of international terrorism. Included with its request were revised "minimization" procedures to guide the department's handling of information obtained through FISA searches that did not relate to foreign intelligence—that is, to minimize the privacy intrusions of keeping information about people that it did not need. Relying on the Patriot Act amendments, the department sought to overhaul these procedures to make it easier to blend the efforts and information of criminal and intelligence investigations and warrants.

The court found that there was enough evidence to support the FISA warrant, but it took issue with aspects of the revised procedures. The court wrote:

> [The revised procedures] mean that criminal prosecutors will tell the FBI when to use FISA (perhaps when they lack probable cause for [regular warrants for] electronic surveillance), what techniques to use, what information to look for, what information to keep as evidence and when use of FISA can cease because there is enough evidence to arrest and prosecute. The 2002 minimization procedures give the Department's *criminal* prosecutors every legal advantage conceived by Congress to be used by U.S. *intelligence* agencies to collect foreign intelligence information, including: a foreign intelligence standard instead of a criminal standard of probable cause; use of the most advanced and highly intrusive techniques for intelligence gathering; and surveillances and searches for extensive periods of time; based on a standard that the U.S. person is only using or about to use the places to be surveilled and searched, without any notice to the target unless arrested and

> prosecuted, and, if prosecuted, no adversarial discovery
> of the FISA applications and warrants.
> (*emphasis added,* In re *All Matters Submitted to the Foreign Intelligence Surveillance Court* 2002, 12, 13)

The court used its powers to modify the Justice Department's motion and to ensure that the minimization procedures satisfy FISA's definition of minimization. It required that three paragraphs of the revised rules be rewritten and wrote two paragraphs of its own. The court allowed broad, unprecedented consultation between agents working on parallel criminal and intelligence investigations, but it drew lines to "ensure that law enforcement officials do not direct or control the use of the FISA procedures to enhance criminal prosecution" (Id., 15). The court also required that Department of Justice staff who work with the court be present at or informed about such cross-wall meetings to share and coordinate information. Finally, the court required that applications for FISA warrants list any criminal investigations against the same target and describe any consultation that has taken place between intelligence and criminal investigators.

However, this unprecedented action was followed by another. The government appealed the decision, as allowed by FISA, to the Foreign Intelligence Surveillance Court of Review— an entity that had never formed because the government never had any reason to appeal. Ordinarily, the public would have never learned of either the lower court's decision or the appeal to the review court. Coincidentally, around that time (September 2002), Senator Patrick Leahy and others wrote the lower court to learn more about the use of FISA. In response, the court sent them its ruling and opinion on the minimization procedures.

The ACLU learned of the appeal and decided to try to file an amicus (friend of the court) brief with the court of review. But ACLU attorney Ann Beeson wondered, "how do you file a brief in a secret court?" (Leone and Anrig 2003, 308). She wrote the judges listed on the lower court's opinion and hoped to hear back. Beeson wrote, "Days went by with no word . . . Then I picked up the phone in mid-September, and an unfamiliar voice said she was our contact for the secret court. My blood raced—it felt like I was talking to Deep Throat. She said the judges had not yet decided whether they would accept our brief but that we could file it with the FISA clerk who it turns out works for the Justice Department. So much for separation of powers!" (Id., 309).

In mid-September 2002, the press reported that the review court was hearing oral arguments on the case—or rather one side of the argument—in secret, within a secure location in the Justice Department. The review court considered amicus briefs written by the ACLU, the National Association of Criminal Defense Lawyers, and others. Nonetheless, on November 18, 2002, the court of review issued an opinion reversing the lower court's orders "to the extent they imposed conditions on the grant of the government's applications, vacate the FISA court's [rule requiring additional information in future warrant requests], and remand with instructions to grant the applications as submitted" (In Re *Sealed Case* 2002, 88).

The ACLU and other groups sought special permission from the U.S. Supreme Court to become a party in the case and to have an appeal of the review court's decision heard. In March 2003, without explanation, the Supreme Court denied the request. The Court's views on whether intelligence tactics can be used in cases whose primary purposes is law enforcement remain unknown. For the time being, therefore, the Justice Department's relaxed rules on intelligence and criminal investigations still stand. The privacy wall is all but dismantled. For those who felt the wall hindered the defense of the United States, it is a significant victory. For those who fear what abuses may result from the government's broader surveillance powers, time will tell.

Privacy at Fault for the September 11 Attacks?

Some people argue that, in August 2001, the privacy wall prevented an FBI investigator from getting additional help to pursue leads that would have led to two of the September 11 hijackers. According to a former senior official at the National Security Agency, "[The United States] couldn't find al-Mihdhar and al-Hazmi in August 2001 because we had imposed too many rules designed to protect against privacy abuses that were mainly theoretical. We missed our best chance to save the lives of 3,000 Americans because we spent more effort and imagination guarding against these theoretical abuses than against terrorism" (Baker 2003). In fact, however, the evidence shows that it was not the rules themselves, but very likely the misinterpretation and misapplication of those rules by the FBI that prevented the sharing of information. The FBI judged the privacy wall to be higher than it actually was and, in some instances, perceived walls where there were none.

The allegation stems from the two months prior to September 11 when FBI and CIA agents were pursuing old leads with renewed interest amid high levels of *chatter* suggesting an attack was in the works. On July 24, 2001, an FBI agent working with an interagency Osama Bin Laden Unit reviewed the FBI's file on a meeting of terrorist suspects in Kuala Lumpur, Malaysia, in January 2000. Other agents had been reexamining events surrounding the attack on the USS *Cole* and the thwarted plans to bomb Los Angeles International Airport at the millennium. Over several weeks, the agent connected several dots that raised grave concerns: the agent discovered that one suspect from the Malaysia meeting, al-Mihdhar, had received a multiple-entry visa to the United States and another suspect, al-Hazmi, had traveled to Los Angeles in January 2000. Discussions with the Immigration and Naturalization Service revealed that al-Mihdhar had also been in Los Angeles in January 2000, around the time of the planned airport bombing. It now seems highly unlikely that either man was meant to play a role in the airport bombing. In August 2001, however, it seemed significant and led to the additional news that al-Mihdhar had since returned to Yemen and reentered the United States on July 4. Regardless, it was known they were connected to al Qaeda and, in all likelihood, the attack on the USS *Cole*. With all the chatter about another attack, it was important to find them. The task was assigned to the FBI's New York City field office. A New York agent requested that the investigation be opened as a criminal case so he might benefit from the assistance of agents from the criminal investigations team. Headquarters denied the request, because the source of the information had come from an intelligence investigation. The field agent protested, e-mailing, "Some day someone will die and—wall or not—the public will not understand why we were not more effective and throwing every resources we had at certain 'problems'" (U.S. Congress 2002, 153). Between August 27 and September 10, 2001, the agent conducted some basic investigation of hotel registries in the New York area and national crime databases but turned up nothing. On September 11, the agent contacted the FBI in Los Angeles, where the terrorists had entered in January 2000, asking that office to investigate further. Of course, it was too late.

The agent's request to headquarters came at a time when the FBI was nervous about the quality of the requests it was making to the secret Foreign Intelligence Surveillance Court. In the summer of 2000, the court had admonished an FBI agent who was found to have submitted several warrant requests with blatant inaccuracies that blurred the line between intelligence operations and criminal investigations. Accordingly, the FBI audited its requests, revised its rules, and implemented them more stringently. Agents got the impression that FISA warrants were too difficult or professionally risky to pursue, even though the court had never denied any and only modified five warrant requests among thousands since its creation in 1978.

It is undeniable that, in this instance and others, FBI officials wasted precious time and energy arguing whether the privacy wall prevented certain actions and collaboration. Unfortunately, these arguments were misguided in several ways. First, in the New York example, the debate was not so much about the privacy wall as about the resource wall between criminal and intelligence investigations. The agent making the request was not motivated by wanting a criminal prosecution but rather by wanting the human resources, which at the time were greater on the criminal side of the wall. Next, FBI headquarters brought both poor and overly cautious legal analysis to its interpretation of the wall. Indeed, according to the 9/11 Commission, there was no wall to overcome in this particular controversy. "Because Mihdhar was being sought for his possible connection to or knowledge of the *Cole* bombing, he could be investigated or tracked under the existing *Cole* criminal case. No new criminal case was needed for the criminal agent to begin searching for Mihdhar" (National Commission 2004, 271). As proven by the 100 percent approval rate of FISA warrant requests, the privacy wall—when properly interpreted—provided the government sufficient flexibility to conduct operations and share information while allowing some minimal oversight by an independent court.

Even assuming the privacy wall was an obstacle in late August 2001, there were many opportunities much earlier in the same investigation of these two terrorists that might have prevented the attacks. And they had little to do with privacy. Rather, as the Center for Democracy and Technology argues, "Intelligence and law enforcement officials weren't effectively sharing information and using their existing powers not because of legal barriers, but because of their overly strict interpretation of then-existing law, cultural problems, and turf wars among agencies" (CDT 2003).

Missed Opportunities

Every place that something could have gone wrong in this over a year and a half, it went wrong. All the processes that had been put in place, all the safeguards, everything else, they failed at every possible opportunity. Nothing went right.

—A CIA agent working with the FBI, referring to the missed leads and opportunities to identify al Qaeda operatives who came to the United States to participate in the September 11 attacks (U.S. Congress 2003, 151)

Both the *9/11 Commission Report* and the July 2003 report of the House and Senate Intelligence Committees of Congress found several missed opportunities to identify, track, and intercept two, possibly three, of the September 11 hijackers.

As of January 2000, the CIA had information linking one of the September 11 terrorists to a known al Qaeda operative (later responsible for planning the attack on the navy ship USS *Cole* in October 2000). They attended a meeting together in Malaysia. According to CIA director George Tenet, "We had at that point the level of detail needed to watchlist [September 11 hijacker Khalid al-Mihdhar]—that is, to nominate him to State Department for refusal of entry into the U.S. or to deny him another visa." However, they chose not to—missed opportunity number one. "Our officers remained focused on the surveillance operation and did not do so" (U.S. Congress 2003, 145). The decision to monitor rather than "watchlist" al-Mihdhar proved to be a mistake with serious consequences. The CIA lost track of al-Mihdhar when he traveled to Thailand because, according to one CIA agent, "we were unable to mobilize what we needed to mobilize" (U.S. Congress 2003, 147). If CIA agents had kept track of al-Mihdhar, it is likely they would have acquired more information and followed him to the United States—missed opportunity number two.

Also in January 2000, the CIA tentatively connected al-Mihdhar to Nawaf al-Hazmi, who would also turn out to be a

September 11 hijacker. He was at the same meeting in Malaysia and traveled with al-Mihdhar to Thailand, but the CIA had difficulty confirming his full name and identity. The National Security Agency, another U.S. intelligence agency, had some information about al-Hazmi. It was minimal but enough to connect al-Hazmi to al Qaeda and confirm the CIA's thread on al-Hazmi. Also, the information was sitting in the NSA's database. But the NSA did not share this information with the CIA or other U.S. agencies, and the CIA did not ask for it. There has never been any privacy wall between NSA and CIA sharing. NSA director Michael Hayden explained, "We did not disseminate information we received in early 1999 that was unexceptional in its content except that it associated the name of Nawaf al-Hazmi with al-Qa'ida" (Ibid., 145). If the NSA and CIA had shared, this "unexceptional" fact might have led to another September 11 hijacker being placed on a watch list, tracked, and intercepted—missed opportunity number three.

This sharing, had it taken place, might have led to the identification of a third hijacker, Nawaf's brother Salem al-Hazmi. In yet another distinct database, the U.S. State Department had records showing that the two brothers obtained visas to travel in the United States from the same consulate in Jeddah, within the same time period that al-Mihdhar did—missed opportunity number four.

In March 2000, the CIA's Osama bin Laden unit learned that Nawaf al-Hazmi (who at this point, as far as the CIA knew, was only tentatively connected to the more definitive al Qaeda member Khalid al-Mihdhar) had flown into Los Angeles in January. An agent pointed out to the unit that it was interesting that someone connected to al-Mihdhar followed a trip to Malaysia with a trip to the United States. But the CIA did not investigate further, put the name on a watch list, or inform the FBI that a potential "terrorist operative" had entered the country. If any agents had investigated, they would have discovered that Nawaf arrived with Khalid, the same terrorist they lost track of in Thailand. The CIA claims its agents "missed" the March warning; they somehow did not read it. Director Tenet said, "During the intense operations to thwart [other] threats, the watchlist task in the case of these two al-Qa'ida operatives slipped through. The error exposed a weakness in our internal training and an inconsistent understanding of watchlist thresholds" (Ibid., 148). Missed opportunity number five.

Nawaf al-Hazmi and Khalid al-Mihdhar settled in southern California, securing a lease and driver's licenses in their real names and taking flight lessons. In June 2000, al-Mihdhar flew to Oman, Jordan, where he applied for a visa extension with the Immigration and Naturalization Service (INS), using his address in southern California. A year later, on June 13, 2001, he circumvented the visa extension requirements and got a new U.S. visa in Saudi Arabia merely by using a new passport (albeit with the same name) and checking a box saying he had not been to the United States before. He returned to the United States on July 4, 2001—missed opportunity number six.

In January 2001, the CIA finally confirmed the connection between Nawaf al-Hazmi and Khalid al-Mihdhar. Following the USS *Cole* attack the agency knew al-Mihdhar was an important, or at least dangerous, player in al Qaeda. The CIA insists it then shared this information with the FBI, but FBI records indicate there was no notification until August 30, 2001. Missed opportunity number seven.

In May 2001, a CIA agent pursuing leads on al Qaeda members met with an FBI agent working on the USS *Cole* investigation. The CIA agent wanted to see if the latter recognized a photo of al-Mihdhar as someone who was, or was connected to, a suspect being held by an unnamed country in the *Cole* investigation. The CIA agent shared nothing more than the photo and the name, even though further information—such as the man's U.S. visas—might have revealed other connections or sparked further investigation and would not have been barred by the privacy wall. According to the CIA agent, he did not share more information because the information was operational in nature, and he would not share operations information unless expressly permitted to do so. His motivation is not clear. It would seem he was acting out of the insular, territorial instincts thought to prevail among the agencies, but perhaps he was simply not interested, given his particular focus at the time on Yemen. There were no laws, rules, or orders preventing him from sharing more information. It was the eighth missed opportunity in the investigation.

The agencies did not pull together and make the critical connections until late August 2001. An FBI agent working for the joint Counterterrorist Center saw the connection between al-Mihdhar and al-Hazmi and checked with an INS agent, who discovered that the two had entered the country. The two terrorists were immediately put on a watch list, al-Mihdhar's visa was revoked, and the FBI was warned to investigate their presence as "a risk to the national security of the United States" (U.S. Congress 2002, 153). FBI headquarters assigned the case to its New York field office, because al-Mihdhar had last entered the United States through a New York airport. The FBI did not, however, inform its southern California offices, which happened to be working with informants who knew the two men and likely would have made the connection more quickly—the ninth opportunity missed.

Finally, there came the problem, described earlier, that arguably resulted from the existence of a wall of privacy between intelligence and law enforcement. The field office wanted to open a criminal investigation, rather than an intelligence investigation, because the crime team had more resources and could move more quickly. But the legal unit, citing the rules that prohibited the FBI from using information garnered purely from intelligence operations rather than investigations of crimes, instructed the agent that it could be pursued only as an FBI intelligence operation.

However, as the 9/11 Commission Report states,

> It is now clear that everyone involved was confused about the rules governing the sharing and use of information gathered in intelligence channels. Because Mihdhar was being sought for his possible connection to or knowledge of the *Cole* bombing, he could be investigated or tracked under the existing *Cole* criminal case. No new criminal case was needed for the criminal agent to begin searching for Mihdhar. And as NSA had approved the passage of its information to the criminal agent, he could have conducted a search using all available information. As a result of this confusion, the criminal agents who were knowledgeable about al Qaeda and experienced with criminal investigative techniques, including finding suspects and possible criminal charges, were thus excluded from the search. (National Commission 2004, 271)

As mentioned earlier, between August 27 and September 10, 2001, an FBI agent conducted some basic investigation in the New York area but turned up nothing. On September 11, 2001, the same day of the attacks, the agent contacted the FBI in Los Angeles, asking them to investigate further.

It is important not to understate the difficulty of counter-terrorism investigating. It can be like looking for a needle in a haystack. That is, the agencies have to respond to multiple threats, suspicious leads, diversionary maneuvers, and false alarms all over the world—investigative clues that at the earliest stages look remarkably similar to one another—whereas a terrorist needs only to slip past their guard once. Where the September 11 trail began (at the January 2000 Malaysia meeting), the intelligence agencies were focused on other threats, including what became the October 2000 attack on the USS *Cole.* However, as the narration of missed opportunities above suggests, it is also important not to understate the other problems that need to be fixed besides those that tear down privacy protections in the United States.

Other Culprits

Other factors contributed to the failure to prevent the September 11 attacks as well. Fixing these problems may not guarantee the prevention of future attacks, but they are managerial improvements that will reduce the risk and promote efficiency without eroding a valued right of democratic societies.

Prior to September 11, the FBI had too few translators—only forty Arabic speakers and twenty-five Farsi speakers—to translate communications it was intercepting. The FBI had a backlog of millions of hours of untranslated interceptions. One interception, received on September 10 but not translated until September 12, recorded an al Qaeda operative stating, "Tomorrow is zero hour." Another, also from September 10, stated, "The match begins tomorrow" (Klaidman and Isikoff 2003, 29). Intelligence operatives have dismissed the portent of these two recordings, saying it was not specific enough to constitute actionable intelligence. However, the point remains that it is impossible to know what is valuable and important intelligence if it is not translated in time.

As of November 2003, although the FBI had increased the number of translators to 200 for Arabic and 75 for Farsi, it still could not translate hundreds of hours of surveillance recordings each week. The language barrier is a problem the agencies are addressing and one that does not require any reduction in privacy rights.

In addition to improving their ability to understand foreigners, intelligence agencies could afford to improve the ways it listens and responds to agents in the field. On July 10, 2001, an FBI agent in Arizona noticed terrorist suspects were attending flight schools and warned headquarters that it should investigate whether al Qaeda operatives might be taking flight training. Headquarters said it was interested, but it pursued the idea lethargically and failed to share the observation with other field offices.

Another element—which can be improved only so much— is human fallibility. In law enforcement, intelligence investigations, and border control, there is inevitably a degree of discretion involved in the decisions made by agents. Sometimes, the judgments made are proper, sometimes they are improper, and sometimes it is impossible to know until after the critical moment. For instance, Jose E. Melendez-Perez, an immigration agent, stopped Mohamed al-Quatani from entering the United States because al-Quatani did not have a return ticket or hotel reservation, would not say who would be picking him up or supporting him during his stay, and "bottom line . . . he gave me the creeps" (Arena et al. 2004). Authorities now believe that al-Quatani was going to be picked up by September 11 hijacker Mohammed Atta to be the fifth hijacker on the plane that crashed in Pennsylvania en route to Washington, D.C. If so, the humble functionary Melendez-Perez may have saved many lives and the White House or U.S. Capitol; presumably, the passengers on that plane were able to overcome or intimidate the four hijackers but might not have succeeded with a fifth hijacker. Similarly successful, U.S. consular officials stationed abroad denied visas for four other potential terrorists.

On the other hand, another hijacker, Saeed Alghamdi, presented a similar lack of credentials for entering the United States, was questioned by an immigration agent but was allowed to enter because he persuaded the agent he was a tourist. Also, U.S. officials permitted hijackers to enter despite the fact that between two and eight of them had passports that showed evidence of manipulation or suspicious travel histories and despite five being sent to agents for questioning who, unlike Melendez-Perez, made a different judgment call. According to the National Commission on Terrorist Acts against the United

States, none of the terrorists filled out their visa applications correctly, and three lied that they had never applied for a visa before—a fact that could have been easily checked if better systems were in place (2004b).

Finally, circumstantial evidence suggests that the computer systems used by related agencies were—both before and well after September 11—woefully inadequate. In March 2002—six months after the attacks, while intelligence and law enforcement agencies were still operating at peak capacity to investigate the attacks—the U.S. Immigration and Naturalization Service sent official notices to a Florida flight school that two of the hijackers had valid, approved student visas. "It certainly showed how incompetent the INS is," said Republican congressman James Sensenbrenner. "Congress in 1996 told them to get a student visa tracking system and provided the money for it, and they never got around to doing it" (CBS 2002). Later that same month, the Federal Aviation Administration still had one of the terrorists in its pilots' database and mailed a newsletter to his former address.

The Privacy Rights of Young People

Youth Privacy in the Era of Criminalized Youth and Fortified Schools

On April 20, 1999, two students at Columbine High School in Colorado terrorized the school, shooting shotguns and semiautomatic weapons and detonating homemade bombs. The two youths killed twelve children and one adult, wounded twenty-three others, and traumatized countless other children, families, and community members.

The incident was the worst in a series of ten unrelated multiple-victim school shootings from 1997 to 2001 in the United States. (Similar tragedies have since been repeated in Erfurt, Germany, where a nineteen-year-old shot and killed seventeen people at school on April 26, 2002, and in Red Lake, Minnesota, where a sixteen-year-old killed ten people at his high school on March 21, 2005.) Although these high-profile shootings were unlike other school violence, which had been concentrated in poor, urban districts, they fueled the perception that youths everywhere were more violent and schools were less safe than ever before. Immediately after Columbine, many schools added metal detectors and cameras, hired or increased the number of school security guards patrolling the schools, reduced the number of accessible entrances to the schools, required students to carry their possessions in backpacks made of see-through plastic, and required students to wear identity cards.

The incidents led to the fortification of suburban schools, as well as new policies and practices to aggressively monitor and address student misbehavior. Fear of violence in schools, along with increased surveillance in greater society, has led to the erosion of privacy for young people in the place where they spend much of their day and start to develop their expectations of the world. Principal Deborah Williams of Annapolis High School in Maryland instituted a see-through backpack policy in 2003, saying, "We will not allow students the opportunity to engage in any activity that will not lend to a safe and orderly environment" (Reimer 2003, B2). Is this new aggressiveness necessary or an overreaction? It is debatable. But it cannot be disputed that the privacy of young people has taken a beating in the post-Columbine era.

In many ways, the post-Columbine policies merely brought suburban schools in line with the high security and privacy depravations that urban schools had been experiencing since the early 1980s due to high-profile crimes involving mainly urban young people of color.

A decade and a day before the Columbine shootings, one such incident seared itself into the American imagination of youth, particularly urban minority youths, and led to the widely held impression that young African Americans and Latinos were increasingly dangerous and predatory. On April 19, 1989, a number of robberies and assaults occurred in New York's Central Park, purportedly committed by a "wolf pack" of "wilding" teens. As the *New York Post* described it three days later, "packs of bloodthirsty teens from the tenements, bursting with boredom and rage, roam the streets getting kicks from an evening of ultra-violence" (Hancock 2003, 38). On the same night, a twenty-eight-year-old white woman was attacked, raped, and left for dead while jogging in the park. Five African American and Latino teens, ages fourteen to sixteen, were arrested for both the marauding and the attack on the Central Park jogger. After twenty hours of questioning, the boys admitted to the attack. They later recanted. They were convicted and spent many years in prison, based almost entirely on their confessions. In 2002, however, the "bloodthirsty" teens' convictions were overturned. A serial rapist in prison admitted that he alone committed the crime, DNA evidence confirmed that he had raped her, and a review of the confessions and physical evidence revealed a version of events much closer to his version than that of the young boys' confessions.

Meanwhile, in the intervening thirteen years, the image of the wilding teens from Harlem became an exaggerated, racist symbol for the problem of youth violence in the United States. In 1996, Professor John DiIulio elevated this image to the realm of credible science. DiIulio predicted that, due to the depravity of youth upbringing and the rise in the youth population, a new breed of superviolent youth—which he dubbed "superpredators"—would beset our communities. To Congress, he described these children as "a new horde from hell that kills, maims and terrorizes merely to become known, or for no reason at all" (K. Roberts 2001). DiIulio has since recanted. "If I knew then what I know now, I would have shouted for prevention of crimes," he said in 2001 (Becker 2001, A19). But too late. The idea caught hold. Magazines put it on their front covers: "Superpredators Arrive: Should We Cage the New Breed of Vicious Kids?" asked *Newsweek* on January 26, 1996; "Teenage Time Bombs," printed *U.S. News and World Report* a few months later. Even President Bill Clinton rehashed the theory in 1997, saying, "We know we've got about six years to turn this juvenile crime thing around or our country is going to be living with chaos," despite acknowledging the steady drop in violent crime (Hunt 1997, 5A).

Starting in 1983, there was a substantial increase in youth violence coinciding with the increased possession of firearms by young people. But the "epidemic of youth violence" peaked in 1993, and, despite an increased population of 3 million teens since 1990, violent crime by youths has decreased ever since. According to a 2001 report of the U.S. surgeon general, "By 1999, arrest rates for homicide, rape, and robbery had all dropped below 1983 rates. Arrest rates for aggravated assault, however, were nearly 70 percent higher than they were in 1983, having declined only 24 percent from the peak rates in 1994" (Satcher 2001).

The Central Park Jogger case and the superpredator theory fueled new "tough-on-crime" policies metal detectors and po-

**"Myths about Youths" from
the Surgeon General's Report
on Youth Violence**

- Most future offenders can be identified in early childhood
- Child abuse and neglect inevitably lead to violent behavior later in life
- African American and Hispanic youths are more likely to become involved in violence than other racial or ethnic groups
- A new violent breed of young superpredators threatens the United States
- Getting tough with juvenile offenders by trying them in adult criminal courts reduces the likelihood that they will commit more crimes
- Nothing works with respect to treating or preventing violent behavior
- Most violent youths will end up being arrested for a violent crime

lice in schools, newer and tougher juvenile prisons, boot camps, the prosecution and punishment of minors in adult courts and prisons ("adult time for adult crime")—that disproportionately impacted poor, urban youths and hence African American and Hispanic young people. At every moment in the criminal justice system when a decision could be made to treat a young person more harshly or less harshly—whether to arrest or warn, what to charge a youth with, whether to refer to juvenile court or divert to alternatives, whether to lock up or release prior to the court hearing, whether to transfer the youth to adult court, whether the youth is found guilty or innocent, whether to commit to juvenile prison or incarcerate in adult prison, and even how long the youth remains committed or incarcerated—white youth were more likely to receive easier treatment and African American youth were more likely to receive harsher treatment, even when charged with similar offenses. Among black and white youth with no prior commitments to state facilities, six times as many black youth were admitted than white youth. Of those admitted for the first time for violent offenses, black youth were committed at nine times the rate of white youth; for property crimes, four times as much; and for drug offenses, forty-eight times as much (Poe-Yamagata and Jones 2000).

In the first years of the millennium, there was some movement away from the harshly punitive approach and back toward a rehabilitation model in the juvenile justice system. Notably, the Supreme Court ruled in 2005 that the execution of people for crimes committed when they were under eighteen is unconstitutional, bringing the United States in line with most of the rest of the world. (Between 1990 and 2003, of the seventy-eight countries that have capital punishment, only eight executed a minor—China, Democratic Republic of Congo, Iran, Nigeria, Pakistan, Saudi Arabia, the United States, and Yemen.) Following a high-profile murder spree in which a teen and his father-figure friend used a sniper rifle to kill ten people, wound three others, and terrorize the region around Washington, D.C., over the course of three weeks in October 2002, a Virginia jury refrained from sentencing the youth to death.

Nonetheless, the disproportionate impact of juvenile and criminal justice policies fell on the backs of minority youth. Moreover, despite the overturning of the Central Park verdicts and the debunking of the superpredator theory, popular perception and images of youth as more evil than ever persisted, and much of the punitive approach and privacy invasions they engendered also remain. Combined with the reaction to the Columbine shootings and the general growth in surveillance, American youth across a wide spectrum of demographics and geography enjoy less privacy today than in the past.

As a matter of U.S. constitutional law, students do not shed their constitutional rights at the schoolhouse gates. In the area of First Amendment free expression, for example, school officials need more than an "undifferentiated fear or apprehension of disturbance" to restrict the expression of students in activities not sponsored by the school. However, students' rights, particularly their right to privacy, are significantly diminished the moment they enter school.

Searches by Police and School Officials

A magazine article for U.S. school principals touts, "Perhaps the most significant tool that educational leaders rely on to stem the flow of weapons and drugs in schools is searches of students, their lockers, and property" (Russo and Mawdsley 2004).

Yet school officials and police must themselves obey the law when conducting searches. Recently, school video cameras caught the principal and police possibly breaking the law. In November 2003, a high school principal in Goose Creek, South Carolina, received reports of marijuana being sold in the hallways. He called the local police, who came in, observed students on the surveillance camera, and planned a raid. Three days later, at 6:40 AM, guns drawn and yelling, twelve police officers in helmets and riot gear raided an otherwise peaceful hallway and forced 107 students onto the ground. They handcuffed twelve students who were slow to get to their knees and, according to some sources, put their guns to the heads of other students. Drug dogs sniffed and pulled at the students' backpacks, and the officers searched their pockets, socks, and wallets.

The police found no drugs and made no arrests. One officer was caught on tape threatening, "If you're an innocent bystander to what has transpired here today, you can thank those people that are bringing dope into this school. Every time we think there's dope in this school, we're going to be coming up here to deal with it, and this is one of the ways we can deal with it" (Associated Press 2003a, B3). Although the school is 80 percent white, three-quarters of the students targeted were African American. "Funny how that happens, isn't it?" remarked one parent (Drug Reform Coordination Network 2003).

This school apparently lost sight of the warning of Supreme Court Justice William Brennan, "Schools cannot expect their children to learn the lessons of good citizenship when the school authorities themselves disregard the fundamental principles underpinning our constitutional freedoms" (*Doe v. Renfrow* 1981, 1027–1028).

Typically, when school officials suspect a student has a weapon or drugs, they call the police. But the laws regarding when the police and when the school can search a student are different. Police have to abide by the same rules for police searches inside the school as out on the street. There are several circumstances under which police may conduct a lawful search. In general, police have to have "probable cause" that a person has committed a crime or is committing a crime. "Probable cause" is created by reliable facts and circumstances that suggest to the common sense of a reasonable person that criminal activity is afoot. It is more than mere rumor, innuendo, or even a "strong reason to suspect." Specifically, police officers may search when:

- They ask a student if they may search and the student consents
- They have a warrant from a judge or magistrate that is based on probable cause
- They have made a lawful arrest based on probable cause
- They learn or see things that create probable cause to believe criminal activity is afoot
- There are exigent circumstances (emergencies or life-threatening situations) that justify an immediate search
- They have a reasonable suspicion that a student possesses a weapon that endangers them, in which case they may conduct a pat-down search on the outside of the student's clothes to feel for anything that might reasonably be a weapon

According to the Supreme Court, school officials—including school security guards or resource officers—are responsible for the well-being, control, and education of a large number of children. These responsibilities allow schools to be more intrusive than police officers. In practice, therefore, schools often call police officers to "stand by"—literally to stand next to the school official and student—as the school official conducts searches. If a student has guns or drugs—or "contraband," which is widely defined and may include items that have innocent uses but that police associate with drug use—the police can arrest the student on the spot and take possession of the evidence.

In *New Jersey v. T.L.O.* (1985), the Supreme Court held that, although the Fourth Amendment applies to students and protects them from unreasonable searches and seizures, the schools are held to a lower standard than police officers. A school official may search a student's bag if the official has "reasonable suspicion" that the student violated a school rule or criminal law and that evidence of the activity may be found in the place to be searched. If a school official sees a student smoking cigarettes but the student denies it, it is reasonable for the official to search the purse or backpack the student is carrying for cigarettes. If, while looking for tobacco cigarettes, the official also discovers marijuana, the student is in big trouble. Or if the official discovers rolling paper often used to wrap marijuana cigarettes, he may lawfully dig deeper to look for further evidence of marijuana and has still acted within the bounds of the law. In either scenario, the school official has committed a lawful search based on reasonable suspicion. These general principles apply to almost all searches at schools other than drug testing.

What is "reasonable" depends on the circumstances. There are no bright-line rules, and courts' interpretations of reasonableness differ. Consequently, the law on school searches varies in different states and federal jurisdictions. Generally, the more serious the threat, the more intrusive a search can be, although it must still be reasonable.

For locker searches, for example, there are generally two categories of searches with many variations within each category. The first category is particularized searches, when schools suspect a particular individual or individuals of wrongdoing. Searches based on particularized suspicion must be reasonable, both at their inception and in their scope. In other words, the search must be based on commonsense facts supporting the suspicion of the person and place to be searched—it must be more than a hunch. And the search must not be more intrusive than necessary. It would not be reasonable to search for a semiautomatic weapon in a wallet, because it would not fit. It would not be reasonable to search a student's locker for a stolen pencil sharpener if the pencil sharpener was already found in her bag. But what happens if a school official is not sure who precisely may be the wrongdoer? For example, what if a principal receives reliable information that two students were just in a knife fight in the cafeteria, but upon arriving in the cafeteria he finds seven students standing in a circle looking sheepish, no knives visible, and no clear indication of which of the seven were in the fight? Many courts would allow the principal to search a number of students who might be guilty of misconduct so long as there are facts that make them likely to be among the guilty parties. On the other hand, most courts will not allow a search to be conducted *solely* because a student is a member of a clique, gang, or other group. It most certainly would be unlawful for an official to search someone solely because the official did not like her or because of her race.

The second category is locker sweeps that are not based on particular suspicion of wrongdoing by certain students. Courts in some jurisdictions have held that, because the schools own the lockers and put up notices that they may search at any time, students have no expectation of privacy and that routine sweeps are constitutional. Other courts have struck down laws permitting routine sweeps based solely on ownership and notice. These jurisdictions generally require schools to document the reason for conducting a sweep and then to employ a neutral method, such as truly random selection of a number of but not all lockers.

More and more, school officials are calling in police officers to conduct exterior sweeps of lockers with drug-sniffing, gun-sniffing, or bomb-sniffing dogs. The U.S. Supreme Court has held that such sweeps when conducted in a public area are not searches but, at most, a "minimally intrusive act." (Pennsylvania, however, has held that its state constitution grants greater protection and that dog-sniffing searches require reasonable suspicion.) It is generally viewed as more intrusive to have dogs sniff students themselves or their bags. And states and federal jurisdictions generally hold that a dog's alert that a particular locker, bag, or clothing item might contain drugs is not enough *by itself* to create probable cause to justify a further search by police. Ordinarily, police will seek more information and a warrant before searching the locker. Another gray area in the law is what school officials (rather than the police) can do when a police dog sniffs out possible contraband. Some jurisdictions allow schools to search the locker in this instance, because the dog's alert satisfies the lower standard of reasonable suspicion. Other court jurisdictions view this cooperation between police and schools as "subterfuge," a way for the police to sneak around the protections of the Fourth Amendment.

Drug Tests at School

The use of illegal drugs by young people decreased by 11 percent between 2001 and 2003, to 17.3 percent of all eighth, tenth, and twelfth graders, according to a U.S. government survey (Associated Press 2003b, A9). The drop is likely related to television advertising campaigns. Despite the drop, many school officials and community leaders feel that a more aggressive approach is required. So schools are turning to drug testing, surveillance, and aggressive searching of students.

It used to be that school officials were required to have "individualized suspicion" that a particular student was breaking school rules in order to conduct a drug test of that student. If school officials did not have a good reason to suspect a particular student, the test would be a violation of the Fourth Amendment to the Constitution, which protects against unreasonable searches and seizures.

However, in two decisions over the past decade, the U.S. Supreme Court opened the door to suspicionless drug testing of students involved in competitive school programs. In *Veronia School District 47J v. Acton* (1995), the Court allowed random drug testing of student athletes, ruling that the school's interest in protecting young people from drugs outweighed the students' interest in the privacy of their bodies. In *Pottawatomie v. Earls* (2002), the Court extended this ruling to apply to testing of students involved in competitive extracurricular programs, such as academic teams, cheerleading, band, and choir. The Court considered it a "negligible" intrusion of privacy to have "a faculty monitor [wait] outside the closed restroom stall for the student to produce a sample and . . . 'listen for the normal sounds of urination . . .' then pour . . . the sample into two bottles that are sealed and placed into a mailing pouch along with a consent form signed by the student" (Id., 824).

The Court's language in the case was quite broad and, therefore, may be used in the future to uphold random suspicionless drug testing of all students in a school or other types of biological tests or sampling of students. "While schoolchildren do not shed their constitutional rights when they enter the schoolhouse . . . Fourth Amendment rights . . . are different in public schools than elsewhere; the 'reasonableness' inquiry cannot disregard the schools' 'custodial and tutelary responsibility for children.'" Approximately 19 percent of schools in the United States have some form of drug testing, according to a University of Michigan study completed in May 2003.

A private school in Chicago instituted drug testing of all its students in fall 2004. Because it is private, it is not bound by constitutional protections against government (that is, public school) invasions of privacy.

Critics of the U.S. approach to fighting drugs discount the dip in drug use and say aggressive policing drives up the price of

The most comprehensive study of school drug testing ever conducted found that there was no less drug use at schools that conducted drug tests than at schools that did not. The rates were the same even at the few schools that randomly tested their entire student populations. One of the surveyors, Dr. Lloyd Johnston of the University of Michigan's Institute for Social Research, commented, "The way that drug testing has been carried out in the schools looks very unpromising. I have no doubt that one could design a drug testing program that could deter teen drug use, but at what monetary cost and at what cost in terms of intrusion into the privacy of our young people?" (University of Michigan 2003; Yamaguchi 2003).

drugs, which leads to a violent, lucrative underground market that perpetuates the lure of drug selling and drug use. At the same time, the aggressive policing leads to violent intrusions of privacy and other rights. Some argue that the government should focus more on education and treatment. Others argue that the government should legalize and regulate the use of drugs in order to eliminate the underground market for drugs. Dr. Marsha Rosenbaum of the Drug Policy Alliance says, "Teenage use of alcohol and other drugs is cyclical, and has gone up and down and then up and down again . . . While we'd all like to see a reduction in drug use among teens, it is a mistake to evaluate the success of American drug policy simply on current prevalence, when we continue to see alarming rates of death, disease and crime resulting from our misguided War on Drugs" (2003).

The 2003 "State of Our Nation's Youth" survey found that only 8 percent of teens, ages fourteen to eighteen, felt that pressure to use drugs and drink was a major problem in their lives. Of those surveyed, 75 percent of teens reported good relations with their families, and most said they would prefer to spend free time with family than hanging out with friends or doing other activities. According to the surveyor, Peter Hart, "The kids who are in high school are telling parents, 'We're listening to you, we care about what you think, and we'd like to spend more time with you'" (Feller 2003, A1).

Security and Surveillance in School and at Home

Both at school and at home, adults are increasing the ways they monitor young people. There are even efforts to allow children to be monitored at school from home. Arizona is pioneering the use of facial-recognition cameras in schools—not to catch kids skipping homeroom, at least not yet. Rather, the cameras are being installed in a Phoenix-area middle school to find lost children and detect sex offenders and suspected abductors who pass by the cameras. Despite the known inaccuracies of the cameras, the chief superintendent in the state would like to see the program expand to every school in the state.

Meanwhile, starting in 2002, schools in Biloxi, Mississippi, pioneered a new level of school surveillance by being the first to install surveillance cameras in every classroom, including the classrooms of six year olds. "It's a deterrent to misbehavior because students know if they make the wrong choice, it's been recorded" (Solomon 2004, A1). The schools have used the cameras to catch a child sleeping in class, horseplaying behind the teacher's back, cheating, and stealing ice cream money. However the live feed is available not only in-house, but also on the Internet, protected by a password that is available, at this point, only to school administrators. Students or parents who wish to dispute a teacher's discipline or reports do not have access to the video recordings without a court order.

The schools in Escambia County, Florida, are planning to make it easier for police to monitor the school. The system's engineer explained, "There are plans for a wireless network on the front of the school. And police cruisers can have a wireless device in them and log into video that's in the school." This decrease in privacy is driven not by local problems but by fear of that historic school shooting. The engineer continues, "If a Columbine incident were to ever happen again, a police cruiser could pull up to the school and have a better idea of what's happening in it" (Pace 2004, 1C).

Schools elsewhere in the United States and the United Kingdom are likely to follow the lead of Biloxi. Some teachers and parents want to give parents access to the live Internet stream of their kids in class, which is already available on certain U.S. military bases.

Parents have increasing power to track their child's every move, through GPS devices in bracelets, car-tracking magnet boxes, cell phones, and implantable chips. With U.S. law requiring all new cell phones to permit tracking through the nearest cell towers by 2005, this surveillance will only increase. It is predicted that 42 million Americans will have some type of technology product that tracks location by the end of 2005. Tracking services permit parents to watch their children's location on mapping software or receive an e-mail alert when a child travels outside a parent-designated boundary. Many teens are not excited about this particular development. "I think if your parents really care that much they should just put a leash on you," said one teen from Seattle (Harmon 2003, A1).

Bodily and Sexual Privacy in a Genetic Age

The privacy of our bodies presents some of the most socially and politically contentious issues in the already fraught battlefields of privacy. What others do to our bodies, such as police strip searches or drug-sniffing dog searches of students, is a source of strong emotion. What we do to our own bodies also touches a nerve with others. Although it appears to be less true in Europe and certain other parts of the world, how we use our bodies sexually is another contentious aspect of the body, what is or should be private, and what is subject to public inspection and control. In this section, we touch on the issues of the privacy of sexual minorities and abortion and contraception (whose histories were briefly described in Chapter 1) and focus on the implications for bodily privacy of the new genetic era as symbolized by the successful completion of the mapping of the entire human genome in April 2003.

The Privacy Rights of Sexual Minorities

In 2003, the U.S. Supreme Court held that laws prohibiting sodomy violate the constitutional right to privacy. The decision in *Lawrence v. Texas* overturned the court's 1984 decision in *Bowers v. Hardwick*. Although the Court based its decision on the right to privacy of sexual relations between consenting adults behind closed doors, there had been speculation that the Court might instead use the right to equal treatment under the law as the basis for overturning the sodomy law. Under an equality rationale, the Court could have established that the law prohibiting sodomy subjected gay men and lesbians to unequal treatment. Indeed, one justice who wrote separately but supported the majority said both rationales were valid and part of why the law was unconstitutional.

Often, the right to privacy overlaps with other protections, such as the right to equal treatment, the right to religious freedom, or the right to free association. This overlap results when—as has so often happened throughout history and throughout the world—a definable group is singled out for discrimination or mistreatment. For example, as discussed in Chapter 1, when Hitler and the Nazis deemed Jews and other minorities impure, these groups were subjected to violations of their associational, bodily, communication, data, and spatial privacy. Their meetings and religious services were disrupted; their bodies were sterilized, experimented on, and gassed; their communications were monitored; their data were collected, stored, and used for unlawful purposes; their homes were invaded; and, in the street, they were regularly stopped and searched. Of course, these violations of privacy also violated other rights and, because they were also persecuted on the basis of religion, race, political belief, sexuality, and nationality, they amounted to something even more serious—genocide.

Yet, arguably, among the rights violated by Nazis, privacy stands out. If these groups' privacy rights—to hold and practice their faith in private, to have their bodies respected, to control medical decisions about their bodies, to not disclose information about themselves, and to be secure in their persons, homes, and papers—had remained intact, the bigotry, torment, and violence directed at the Jews and other targeted minorities would have been limited. Of course, it is impossible to know what history would have held if one thing or another had been different. But the argument makes an important point about privacy: often, privacy is a safeguard to protect people from discrimination and violations of other rights, at least within a protected sphere. It may not protect a gay high school student from harassment at school, but it will, in the privacy of his home, protect his right to exclude harassers, read about issues important to gay teens, and even associate with other gay teens. *Bowers v. Hardwick,* by allowing police officers to arrest a couple in the privacy of their own home, erased this hope for gay men and women in the United States. The overturning of *Bowers* restores the hope of such protection, although it remains to be seen how far privacy will protect other minorities and sexual minorities.

Justice Antonin Scalia worries that, after *Lawrence,* the right to privacy will do too much to protect sexual minorities. In his dissent in *Lawrence,* he wrote:

> State laws against bigamy, same-sex marriage, adult incest, prostitution, masturbation, adultery, fornication, bestiality, and obscenity are likewise sustainable only in light of *Bowers'* validation of laws based on moral choices. Every single one of these laws is called into question by today's decision; the Court makes no effort to cabin the scope of its decision to exclude them from its holding. See *ante,* at 11 (noting "an emerging awareness that liberty gives substantial protection to adult persons in deciding how to conduct their private lives *in matters pertaining to sex*"). The impossibility of distinguishing homosexuality from other traditional "morals" offenses is precisely why *Bowers* rejected the rational-basis challenge. "The law," it said, "is constantly based on notions of morality, and if all laws representing essentially moral choices are to be invalidated under the Due Process Clause, the courts will be very busy indeed." (2490)

Indeed, Scalia is right that it is unlikely that the right to privacy will protect the private sexual behavior of only lesbians and gay men. Other sexual minorities may also be entitled to such privacy, if society and the courts will allow it. These future conflicts—such as the rights of cousins to marry, questions at the margin of sexual and marital age of consent laws, and the rights of intersex or transgendered individuals—are likely to raise the same moral concerns contested in *Bowers* and *Lawrence.*

In April 2002, the *New York Times* reported, "Contrary to widely held beliefs and longstanding taboos in America, first cousins can have children together without a great risk of birth defects or genetic disease, scientists are reporting today" (Grady 2002, A1). In the general population, 3 to 4 percent of births produce children with serious problems. Among first cousins, this rate is 1.7 to 2.8 percentage points higher. Although the rate of problems is slightly higher than in the general population, it is still quite low, and it is lower than other couples and groups whom laws do not regulate, such as parents with Huntington's disease, which has a 50 percent transmission rate.

Although past studies have produced similar conclusions, according to genetics doctor Arno Motulsky of the research panel convened by the National Society of Genetic Counselors, "Somehow this hasn't become general knowledge" (Ibid.). Twenty-four states forbid first-cousin marriages; six others require genetic counseling or other hurdles prior to marriage. Such laws are particular to the United States; European nations do not have them, and marriage among cousins is common practice on parts of other continents. The lack of information has led to misinformation and worse: doctors involved in the study cited one case of a woman receiving an abortion and another a tubal ligation based on bad information about the risk of first-cousin procreation. The research panel concluded that first cousins do not need to have any special genetic testing done prior to marrying or reproducing. They should follow the same precautions and seek the same tests that unrelated couples do.

The parameters of sexual age of consent laws are another issue at the cutting edge of privacy that is likely to become more contested in years to come. In 2002, the ACLU challenged a law that punished gay teens significantly more than heterosexual teens for the same sexual activities. Matthew Limon turned eighteen a week before having oral sex with a boy who was about to turn fifteen. The affair was entirely consensual, except that Kansas law deems a person under eighteen years old unable to consent. In this way, the law aims to protect young, impressionable people from the persuasion or manipulation of adults. Nonetheless, in recognition that relations between young people only a few years apart in age are less morally unacceptable than, say, a forty-year-old man and a fifteen-year-old, many states' laws provide for a lesser sentence for young adults in so-called Romeo and Juliet sexual relationships (ACLU 2002).

In Kansas, the law provided a lesser sentence for an adult under age nineteen who had consensual oral sex with a minor between ages fourteen and sixteen, so long as, in addition, the teenagers "are members of the opposite sex." (In Kansas, the Romeo and Juliet law also allowed the guilty eighteen-year-olds to stay off the sex-offender registry.) As a result, Matthew Limon was sentenced to seventeen years in prison, rather than fifteen months or less. The ACLU appealed the sentence to the U.S. Supreme Court, which, two days after its *Lawrence* decision, vacated the judgment and sent the case back to the Kansas courts. In January 2004, a Kansas appellate court again upheld the seventeen-year sentence, and the case is being appealed (*Windy City Times* 2004).

In 2000, the United Kingdom lowered the age of consent for sexual activity for same-sex couples from eighteen to sixteen. The consent age had already been sixteen for heterosexual couples. The change was required by a decision of the European Commission, which, on equality grounds, found the disparity to violate the European Convention on Human Rights. Members of the House of Lords vetoed the change several times, but the government used special powers to overcome the opposition (BBC 2000).

Yet another bodily privacy issue at the cutting edge for sexual minorities is the rights of transgendered or intersex people to determine their own physical sexual identity. In 1993, Anne Fausto-Sterling published an article in *The Sciences* titled "The Five Sexes," arguing that, rather than male and female, there ought to be five gender categories based on the diverse range of genes and genitalia that people are born with. "Chromosomes, hormones, the internal sex structures, the gonads and the external genitalia all vary more than most people realize" (2000, 20). Besides classic male and female categories, there would be true hermaphrodites who are born with one testis and one ovary, male pseudohermaphrodites born with testes and some aspect of female genitalia, and female pseudohermaphrodites born with ovaries and some aspect of male genitalia. In 1993, based on a medical expert's estimate, Fausto-Sterling reported that 4 percent of births fall outside the classic male-female duality and instead are better characterized as intersex (2000, 19). In 2000, she reported, after an exhaustive study of her own, that a more accurate estimate is that 1.7 percent of births are intersex, and only a small subset of this group have ambiguous genitalia that would require surgery if the parents wished to make the genitalia more traditional.

Since the 1950s, according to Fausto-Sterling, it has been standard practice to advise the parents of a child born with ambiguous genitalia to approve "corrective" surgery to craft the child's genitalia into an approximation of either a penis or a vagina, whichever the genitalia most resembles at birth, then to raise the child as the surgically assigned sex. The gender assignment could be made "solely on the basis of what made the best surgical sense" (2000, 20). However, dissenting voices are now being heard, notably from grown adults who were themselves subject to this surgery as newborns and who object to the practice. According to a *New York Times* article, affected people testified to the San Francisco Human Rights Commission about "lives burdened by secrecy, shame and medical complications: some said the surgeries robbed them of sexual sensation and likened the procedures to mutilation; others said they were made to feel like freaks when nothing was really wrong with them" (Navarro 2004, Sec. 9, 1). Katrina A. Karkazis, a Stanford University anthropologist, found that most of the adults she interviewed who had undergone a surgical change as babies were now unhappy. They "complained of lack of sensation or pain, of the need for repeated surgeries and of the fact that they had thick scarring and the genitals never looked 'normal.' Few were in intimate relationships" (Ibid.).

Some intersex advocates argue that society should tolerate a range of sexual identities and anatomies and that the person affected should be the only one making the decision about whether to have surgery and what kind. It is not an easy decision for parents of a newborn who must consider, first, what is physically and medically necessary based on little research and, second, what is psychologically best for the child based on their instincts. Is it better for the child to make the decision herself when she is grown? Will the potential teasing and embarrassment in the meantime cause more harm than making a choice now? If the surgery is conducted, do you ever tell the child about it?

Parents are coming to different conclusions. One parent, who chose not to authorize surgery, stated, "I just came to the conclusion that we'd raise her with as much confidence as we can. If she chooses as an adult to have the surgery, I'll support her." A different parent, who dismissed waiting for the child to grow older and give consent, stated, "You're the parent, you make the decisions. We felt this needed to be done right now" (Ibid.).

Contraception

Among the most contested issues of bodily privacy have been those relating to reproduction, particularly whether and how people have access to contraception and abortion. A more recent question, also discussed later, has emerged around maternal-fetal relations. But the first of these issues to come to the fore was contraception.

By the mid-1930s, contraceptives, or methods of birth control, were common in the United States. Although the Comstock Act of 1873 made it a crime to transport contraceptives or information about contraceptives through interstate commerce, private doctors routinely prescribed contraception, and some types of contraception were available without prescription at neighborhood pharmacies (McCann 1994, 64). In Connecticut, however, an 1879 law strictly forbade the use or prescription of any form of contraception—even by married couples. Although there were bans on contraception in other states, Connecticut's law was unique because it criminalized not only the prescribing but also the use of contraceptives, thus allowing prosecution of doctors *and* their patients. The law was widely ignored by doctors in private practice, who continued to prescribe contraceptives, but it reduced significantly prescriptions of contraception by doctors in public clinics and hospitals, places that provided services to predominantly low-income patients. Connecticut's strict law made the state a proving ground for the debate about whether contraceptives should be legal.

Aware of the risk of prosecution, the newly formed Connecticut Birth Control League opened a clinic in Hartford, the state capital, in 1935. In defiance of the 1879 law, doctors in the Hartford clinic prescribed contraceptives to married women, the majority of whom were low-income women. The Hartford clinic was such a success that the league opened clinics in other cities around the state. In 1938, the league met its first significant resistance, however, when it opened a clinic in Waterbury, a predominantly Catholic town. Leaders of Waterbury's Catholic community demanded an investigation into the health center's activities. Within a year, the Waterbury clinic was shut down, and two doctors who worked in the clinic were arrested. The Connecticut Birth Control League saw the Waterbury incident as an opportunity to bring a case to challenge the 1879 law. The case, the *State of Connecticut v. Roger B. Nelson* (1940), made it to the Connecticut Supreme Court, which found that the 1879 law did not allow an exception for doctors to prescribe contraception in order to preserve the health of the patient. The Nelson ruling effectively closed every clinic in the state for two decades (Cushman 2001, 183).

For the next twenty years, the Connecticut Birth Control League tried to build a legal case that would force a reconsideration of *Nelson.* In 1961, the league was optimistic that it had found its case. *Poe v. Ullman,* in which Dr. Lee Buxton and several of his patients filed suit to establish a need for contraception. The case went all the way to the U.S. Supreme Court. In a petition on behalf of the plaintiffs, the lawyer for the Planned Parenthood League of Connecticut (formerly the Connecticut Birth Control League) asserted that Dr. Buxton's patients insist that "it is precisely their privacy in their homes, and indeed, in the most private part thereof that is invaded. They want to be left alone in their bedroom" (Ibid., 184). Planned Parenthood of Connecticut intended to argue that the 1879 law was invalid because it unfairly restricted the privacy of Connecticut married couples. The Supreme Court refused to hear the case, however, because it found no "substantial controversy"; the plaintiffs in the case had not been prosecuted for violating the law.

In hopes of provoking yet another legal controversy, Connecticut's Planned Parenthood opened a clinic in the city of New Haven. Ten days after a public ceremony that marked the clinic's launch, Dr. Buxton and Estelle Griswold, the executive director of the state's Planned Parenthood, were arrested. The appeal of their convictions reached the U.S. Supreme Court in the case *Griswold v. Connecticut* (1965). Twenty-five years after *Nelson,* Connecticut would see the 1879 law overturned. In the Court's 7–2 decision, it struck down the law on the grounds that it infringed on the constitutionally protected privacy of married persons. Writing the majority opinion in *Griswold,* Justice William O. Douglas allowed that the right to privacy was not specifically enumerated in the Constitution, but that the right to privacy was indeed implicit in the penumbras emanating from other rights in the Bill of Rights. He called on previous cases that suggest "that specific guarantees in the Bill of Rights have penumbras, formed by emanations from those guarantees that help give them life and substance . . . Various guarantees create zones of privacy . . . The present case, then, concerns a relationship lying within the zone of privacy created by several fundamental constitutional guarantees" (484–485). Later in the opinion, Douglas found the idea of the police searching married people's bedroom "repulsive" and linked the right to use contraception with the protection of the marital bond.

The U.S. Supreme Court overturned the convictions and ruled that Connecticut's law was unconstitutional based on rights set down in the Fourth and Fifth Amendments that protect an individual's home and private life from government interference. The Court considered marriage to be a sacred and private bond that lies within the zone of privacy and held that citizens of the state of Connecticut should be able to enjoy the freedom to use birth control within the bond of marriage.

Griswold was a landmark ruling about privacy, but it did not yet extend the right to use contraception to people who were not married. Six years later, the Supreme Court heard a case about contraceptive use by unmarried people in *Eisenstadt v. Baird* (1971). Reproductive rights activist Bill Baird was arrested for handing out a package of contraceptive foam to an unmarried woman after a lecture about population control at Boston University; a Massachusetts law held that distributing contraceptives without a doctor's or pharmacist's license was a felony. In *Eisenstadt,* the Court struck down the Massachusetts law on equal-protection grounds. The majority found that there was no rational basis underlying a law that made an unwanted pregnancy the penalty for sexual activity by unmarried people. The majority held that under the equal-protection clause, unmarried people should have the same access to contraceptives as married people.

Although equal protection was the motivating factor for the finding, the right to privacy played a role in the *Eisenstadt* decision. In the plurality opinion, Justice William J. Brennan Jr. wrote:

It is true that in *Griswold* the right of privacy in question inhered in the marital relationship. Yet the marital couple is not an independent entity with a mind and heart of its own, but an association of two individuals each with a separate intellectual and emotional makeup. If the right of privacy means anything, it is the right of an individual, married or single, to be free from unwarranted government intrusion into matters so fundamentally affecting a person as the decision whether to bear or beget a child. (453)

The reference in *Eisenstadt* to "the decision whether to bear or beget a child" would look ahead to the most important and controversial case to consider women's reproductive health and her right to privacy.

Abortion

In the mid-twentieth century, American women were not legally free to decide whether to carry a fetus to term or to terminate a pregnancy. Most states had laws that severely restricted abortion, allowing it only when a woman's health was in danger or if she had been raped (Solinger 1998, 17). Like laws prohibiting the use of contraceptives, however, laws prohibiting abortion were routinely circumvented by women of means. If abortion were illegal in the state in which she lived, a woman of means could travel to another state or to a foreign country where abortion was legal, or she could hire a private doctor to perform the surgery in secret. Poor women did not have as many options for seeking abortion, and many women died from botched abortions performed by less skilled doctors. Abortions were sometimes performed in unsanitary alleys (Hadley 1996, 33). Coincident with the women's liberation movement in the 1960s, campaigns arose in many states to rewrite or repeal entirely abortion laws. Between 1967 and 1970, twelve states enacted laws that permitted abortions in limited cases.

While women across the country continued to push for legislative reform, two Texas women brought about a watershed judicial decision—*Roe v. Wade*. Two recent graduates of the University of Texas Law School, Sarah Weddington and Linda Coffee, had graduated near the top of their class but had not received the kind of job offers for which they had hoped. They were looking for a case both to challenge the Texas law on abortion and give them some practice in the courtroom. Norma Mc-Corvey, the woman who would become known by the alias Jane Roe, asked her doctor about the possibility of having an abortion and eventually was referred to Weddington and Coffee. Twenty-three years old and pregnant for the third time, Mc-Corvey did not want to have another child. Texas law, however, prohibited abortion in all instances except when the life of the woman was at risk. Coffee and Weddington filed suit in Dallas against Henry Wade, the district attorney of Dallas County; they sought an order to restrain Wade from enforcing the Texas abortion law.

In the 7–2 decision of *Roe v. Wade* (1973), the U.S. Supreme Court struck down the Texas law. Justice Harry Blackmun wrote the majority opinion for the Court. Blackmun concluded that the right to privacy was "broad enough to encompass a woman's decision whether or not to terminate her pregnancy" (153). He noted that abortion had been both common and legal in ancient times; U.S. laws began to limit abortion in the nineteenth century because it was thought to be an unsafe medical practice. Now that the practice was considered safe, Blackmun argued, this reason for restricting abortion no longer had merit.

Although Blackmun defended a woman's right to privacy and so a woman's right to obtain an abortion, he did allow that the balance of a woman's right and the state's right changed as the pregnancy progressed. In the first trimester of pregnancy, he held, the state could not regulate or prohibit abortions at all; the decision whether to have an abortion was to be made by a woman with the counsel of her doctor. In the second trimester, the state could regulate abortion in ways that "are reasonably related to maternal health." By the third trimester, or when the fetus can be viable outside of the womb, Blackmun insisted that the state's interest in preserving life could justify regulating or banning abortion altogether.

Roe v. Wade ignited a firestorm of political debate about a woman's right to choose and the need to protect the life of the fetus in the womb. After *Roe*, political opposition to the decision grew into the prolife movement. Among the movement's goals is to have the Supreme Court overturn the *Roe* decision.

In 1992, the Supreme Court considered a significant test for *Roe*. In *Planned Parenthood v. Casey* (1992), Planned Parenthood of

Pennsylvania appealed a 1989 law that required several things: that there be a twenty-four-hour waiting period for a woman who wanted to have an abortion, that women be given state-mandated information on fetal development, that a married woman inform her husband of her intention to have an abortion, and that a minor get a parent's consent or a judicial waiver. (A minor procures a judicial waver by appearing before a judge and convincing the judge that she is able to make the decision to have an abortion and that she is not able to tell her parents.)

In the jointly written majority opinion, Justices Sandra Day O'Connor, Anthony Kennedy, and David Souter held that "the essential holding of Roe v. Wade should be retained and once again affirmed." They affirmed that "the Constitution places limits on a State's right to interfere with a person's most basic decisions about family and parenthood" (849).

Yet the justices in the majority allowed that states are "free to enact laws to provide a reasonable framework for a woman to make a decision that has such a profound and lasting meaning" (873). The majority opinion upheld, therefore, all of Pennsylvania's provisions except that a woman must inform her husband. The Court concluded that it would present a woman with an "undue burden" to inform her husband of her intention to have an abortion. Recognizing the possibility of an unsafe home situation or the potential for a husband to prevent a woman from having an abortion, the Court found unconstitutional Pennsylvania's requirement that a woman inform her husband. The Court's decision in Planned Parenthood v. Casey affirmed a woman's right to make a decision about abortion while recognizing that it is "not a right to be insulated from all others in doing so" (877).

On November 5, 2003, President George W. Bush signed into law the Partial Birth Abortion Ban Act of 2003. The law defines partial-birth abortion as when a physician "deliberately and intentionally vaginally delivers a living fetus until, in the case of head-first presentation, the entire fetal head is outside the body of the mother, or, in the case of the breech presentation, any part of the fetal trunk past the navel is outside the body of the mother, for the purpose of performing an overt act that the person knows will kill the partially delivered living fetus" (Schneider 2003, 1). The law does not refer to the gestational age of the fetus. According to the law, if a physician performs a partial-birth abortion, the physician can be fined, sentenced up to two years in prison, or both. A physician cannot be penalized when the procedure is undertaken to save the life of a woman.

Nearly thirty states passed variations of such laws, and many were overturned by the courts. Most significantly, the U.S. Supreme Court overturned a Nebraska law in 2000 because it was too vague and did not allow an exception to the ban to protect the health of the mother (*Stenberg v. Carhart* 2000).

Critics of the Partial Birth Abortion Ban Act charge that the term *partial-birth abortion* is a political term and not a recognizable medical procedure (Stetson 2001, 261). Late-term abortions are undertaken by a variety of procedures, including third-trimester dilation and extraction, a procedure similar to dilation and evacuation that is performed in a woman's first or second trimester. The bill does not reference these particular medical procedures. Two leading medical associations, the American Medical Association and the American College of Obstetricians and Gynecologists, oppose the law, in part for this reason.

Legal challenges to the Partial Birth Abortion Act occurred right away. By September 2004, three federal district courts had found the federal law unconstitutional.

Maternal-Fetal Relations

In addition to contraception and abortion, "maternal-fetal relations" is another controversial area within the category of reproduction and bodily privacy that is receiving growing attention. Maternal-fetal relations describes a variety of medical issues affecting both the pregnant woman and her fetus and asks who gets to decide what treatments or actions will be taken—the mother, her doctor, or the state. There are three major types of conflicts in maternal-fetal relations: (1) pregnant women are charged with prenatal child abuse for use of illicit drugs during pregnancy; (2) doctors recommend fetal therapy, including surgery; and (3) doctors procure court orders for cesarean deliveries.

Legal appeals to the woman's obligation to protect the fetus are often made using an analogy to other parental obligations to children. For example, a woman who does not allow the proper medical intervention is analogous to a woman abusing her child.

Of course, unlike two legally and physically separate persons such as a mother and her child, this analogy implicates a pregnant woman's legal and physical autonomy and privacy.

The rise of cesarean sections illustrates the problem. As a result of more technologically advanced prenatal detectors, doctors are increasingly recommending cesarean sections to benefit the health of the fetus when the woman is in late stages of pregnancy. Although it might seem that a woman in her eighth or ninth month of pregnancy would likely endorse the doctor's recommendation that she undergo a cesarean section, women may refuse cesareans for a number of reasons, including religious beliefs that oppose surgery or disagreement with the doctor's prognosis. When a woman refuses a cesarean, doctors are increasingly seeking court intervention to protect the fetuses (Annas 1986, 182).

Nurse Nancy Rhoden argues that court-ordered cesarean sections constitute a "significant intrusion into women's conduct during pregnancy or birth" (1987, 119). She argues that courts should not order competent women to have cesarean sections, despite potentially tragic consequences to the fetus. The patient's consent to treatment is one of the core principles underlying medical ethics and, in most cases, informed consent is a legally required precedent to lawful medical procedures. Since the patient is the one who has to live with the outcome of medical procedures, medical ethics holds that he or she is in the best position to assess a procedure's risks and benefits. Rhoden notes that, by undermining the principle of consent, court-ordered cesarean sections sow the seeds of unprecedented discriminatory treatment of women.

It is important to highlight that court-ordered interventions in the medical treatment of pregnant women occur most frequently in cases of poor women, particularly poor African American women. In *Killing the Black Body: Race, Reproduction and the Meaning of Liberty,* Dorothy Roberts, a law professor at Northwestern University, argues that "states have recently turned their attention to reproduction as a focus for criminal punishment" (1997, 152). She highlights an attempt by a county in South Carolina to systematize the prosecution of women for maternal drug use. A nurse at the Medical University of South Carolina, the local state hospital that served primarily an indigent minority population, approached a local prosecutor with her concerns that an increasing number of women were using illicit drugs, particularly crack, while pregnant. The hospital began to administer nonconsensual drug tests to pregnant women. If a woman tested positive for illicit drugs at the time she gave birth, she was immediately arrested and jailed. Roberts reports cases of women still bleeding postpartum when they were taken away in leg shackles and jailed; their babies were taken into state child-protective custody. The collaboration of Charleston law enforcement officials and the state hospital resulted in the arrests of forty-two women, all but one of whom were African American (164–167).

In Roberts's estimation, these women were not being arrested for drug use alone but were arrested for being pregnant. She notes that "prosecutors charge these defendants, not with drug use, but with child abuse or drug distribution through the umbilical cord—crimes only pregnant users can commit" (180). Pregnant women also received harsher sentences than nonpregnant drug users. Ironically, under such a policy, as Roberts points out, pregnant women could escape criminal charges by having an abortion. Even an illegal late-term abortion would have less serious legal consequences than the drug charges.

Our Genetic Makeup, Our Essence, Our Privacy

In an all-out sprint watched by the whole world, two groups of scientists raced to be the first to complete the map of the human genetic code. In June 2000, the rival groups—a U.S. corporation, Celera Genomics, and a publicly funded international consortium called the Human Genome Project—crossed the finish line together, announcing a rough draft of the human genome at press conferences in London and Washington (CNN 2000). Both published their draft blueprints in science journals in February 2001, and the entire map was completed in April 2003 (Spotts 2003). Like the terrorist attacks of September 11 or the Columbine shootings, this historic event has profound and complicated implications for privacy.

Knowing the makeup of our genetic code will help to identify the sources of nearly all disease and, it is hoped, lead to cures for these diseases. "It's hard to overstate the importance of reading our own instruction book," said Dr. Francis Collins, one of the lead scientists in the effort. Indeed, the mapping of the genome has been described as one of the most important scientific undertakings of all time, comparable to Charles Darwin's theory of evolution or landing on the moon (Clark 2000).

However, the map takes humankind only so far. There remain tremendous scientific hurdles—for example, identifying the genes associated with certain diseases as well as how to "fix" these genes. There is also the distinct possibility that knowing so much more will prove how little we yet know about the genetic, environmental, and mixture of causes of diseases.

Then there are the moral, social, and legal questions that remain unsolved. "Politicians and medical policy makers are going to have to do a lot of catch-up to keep pace with the science of genetic research," one geneticist said (Ibid.). The Human Genome Project laid out some of these difficult questions:

- Should employers, insurers, courts, law enforcement, or others have access to an individual's genetic information, and, if so, what controls should be put on its use?
- Should people be tested for propensity to diseases if no cure exists for that disease?
- Should testing of fetuses check for not only dangerous health conditions but also individual traits thought to be desirable or undesirable by parents? (Ibid.)

A. M. Capron, a professor at the University of Southern California, identifies why genetics conjures up such strong worries about privacy. Genetics and privacy are fundamentally in tension with one another. The various definitions of privacy can be "woven together in support of a basic interest of all persons to control their own lives: the direction and control of that life, the way in which they experience it, and the way it is perceived by others." This sense of being "authors of our own fate" conflicts with the power of genes to influence "which existing or potential paths are available to us and how we go about choosing among them" (2000, 245). Thus, if genes determine aspects of our being and we cannot control our genes, we feel the more dire need to control others' access to our genes and the information contained in them.

DNA Identification

As discussed in Chapter 2, there is already quick, steady growth in the number and size of DNA databases around the world. These databases are used primarily for law enforcement purposes. A government will collect the DNA of people who are convicted of a crime or even of those merely arrested and charged with a crime, store their DNA or DNA code in a database, and compare the DNA in the database to DNA from crime scenes—not just for the criminal incident of which they are suspected but any crime scene where genetic material was collected.

In the United States, DNA collection for law enforcement is coordinated and supported by the federal government. The federal government collects and analyzes the DNA of people convicted of federal crimes and provides funding to the states to run similar programs. The FBI runs a database called the Combined DNA Index System (CODIS), which contains the DNA codes from those identified by both the federal and state governments. As of mid-2004, CODIS contained DNA records from approximately 1.7 million people and 79,000 crime scenes. When a law enforcement agency has DNA evidence from a crime scene, it runs the DNA code through CODIS to see if it matches any person in the database or any evidence from other crime scenes.

For example, in 2001, DNA evidence linked crimes in Philadelphia, Pennsylvania, and Fort Collins, Colorado, which helped police to locate and convict Troy Graves who had committed several rapes and a murder in downtown Philadelphia between 1997 and 1999 and six rapes in the university town of Fort Collins in 2001. Evidence from the crime scenes was run through CODIS, linking the two crime sprees. Then, at the scene of the fifth rape in Fort Collins, a crime scene analyst lifted a fingerprint from a handrail on the deck where a rape took place. The print matched Graves's, which allowed the police to detain him while his DNA was checked against the DNA from the multiple crime scenes (Porter 2004). In Ohio, DNA analysis of twenty-year-old evidence led to the release from prison of Steven Avery who had served eighteen years after being wrongly convicted of sexual assault and attempted murder. Only two hairs with roots remained from the crime scene—one was the victim's, the other was the true assailant's (Ross 2003, 2B). From these examples, and thousands more that exist, it is clear that DNA identification can be invaluable both for solving cases and for identifying people who were wrongly convicted.

DNA databases are growing, as is the ability to use them. The DNA system is becoming more and more efficient by the day. For instance, in the Troy Graves case, the local police had to wait for the state police to run its requests through CODIS. Now, the Philadelphia Police Department has its own access to CODIS, making it possible to run DNA checks far more frequently (Porter 2004). Meanwhile, in 2004, the state of Michigan cleared up its "DNA backlog," the DNA that had been collected from convicts but not yet analyzed and databased. In Michigan, a federal grant allowed the state to send 80,640 DNA samples dating back ten years to a Virginia company to analyze and record them. Michigan already had 100,000 DNA profiles in its database (Bailey 2004).

The legal right to privacy does not prevent police from searching a person or taking his DNA where there is probable cause to suspect him of committing a crime and the search is relatively unintrusive. Taking someone's DNA no longer requires a blood sample; it can be taken by merely rubbing a person's cheek with a cotton swab, which the courts view as minimally intrusive. Under the U.S. Constitution, the right to be free from such searches and seizures is a limited one. The Fourth Amendment states: "The right of the people to be secure in their persons, houses, papers, and effects, against unreasonable searches and seizures, shall not be violated." Searches and seizures that are reasonable are permitted. Nor does the Constitution prohibit absolute efficiency—the ability of the government to have total perfect information, instantly accessible anywhere in the country, that it can act on immediately.

Nonetheless, having a superefficient law enforcement mechanism with huge databases of DNA records, although technically not in violation of the Constitution, may make the United States seem less like the land of liberty the founders imagined and more like a police state, especially in light of two present trends: the expansion of reasons for collecting DNA and the ever increasing ability to collect a person's DNA from anything he or she touches.

As discussed in Chapter 2, the United States started collecting DNA from convicted sex offenders only. By 2003, all fifty states and Puerto Rico collected DNA from people convicted of violent felonies, thirty states collected from juveniles convicted of certain felonies, twenty-eight states collected from all convicted adult felons, fourteen states collected for both felony and certain misdemeanor convictions, three states (Louisiana, Texas, and Virginia) collected from certain felony arrestees, and Utah collected from people charged with immigration violations. And all fifty states and the federal government are moving toward collecting DNA under more circumstances and allowing DNA from other jurisdictions that have different standards. In 2004, Californians voted on a ballot initiative to, within five years, collect DNA from *all* felony arrestees (again, people accused but not yet found guilty of any crime) (*United States v. Kincade,* 819).

If all fifty states move to collecting DNA for all arrestees, it is easy to see how—without meaningful safeguards—anyone's becoming part of the database would depend on the whim of a police officer. Getting in a fight at a bar, objecting to police behavior, or participating in a sit-in or other political protest could lead not only to a person's being arrested for disorderly conduct or another low-level charge but also to his or her being swabbed for DNA.

At the same time, increasingly powerful DNA technology allows DNA material to be found wherever the tiniest human cells are left, which is to say almost everywhere. A "high-sensitivity crime lab" in New York City is completing a system that will allow DNA profiles to be generated from as few as six cells—a smudged fingerprint or saliva in a ski mask (Dewan 2004). A government guide for victims explaining some possible sites of DNA evidence and their sources is listed in Table 3.1.

This creates the likelihood that once the technology improves to make collection even easier, processing times faster, and costs lower, the government will use DNA evidence not only to identify perpetrators of past crimes but also to track the movements of people they suspect will commit crimes. Of course, lawfully or unlawfully, the government could track political opponents or protesters.

Surprisingly, so far, few U.S. courts are troubled by the broader implications for democratic society of the government's DNA profiling. In August 2004, in the case of *United States v. Kincade,* the Ninth Circuit Court of Appeals upheld the taking of DNA from federal convicts released on parole. Five of the judges focused narrowly on the case at hand—in which a former prisoner released on supervised parole refused to give a blood

Table 3.1
Possible Sites of DNA Evidence and Their Sources

Possible Location of DNA Evidence	Source of DNA
Bite mark or area licked	Saliva
Fingernail scrapings	Blood or skin cells
Inside or outside surface of used condom	Semen or skin cells
Blankets, sheets, pillows, or other bed linens	Semen, sweat, hair, or saliva
Clothing	Hair, semen, blood, or sweat
Hat, bandanna, mask	Sweat, skin cells, hair, or saliva
Tissue, washcloth, or similar item	Saliva, semen, hair, skin cells, or blood
Cigarette butt, toothpick, or rim of bottle, can, or glass	Saliva
Tape or ligature	Skin cells, saliva, or hair
Dental floss	Semen, skin cells, or saliva

Source: National Institute of Justice 2001.

sample for DNA databasing—and found that society's interest in supervising ex-offenders outweighed a parolee's diminished expectation of privacy (836–838). One of those five wrote separately that he might feel differently if the case had arisen after Kincade had been released from parole and if he had demanded that his DNA record then be removed from CODIS (841–842).

The four judges in the minority worried about the standard adopted by the majority, which, they argued, was so broad it will put all Americans "at risk, sooner rather than later, of having our DNA samples permanently placed on file in federal cyberspace, and perhaps even worse, of being subjected to various other governmental programs providing for suspicionless searches conducted for law enforcement purposes" (843). Judge Stephen Reinhardt accused the majority of dispensing with the "traditional Fourth Amendment requirement that law enforcement officials conduct searches only when predicated on some level of suspicion that the individual being searched has committed a crime" in favor of an opaque "totality of the circumstances test." He argued, "Under the test the plurality employs, any person who experiences a reduction in his expectation of privacy would be susceptible to having his blood sample extracted and included in CODIS—attendees of public high schools or universities, persons seeking to obtain drivers' licenses, applicants for federal employment, or persons requiring any form of federal identification, and those who desire to travel by airplane, to name just a few" (844).

Nonetheless, the majority believed that the case sufficiently distinguished between profiling those convicted of crimes who had a lower expectation of privacy and those who were merely charged with a crime and enjoyed the presumption of innocence. Further, the majority believed that courts would act appropriately if Judge Reinhardt's fears came to pass (838). Like the majority in *Kincade*, DNA collection advocates argue that there are safeguards in place to limit the threat to privacy. First, many statutes provide for removal of a person's DNA from government databases if the person is exonerated of the crime or all charges are dropped. Second, typically, only *junk DNA* is decoded and digitized into the database. Junk DNA means pieces of DNA that are currently believed to have no bearing on one's physical makeup but nonetheless are unique to the individual. In other words, these advocates argue that the DNA being databased can reveal only a person's identity and not, for example, whether he or she is prone to developing cancer.

Privacy advocates, on the other hand, point out that some statutes do not provide for removal and these DNA records are being filtered into other databases. Even where removal is permitted, they argue, it is much more difficult to get one's record out than in. Innocent people end up carrying an administrative burden to ask for something back that should never have been taken. As to junk DNA, they note that experts are not yet certain what is junk and what is not. Also, the actual samples—not just the digital record of them—are often being kept by the jurisdiction that secured them, creating the risk that other parts of the DNA could be sampled. Finally, they fear that law enforcement will continue to expand what it does with DNA, especially as researchers identify genetic markers for body features such as race, sex, height, and hair color.

DNA Dragnets

DNA's ability to identify an individual with unprecedented precision has led to a law enforcement tactic, first used in the United Kingdom in the late 1980s—the DNA dragnet. In DNA dragnets, the police have found genetic material left by a criminal at the scene of a crime, and the police collect the DNA of a large number of people from the surrounding neighborhood, area, or town or of people who match the general description of the criminal, in hopes of finding a match. Typically when DNA dragnets are used, police have given up on the usual investigation techniques of collecting clues, following leads, and developing individualized suspicion. In the first known DNA dragnet, in Leicester, England, the police found DNA they suspected belonged to the perpetrator of a rape and strangulation of two teenage girls and had little other evidence to go on. They knocked on the door of every male in the three nearby villages, explained what they were doing, and asked them to submit to a blood test. They took 4,700 samples. Only one person refused to provide blood. Using this person's refusal as justification, the police obtained a warrant from a judge and forced the man to submit to a blood test. The person's DNA matched that from the crime scene, and the person was tried and convicted (Hansen 2004). It is a clever investigation technique, in part, because it can reveal who is scared of being tested. If a person refuses to hand over his or her DNA, then the police put that person under greater scrutiny. Presumably, an innocent person will hold out only so long before the pressure and hassle from the police outweigh the indignity or worry associated with submitting to the test. Therefore, if the person continues to refuse in face of the increased attention, it seems more likely that he or she is somehow guilty or implicated. Depending on your perspective, DNA dragnets are a recipe either for success or for unjustified police harassment. Even if you are not concerned about police analyzing your DNA, the risk of compliance may be too great if you are concerned about how long they will keep it, for what purposes they will use it, who will be authorized to access it, and how well it will be protected from unauthorized use.

It has been shown that DNA dragnets are more successful when either more information is known about the perpetrator to help narrow the group tested or, as in Leicester, England, it is possible to identify and collect a complete sample of the total population. In other words, DNA dragnets are most effective when either preceded by traditional investigation techniques aimed at developing individualized suspicion or, alternatively, using the total information tactics of a totalitarian state. Even short of the risk of creating a police state through total identification, DNA sweeps pose other risks of abuse, as actual experience bears out.

In Charlottesville, Virginia, there were seven house-invasion rapes between 1997 and 2004 thought to be committed by the same perpetrator, but police have been unable to solve the case. In 2003, one of the victims offered a description, and a vague artist's sketch of a young African American man was posted all over town. Using this sketch and telephone tips, the police cast a DNA dragnet. Between November 2002 and May 2004, the police asked 197 black men for a cotton swab of skin cells from their cheeks in order to check their DNA; of this group, 187 agreed. One of those who agreed, Jeffery Johnson, was forty-seven years old, much older than any of the victims had described the perpetrator. Police came to the restaurant where Johnson worked and, in front of his colleagues and customers, informed the man that he had been reported as a possible suspect in the rapes. They told him he could clear his name by providing a DNA sample. He felt angry and humiliated, yet he allowed the police to swab his cheek in order to get rid of them.

Ten men did not agree to provide a sample. One who refused was Steven Turner, a graduate student at the University of Virginia. The first time he was asked, he was riding his bicycle down the street. Five months later, they came to his apartment. "When they stopped me and they profiled me, it was disturbing in a way I cannot communicate. And after the second time, it was the same feeling all over again. I didn't feel safe here," said the student. "They kept asking, they kept asking. They said since you will not provide a sample, we are going to come to your classes, sit in on them, make sure you really are a student here" (*Religion and Ethics Newsweekly* 2004). When the student and a dean held a community forum, it became clear that there was widespread anger among the African American community; some referred to the long history of racism and racial segregation in Charlottesville. Some, including Turner, accused the police of racial profiling: "The way the police are conducting this investigation—because the suspect is a black man, every black man is a suspect" (Glod 2004, A1).

When faced with the community's strong feelings and when the story was covered in media around the world, the police chief compromised. He agreed that officers would not ask for DNA swabs without a supervisor's authorization and not based solely on a person resembling a vague artist's sketch. He also agreed to destroy all of the samples that had been collected and analyzed (*Religion and Ethics Newsweekly* 2004).

In Louisiana, in 2002 to 2003, a sheriff's office allegedly collected more than 1,200 DNA samples over a ten-month period in its quest to find a serial killer. None of the samples yielded a match with DNA evidence from the crime scene. The perpetrator was later caught when an investigator working on an unrelated killing identified a suspect and secured a warrant to take his DNA—in other words, using traditional investigative techniques to find probable cause that a particular person committed a particular crime (Hansen 2004).

The DNA dragnet, in the meantime, took in people like Shannon Kohler and Floyd Wagster, who matched an FBI serial killer profile, resembled a victim's description, or were identified by anonymous tips on a telephone hotline. According to the sheriff's office, Kohler had a prior burglary conviction, had been identified by an anonymous caller, and had worked on a street where a victim's cell phone was found. But he did not drive a white pickup truck seen near several of the crime scenes, and his phone records showed he was at home at the time of the crime—which eliminated him as a suspect. Unfortunately, a clerical error by the courts caused his name to be publicly released, and he became the center of media attention (Wilson 2003). Wagster, who had a prior conviction for marijuana possession, received a call from a sheriff's deputy informing him that he was wanted not as a suspect but for questioning. He agreed to come into the station but wanted to speak to his lawyer first. His lawyer was in court that afternoon, so Wagster left a message and went on with his day. The deputy called back an hour later, and Wagster explained he had not yet reached his lawyer. When Wagster left on errands, he was stopped, handcuffed, and brought to the sheriff's department for interrogation. According to Wagster, the deputies said they knew he was not the perpetrator but insisted on taking his DNA anyway. If he would not provide a DNA sample, Wagster recounted, they said they would give his name to the media, drug test him, and jail him for violating probation. He relented but felt there was nothing voluntary about it (Hansen 2004).

Wagster and others are suing the sheriff's department for violating their constitutional right to reasonable searches and seizures. They want their DNA samples returned or destroyed, the state DNA collection law that allows samples taken from those accused (rather than convicted) of offenses ruled unconstitutional, and punitive damages. Jim Boren, one of Wagster's lawyers, believes the suit will have an impact on DNA dragnets generally: "Can the police obtain samples from anyone remotely suspected of being involved in a crime without any rules or regulations governing the process?" (Ibid., 37). The sheriff's department, like other proponents of DNA dragnets, emphasize the voluntariness of the request. "Most people were only too happy to have themselves excluded as suspects," said the sheriff's department's attorney (Ibid.). But when the choice is between giving DNA and making yourself a suspect, opponents say, the choice is coerced or not really a choice at all.

Criminologist and historian Samuel Walker studied publicly reported cases of DNA dragnets and found that they are an unproductive use of public funds and an ineffective crime investigation technique. Of eighteen reported sweeps in the United States since 1987, only one succeeded in identifying the perpetrator—a rapist in Lawrence, Massachusetts, who was one of approximately twenty-five people sampled. Significantly, this was the smallest dragnet of the eighteen, suggesting that narrowly targeted investigations remain more effective than large dragnets (2004).

Other dragnets included:

- Wichita, Kansas, 1987; more than 200 tested. Case unsolved.
- Costa Mesa, California, 1988; 113 tested. Case unsolved.
- San Diego, California, 1990; 800 tested. Case solved by unrelated means.
- Ann Arbor, Michigan, 1994; 160 tested. Case solved by separate, individualized, nondragnet identification.
- Miami, Florida, 1994; more than 2,300 tested. Case solved by unrelated means.
- Lawrence, Massachusetts, 1998; more than 25 tested. Case solved.
- Prince George's County, Maryland, 1998; 400 tested. Case unsolved.
- Los Angeles, California, 1999; 186 tested. Case unsolved.
- Costa Mesa, California, 2001; 188 tested. Case unsolved.
- Oklahoma City, Oklahoma, 2001; more than 200 tested. Case solved by separate, individualized, nondragnet identification.
- Simi Valley, California, 2001; approximately 500 tested. Case solved by separate, individualized, nondragnet identification.

- Baton Rouge, Louisiana, 2002; 1,200 tested. Case solved by separate, individualized, nondragnet identification.
- Kearney, Nebraska, 2002; 75 tested. Case solved by unrelated means.
- Miami, Florida, 2003; 120 tested. Case solved by unrelated means.
- Charlottesville, Virginia, 2004; 187 tested. Case unsolved.
- Omaha, Nebraska, 2004; more than 36 tested. Case unsolved. (Walker 9–13)

For those caught up in DNA sweeps—in the street, at work, in front of their families—the experience can be frightening and humiliating. But, as detailed in Chapter 2, the risks are greater than that when genetic material is collected and stored: DNA could be collected without a person's knowledge from the saliva on the back of a stamp or a fallen hair. Even if rules and protections are put in place to protect the privacy of stored DNA samples now, those rules could be changed later. Even if an individual consents to the use of his DNA, that individual's family members who share similar genetic traits may be affected without their consent. Finally, the information may be abused or the protections overcome.

Privacy proponents do not suggest that DNA not be used for forensic investigations and identification. Rather, they urge federal rules that require (1) states to be prohibited from conducting nonconsensual collection of DNA, except when they have a court order to do so; (2) biological samples that are properly collected from suspects be destroyed within a reasonable period after the criminal matter is resolved; (3) the genetic profiles not be entered into a networked database accessible to other jurisdictions unless they are taken from a person convicted of a violent felony; and (4) DNA samples from crime scenes be made available for testing to criminal defendants and convicted criminals who claim they are innocent (Steinhardt 2000).

Genes and Public Health

More than their utility in identifying individuals, genes are the center of public and scientific attention for their potential to decode the components of diseases and possibly, through so-called gene therapy, prevent or cure them. Scientists are careful not to overstate this potential. In many cases, the presence of a gene pattern associated with a particular disease does not mean the carrier will contract the disease. Rather, it reveals the mere possibility or increased likelihood that the disease will form through a process of interaction with other gene combinations and environmental factors that scientists do not yet understand. Also, gene therapy is in its infancy; at this writing, there is little doctors can do to help a person who carries a disease gene.

These limitations put public health in tension with private health or, at least, the privacy of individuals' health information. To learn more about the relationships between genes and disease, scientists need access to both a large sample of "normal" genes and access to every alternative or mutation that exists or develops. Individuals may not want to share their genetic code, which tells so much about them. This reluctance may be justified in light of privacy violations that have already occurred.

The Council for Responsible Genetics tracks such abuses. The organization states, "In as many as five hundred cases, individuals and family members have been barred from employment or lost their health and life insurance based on an apparent or perceived genetic abnormality" (2005). For example, in 2001, the U.S. Equal Employment Commission announced that the Burlington Northern Santa Fe Railroad Company had been testing employees' DNA without their informed consent in order to defeat their worker's compensation claims for on-the-job injuries. The rail workers claimed they had developed repetitive stress injuries, and the company required them to get physical examinations from its doctors, during which the company took or sought to take genetic material for DNA testing. The company stopped the practice and paid $2.2 million to settle the government lawsuit. The company hoped to show that the employees were genetically inclined to the pain they experienced and therefore deserved less compensation (Szekely 2002). In 1997, the American Management Association conducted a survey of more than 6,000 companies and found that 6 to 10 percent of employers considered genetic factors as part of their employment decisions (Council for Responsible Genetics 2005).

The abuse of genetic science—or what was thought to be science—has a long history. Putting modern fears in perspective, a national research group stated, "These privacy concerns are far from abstract. The eugenics movement in this country, which resulted in thousands of involuntary sterilizations, the suggested screening of violent men for extra Y chromosomes, the sickle cell screening tests employed to prohibit marriages, and the current privacy concerns over HIV screening, underlie a national research panel's following recommendation: Use of a data bank for other than law enforcement suspect identification purposes should be expressly prohibited and subject to criminal penalties" (Steinhardt 2000). The eugenics movement in 1920s America called for elimination of the "unfit" from those reproducing and led to the forced sterilization of African Americans, in some places, into the 1970s (Roylance 2004).

Some critics worry that the abuse of genetics runs deeper than the misuse of individuals' genetic information; they question some of the science itself, particularly as geneticists increasingly focus on race and ethnicity. On one hand, modern genetics has shown and proclaimed the scientific meaninglessness of race at the genetic level. "The concept of race has no genetic or scientific basis," stated Craig Venter at the White House event marking the near completion of the human genome map in 2000. Race is one part of the 0.1 percent of genes that distinguishes human beings from one another and, it is argued, are otherwise biologically insignificant. Further, it has been found that there is greater genetic variation among people of the same race than between different races (Henig 2004, 47). On the other hand, scientists are now exploring that last tenth of 1 percent to make sure they are not missing anything. Although they expect that biological differences will best be described by each individual's unique genetic makeup, it is possible there will be some generalizations associated with racial or ethnic groups. In the meantime, pharmaceutical companies are eager to use generalizations to develop and market products to defined, targetable groups, such as racial and ethnic minorities. In 2004, for example, NitroMed, a large pharmaceutical company, neared final approval of BiDil, a pill (beta-blocker) that reduces the chances of heart failure, according to the company's studies, in African Americans but not whites (Ibid.). BiDil is one example of how pharmaceutical companies hope to tailor medicines to particularized genetic conditions.

Although research such as that done on BiDil may appear to be based on the content and structure of genes, in fact it is based on clinical trials, or clinical epidemiology, which chooses particular population groups to test and observe for the effects of medicine and treatment. According to Jennifer Poudrier, "The assumptions in both epidemiological and genetic sciences, particularly in the development and use of categories, are highly problematic" (2003, 113). Epidemiology, according to some critics, uses a broad brush to categorize groups and fails to incorporate the complex subtleties of cultural affiliation and interaction when it comes to health. Genetics, according to some critics, assumes categories, then bases its biological research on those categories (Ibid., 114–116).

These assumptions can lead to misleading characterizations about groups that nonetheless appear to be hard science, such as which groups are "at risk." For example, Dr. Sally Satel told the *New York Times*, "I am a racially profiling doctor . . . I always take note of my patient's race. So do many of my colleagues. We do it because certain diseases and treatment responses cluster by ethnicity. Recognizing these patterns can help us diagnose disease more efficiently and prescribe medications more effectively" (Satel 2002, 56). It sounds persuasive; it comes from an intelligent, authoritative, well-meaning doctor, and she may get lucky, but it is not accurate. Alan Goodman, an anthropologist, stated, "Every disease known has some variation in frequency and prevalence by race . . . But with no firm basis in biology, race isn't a precise indicator of any patient's genetic heritage, and doctors shouldn't rely on it" (Roylance 2004, A1).

Consider sickle-cell disease (including sickle-cell anemia), a blood disease in which the hemoglobin that carries oxygen in red blood cells can become crescent shaped and unable to pass through small vessels, blocking blood flow and causing tissue damage, joint pain, jaundice, gallstones, or other complications. Sickle-cell disease can be managed, especially if caught at a young age, with medicines, vaccines, blood transfusions, and other treatments, but it is often disabling and tends to shorten the sufferer's life span. Also, the moment when blood cells sickle can be agonizingly painful. The risk that blood cells will sickle is inherited through the genes in hemoglobin. If a particular DNA arrangement exists in both a mother and a father, then the chances of their child developing sickle-cell disease are substantially elevated. If it exists in only one parent, then the child is likely to carry (and pass on) the trait but not develop sickle-cell disease him- or herself.

In the United States, most people think of sickle-cell disease as a disease affecting black people. The Wordnet online dictionary, developed by the Cognitive Science Laboratory at Princeton University, defines sickle-cell anemia as "a congenital form of anemia occurring mostly in blacks." In fact, this popular understanding (and this Princeton cognitive dictionary definition) is inaccurate and, worse, potentially harmful both medically and socially. Sickle-cell disease is not a black disease. Nor is it a reflection of biological or genetic differences between blacks and other racial groups. Rather, as with all genetic characteristics that are passed on to children, it is based on individuals and populations, not race. Scientists believe that the unique hemoglobin genes associated with sickle cells may have developed (or been successfully propagated) as a response to malaria. Carrying one copy of the genetic trait seems to provide an advantage to beating malaria. The trait is seen with higher frequency in those parts of the world with high rates of malaria: parts of western Africa, parts of India, parts of Greece and Italy, and parts of the Arabian peninsula. Even naming merely "parts of" these countries is inaccurate, because one village will have a high incidence of the trait and a neighboring group will not. When marriage or migration outside the village is considered, it becomes even more difficult to define what groups are at risk. There are many descendants of western Africa in the United States, and, among them, the incidence of the sickle-cell trait is elevated relative to other groups—but these other groups include African Americans with ancestors from different parts of West Africa and Africa.

The popular (and inaccurate) understanding of sickle-cell disease, which is based on race, has negative consequences. It reinforces biases, first, that African Americans are genetically different and, second, that they are inferior. It also promotes medical surveillance of African Americans and self-surveillance by African Americans that may cause unnecessary stress and distort the statistics on prevalence of the trait in African Americans relative to other groups. To some extent, the disease is detected more in certain groups because there is more surveillance of these groups. This surveillance is a pernicious sort of privacy invasion, because it has beneficent motives and no doubt is received or invited voluntarily. But it may be based on false assumptions that, if known, might negate consent.

As an example of the future of genetic disease detection and treatment, it raises important privacy concerns. If members of the chosen group become skeptical and fail to submit to testing, then further invasions of privacy are likely to result through coercive laws justified by "public health," such as testing of infants without the consent of the parent or, as required in many places in the United States, mandatory blood screening of the minority group for marriage licenses. In New Castle, New York, prior to getting married, "A test is required to determine the presence of sickle cell anemia for each marriage license applicant who is not of the Caucasian, Indian or Asian race" (New Castle, NY, 2004).

Finally, it may lead to misdiagnosis, for instance, of Italian Americans who have the disease due to their ancestors' exposure to malaria. The president of the American Society of Human Genetics tells the story of doctors who failed to diagnose sickle-cell disease in a white patient for eight years, despite bouts of pain characteristic of the disease, because the patient was not black and so the doctors did not think of it (Roylance 2004).

There are other problems with even the most scientifically accurate inquiry into genetics and race. It distracts from the complex interaction of environment, genetics, and health. At the cellular level, scientists still have not figured out how nongenetic factors interact with genes to produce disease—yet credibility, resources, and public attention are being devoted to mapping genes by race. At the societal level, the focus on DNA variations is likely to distract from the numerous environmental factors that adversely affect disadvantaged racial minorities—higher pollution and stress, differences in diet, poorer access to health care, poorer-quality health care. If resources are not limitless, it may be better to tackle these urgent public health issues than decoding genetic variations of diseases or races.

In the same way that the threat of terrorism can be used or abused as a rationale for invading privacy, so too can the risk of health problems. The deeply revealing nature of genetic analysis makes modern risk assessment more powerful and more problematic. When these risk assessments are based on genes and DNA, there would seem to be nothing in this genetic age more incontrovertible. But when scientists switch from the DNA makeup of disease or of individuals to that of poorly defined groups, such as racial minorities, then science must be checked against the lessons of history, particularly the history of discrimination.

Privacy Solutions

This book details the invasions of privacy that have come about due to the advancement of technology and science and in response to major historical events, such as the September 11 attacks, the Columbine shootings, and the mapping of the human genome. If you opened this book concerned about your privacy, you have found much to be depressed about. You have also seen that the issues are complex and that privacy is often in competition with other legitimate interests or rights.

Nonetheless, there is reason for hope. A lot of people care about their privacy, so politicians have to care as well. When people express their concern, new laws are passed or new systems put in place to protect privacy. Technology is not just an enemy of privacy; it is also its closest friend. Already, technology can be used to protect privacy or hold accountable those who would abuse it. Finally, of course, the ever-developing legal right to privacy—which exists in national constitutions and international treaties—is another source of potential protection from new forms of privacy invasions.

The challenge for improving privacy protections is how also to accommodate the (often but not always) legitimate competing interests of protecting security or public health; protecting other rights, such as free expression or freedom of the press; and properly valuing consumer convenience and economic costs. The potential solutions described below aim to achieve this balance or explain why privacy outweighs the competing interests.

Using Technology to Protect Privacy

The ACLU and other privacy advocates propose a compromise on biometric identification systems and smart cards that promotes security while protecting privacy. Currently, biometric systems place identifying information about a person (such as fingerprints, retina pattern, or facial measurements) in a database along with other data about the person. When the person encounters a checkpoint, the database is accessed to confirm his identity and review the data for any alerts or suspicious characteristics. It is this last piece that bothers privacy advocates: the person has no control over what information is collected or stored; the information could be stolen or misused; if the information is wrong, the person is likely to have trouble getting it corrected; and the idea of profiling of suspicious persons based on patterns of data is flawed.

However, the need to confirm that someone is who he says he is and that he is allowed to cross a checkpoint is a basic, important security issue. Barry Steinhardt of the ACLU and others recommend embedding biometric information in the card but not in a central database. For example, at a bank machine, a user would insert his bank card and scan his fingerprint or retina. The machine would check the fingerprint or retina scan against the data in the card (not in a central database); if they match, the machine would allow the person access to his bank account (Krim 2004).

Declan McCullagh does not trust the law, its agents, or the people to devise the best protections for his privacy. Too often, it has been unpopular minorities that have unjustly suffered from the whims or intolerance of these forces. Rather, he recommends the power of technology and algebra to protect privacy. "The combination of two large prime numbers to produce an encryption key that can scramble your conversation is straightforward algebra." Encryption programs and anonymizing services are available on the Internet, some at no cost, and allow users to encrypt their e-mails and online files, hide their Web browsing, and scramble their Internet phone calls. McCullagh recognizes that encryption and anonymity can protect the guilty as well as the innocent, but he believes the benefits outweigh the risks (2000a). "Anonymity has long been a shield from the tyranny of the majority. It protects individuals from retaliation for having unpopular views, and it prevents controversial ideas from being suppressed" (McCullagh 2000b).

Critics of McCullagh's reliance on technology over law argue that encryption, anonymizers, and other such technology are beyond the grasp of the vast majority of people. Others argue that privacy-protective technologies will not evolve unless privacy laws are created to force the demand for such technologies (Rotenberg 2003, 3).

Technology can also protect privacy through the implementation of high-tech accountability systems that monitor the monitors and watch the watchers. Presently, courts issue warrants for surveillance, searches, or arrest when presented with probable cause that a crime is afoot. The court does not know if the limits of the warrant were respected or other abuses were committed unless illegal evidence is offered. If there is no arrest or prosecution, the agents or police officers might invade people's privacy without consequence. If the police frame a suspect during a raid, say, to take drug money for themselves, no one may ever find out. Or, if agents using dragnet software acquire and use information about a nonsuspect, how would anyone outside the agency know? Technology and independent oversight mechanisms could be implemented to solve these problems. For instance, courts could require police officers to record and transmit live video (or, using older technology, simply videotape) of those raids known to be associated with the greatest risk of abuse (such as drug raids where a lot of money is likely to be lying around) for review by the court or an independent entity.

Using or Changing the Law to Better Protect Privacy

To improve the protection of privacy in this high-tech age, the ACLU identifies several goals, most of which involve changing current law. These goals include passage of comprehensive privacy laws, adoption of new laws to regulate powerful, invasive new technologies that continue to appear, and a revival and retooling of the Fourth Amendment to the U.S. Constitution for the new millenium (Stanley and Steinhardt 2003, 14).

Proponents of a comprehensive privacy act for the United States point out that it is the only developed nation not to have one. Instead, the United States has a variety of laws covering different aspects of privacy to different degrees—a law for video rentals, a law for medical records, a law for government records, one for financial data. Other areas are not covered by any existing law. And for issues the Supreme Court has not ruled on, the United States has different interpretations of the constitutional right to privacy depending on a region's or state's court decisions. The ACLU argues, "As invasive practices grow, Americans will face constant uncertainty about when and how these complex laws protect them, contributing to a pervasive sense of insecurity" (Ibid., 15). This sense of insecurity could be relieved by a comprehensive privacy act, according to advocates. In the absence of such a law, the ACLU calls for new protections to keep up with new technologies. "Surveillance cameras, for example, must be subject to force-of-law rules covering important details like when they will be used, how long images will be stored, and when and with whom they will be shared" (Ibid., 16).

Antidiscrimination laws are another type of law that might alleviate abuses stemming from access to private information in the growing number of databases. Antidiscrimination laws make it illegal for employers, landlords, insurers, banks, and others to deny a person a service or benefit because of some characteristic, such as her race, sex, religion, nationality, disability, or, in some places, sexuality. For DNA, for example, the National Human Genome Research Institute concluded that "two pillars of protection [are] necessary to prevent the misuse of genetic information. The first pillar consists of the enactment of anti-discrimination laws, especially in the realm of health insurance and employment, and the second focuses on the assurance of privacy protections for individuals involved in genetic testing" (Capron 2000, 247).

Jeffrey Rosen's preferred solution focuses on the problem of privacy invasions resulting from criminal investigations and civil lawsuits. Like Monica Lewinsky's unsent love letters and Senator Packwood's diaries, Rosen laments, our private papers are more vulnerable than they were 100 years ago, more vulnerable even than when the king's sheriffs raided John Wilkes's house and riffled through his drawers in 1763. The erosion began with the government's need to get at business papers in order to fight corporate crime and monopolies. With the development of powerful computer dragnet programs, there is the further likelihood that nonsuspects' personal "papers" will be dragged in (Rosen 2000a). Somewhere along the way, Rosen argues, human discretion—usually a judge's balancing of the need versus the intrusion—was abandoned. Ironically, "in the brave new world of cyberspace, human judgment turns out to be more rather than less necessary for rebuilding the enclaves of privacy that people long took for granted in real space" (Ibid.).

Rosen is less interested in new laws (except in extreme cases) or relying on technological self-help solutions that are beyond the capacity of the vast majority of people. Rather, he proposes that—in both criminal and civil cases—when courts are called upon to allow the capture and disclosure of data or correspondence, judges appoint agents of the court to oversee the process and separate, for instance, personal e-mails from incriminating material. For more serious crimes (the exact list would have to be developed by legislatures), the courts could allow greater searching and disclosure than for less serious cases. In that way, it will be easier for law enforcement to get ahold of the Unabomber's diary than Monica Lewinsky's love letters (Ibid.).

References

9/11 Commission Report. 2003. Ch. 8. http://www.9-11commission.gov/report/911Report_Ch8.htm.

American Civil Liberties Union (ACLU). 2002. "ACLU Asks Supreme Court to Strike Down Anti-gay Kansas Law." Oct. 10. http://www.aclu.org/LesbianGayRights/LesbianGayRights.cfm?ID=10856&c=41.

———. 2004. "GAO Report Reveals Four Potential Government Data-Surveillance Programs, ACLU Says." May 27. http://www.aclu.org/news/newsprint.cfm?ID=15860&c=130.

Annas, George. 1986. "Pregnant Women as Fetal Containers." *Hastings Center Report* (Dec.): 182–183.

Arena, Kelli, Justine Redman, and Larry Shaugnessy. 2004. "Customs Agent Tells of Stopping '20th Hijacker.'" CNN, Jan. 26. http://www.cnn.com/2004/US/01/26/911.commission.

Associated Press. 2003a. "Raid Might Have Broken Drug-Dog Rules." *Columbia State*, Dec. 8.

———. 2003b. "Teen Drug Use Continues to Decline." *Augusta Chronicle*, Dec. 20.

Bailey, Amy F. 2004. "State Clears a 10-Year DNA Backlog." *Detroit Free Press*, Sept. 1.

Baker, Stewart. 2003. "Wall Nuts: The Wall between Intelligence and Law Enforcement Is Killing Us." *Slate* (Dec. 31.) http://slate.msn.com/id/2093344/.

BBC. 2000. "Gay Consent at 16 Becomes Law." BBC. Nov. 30. http://news.bbc.co.uk/1/hi/uk_politics/1047291.stm.

Becker, Elizabeth. 2001. "As Ex-Theorist on Young 'Superpredators,' Bush Aide Has Regrets." *New York Times*, Feb. 9.

Black, Edwin. 2001. *IBM and the Holocaust: The Strategic Alliance between Nazi Germany and America's Most Powerful Corporation.* New York: Crown.

Blum, Vanessa. 2004. "Playing Politics with the Patriot Act." *Legal Times*, Aug. 11.

Brennan, William. 1981. *Doe v. Renfrow,* 451 U.S. 1022, 1028 (dissenting from denial of certiorari).

Cambanis, Thanassis. 2004. "Resistance to Patriot Act Gaining Ground." *Boston Globe*, Jan. 20.

Capron, A. M. 2000. "Genetics and Insurance: Accessing and Using Private Information." In *The Right to Privacy*, edited by Ellen Frankel Paul, Jeffrey Paul, and Fred D. Miller. New York: Cambridge University Press.

CBS. 2002. "INS Shuffle in Wake of INS Flap." *CBS News,* Mar. 15. http://www.cbsnews.com/stories/2002/03/13/national/main503611. shtml.

Center for Democracy and Technology. 2003. "Setting the Record Straight: An Analysis of the Justice Department's PATRIOT Act Website." Oct. 27. http://www.cdt.org/security/usapatriot/031027cdt. shtml.

Clark, Carol. 2001. "On the Threshold of a Brave New World. *CNN,* Feb. http://www.cnn.com/SPECIALS/2000/genome/story/overview/.

CNN. 2000. "Rough Map of Human Genome Completed." *CNN,* June 26. http://www.cnn.com/2000/HEALTH/06/26/human.genome.03/.

Council for Responsible Genetics. 2005. "About Gene Watch." http://www.gene-watch.org.

Cushman, Claire. 2001. *Supreme Court Decisions and Women's Rights: Milestones to Equality.* Washington, DC: CQ Press.

Dewan, Shaila K. 2004. "As Police Extend Use of DNA, a Smudge Could Trap a Thief." *New York Times,* May 26.

Doe v. Renfrow, 451 U.S. 1022 (1981).

Drug Policy Alliance. 2003. "Fed 'Monitoring the Future' Survey Shows Mixed Teen Drug Use Data." *Drug Policy News,* Dec. 29. http://www. drugpolicy.org/news/12_22_03mtf.cfm.

Drug Reform Coordination Network. 2003. "South Carolina: High School Drug Raid Sparks Incredulity, Outrage." *Drug War Chronicle,* no. 311, Nov. 14. http://stopthedrugwar.org/chronicle/311/stratford. shtml.

Eisenstadt v. Baird, 405 U.S. 438 (1972).

Fausto-Sterling, Anne. 1993. "The Five Sexes." *The Sciences,* 20–25, March/April.

———. 2000. "The Five Sexes Revisited." *The Sciences,* 18–23, July/August.

Feller, Ben. 2003. "Survey Finds Teenagers Get Along with Parents." *Philadelphia Inquirer/Associated Press,* Aug. 6.

Foreign Intelligence Surveillance Act , 50 U.S.C. §§ 1801–1862.

Gingrich, Newt. 2003. "Open Forum: The Policies of War Refocus the Mission." *San Francisco Chronicle,* Nov. 11.

Ginsburg, Faye. 1998. "Rescuing the Nation: Operation Rescue and the Rise of Anti-abortion Militance." In *Abortion Wars: A Half Century of Struggle, 1950–2000,* edited by Rickie Solinger, 227–250. Berkeley and Los Angeles: University of California Press.

Glod, Maria. 2004. "'DNA Dragnet' Makes City Uneasy." *Washington Post*, Apr. 14.

Grady, Denise. 2002. "Few Risks Seen to Children of 1st Cousins." *New York Times*, Apr. 4.

Griswold v. Connecticut, 381 U.S. 479 (1965).

Hadley, Janet. 1996. *Abortion: Between Freedom and Necessity*. London: Virago Press.

Hancock, Lynell. 2003. "Wolf Pack: The Press and the Central Park Jogger." *Columbia Journalism Review*, 38–42, Jan./Feb. 2003, Vol. 45, no. 5 (citing *New York Post*, Apr. 22, 1989).

Hansen, Mark. 2004. "DNA Dragnet." *ABA Journal,* May.

Harmon, Amy. 2003. "Lost? Hiding? Your Cellphone Is Keeping Tabs." *New York Times*, Dec. 21.

Henig, Robin Marantz. 2004. "The Genome in Black and White (and Gray)." *New York Times Magazine*, Oct. 10.

Holmes, Stephen A. 2000. "Census Blamed in Internment of Japanese." *New York Times*, Mar. 17.

Hudson, Audrey. 2004. "Census Bureau Restricts Release of Arab Analysis." *Washington Times*, Aug. 31.

Humanitarian Law Project v. U.S. Department of Justice, 352 F.3d 382, 403 (9th Cir. 2003), *rehearing granted*, 2004 U.S. App. LEXIS 18933 (9th Cir. Sept. 8, 2004); *Humanitarian Law Project v. Ashcroft*, 309 F. Supp. 2d 1185 (C.D. Ca. 2004).

Hunt, Terence. 1997. "Clinton Aims at Juvenile Crime: President Sees Crisis for U.S. Cities." *Detroit Free Press*, Feb. 20.

In re *All Matters Submitted to the Foreign Intelligence Surveillance Court*. 2002. 218 F. Supp.2d 611 (Foreign Intelligence Surveillance Court, May 17, 2002) (en banc).

In re *Sealed Case*. 2002. 310 F.3d 717 (Foreign Intelligence Surveillance Court of Review 2002) (No. 02-001).

Isikoff, Michael, and Daniel Klaidman. 2001. "Access Denied." MSNBC/Newsweek. Oct. 1. http://msnbc.msn.com/id/3067609.

Klaidman, Daniel, and Michael Isikoff. 2003. "Lost in Translation." *Newsweek*, 26-30, Oct. 27.

Krim, Jonathan. 2004. "Passport ID Technology Has High Error Rate." *Washington Post*, Aug. 6.

Lawrence v. Texas, 539 U.S. 558 (2003).

Leach, Susan Llewelyn. 2004. "Passports Go Electronic with New Microchip." *The Christian Science Monitor.* Dec. 9. http://www.csmonitor.com/2004/1209/p12s01-stct.html.

Leone, Richard C., and Gregory Anrig. 2003. *The War on Our Freedoms: Civil Liberties in an Age of Terrorism.* New York: Public Affairs.

Lichtblau, Eric. 2004. "F.B.I. Goes Knocking for Political Troublemakers." *New York Times,* Aug. 16.

McCann, Carole R. 1994. *Birth Control Politics in the United States, 1916–1945.* Ithaca, NY: Cornell University Press.

McCullagh, Declan. 2000a. "The Book Club: *The Unwanted Gaze.*" Review of *The Unwanted Gaze: The Destruction of Privacy in America,* by Jeffrey Rosen. *Slate,* June 6–7. http://slate.msn.com/toolbar.aspx?action=print&id=2000174.

———. 2000b. Testimony before the Democracy Online Task Force (Chairs, Former U.S. House Representatives Patricia Schroeder and Rick White). May 22. http://www.politechbot.com/p-01184.html.

———. 2004. "Database Nation: The Upside of 'Zero Privacy.'" *Reason,* June.

National Commission on Terrorist Attacks upon the United States. 2004a. *The 9/11 Commission Report: Final Report of the National Commission on Terrorist Attacks upon the United States.* Washington, DC: Government Printing Office. http://www.9-11commission.gov/report/index.htm.

———. 2004b. Seventh Public Hearing. Jan. 26–27. http://www.9-11commission.gov/hearings/hearing7.htm.

National Institute of Justice 2001. *Understanding DNA Evidence: A Guide for Victim Service Providers.* Washington, DC: National Institute of Justice. BC000657. http://www.nlectc.org/techbeat/summer2000/DNAevidSum2000.pdf.

Navarro, Mireya. 2004. "When Gender Isn't a Given." *New York Times,* Sept. 19.

New Castle, NY. 2004. "Instructions for Obtaining a Marriage License." http://www.town.new-castle.ny.us/Marriage%20License%20Instructions.htm.

New Jersey v. T.L.O., 469 U.S. 325 (1985).

Pace, Gina. 2004. "Smile—You're on Principal T.V." *Pensacola News Journal,* Jan. 10.

Planned Parenthood v. Casey, 505 U.S. 833 (1992).

Poe-Yamagata, Eileen, and Michael A. Jones. 2000. *And Justice for Some: Differential Treatment of Minority Youth in the Justice System.* Washington, DC:

Building Blocks for Youth. http://www.buildingblocksforyouth.org/justiceforsome.

Porter, Ira. 2004. "Police Get New Way to Match DNA." *Philadelphia Inquirer*, Sept. 17.

Pottawatomie v. Earls, 536 U.S. 822 (2002).

Poudrier, Jennifer. 2003. "'Racial' Categories and Health Risks: Epidemiological Surveillance among Canadian First Nations." In *Surveillance as Social Sorting: Privacy, Risk, and Digital Discrimination*, edited by David Lyon. New York: Routledge.

Reimer, Susan. 2003. "Displaying a Lack of Trust: School's Backpack Ruling Sends a Clear Message." *Pittsburgh Post-Gazette*, Sept. 2.

Religion and Ethics Newsweekly. 2004. "DNA Testing and Crime." *Religion and Ethics Newsweekly*, no. 739, May 28. http://www.pbs.org/wnet/religionandethics/week739/cover.html.

Rhoden, Nancy K. 1987. "Cesareans and Samaritans." *Law, Medicine and Health Care* 15, no. 3: 118–125.

Roberts, Dorothy. 1997. *Killing the Black Body: Race, Reproduction and the Meaning of Liberty*. New York: Vintage Books.

Roberts, Kristin. 2001. "Exposing the Myth of Youth Predators." *Socialist Worker Online*, May 25. http://www.socialistworker.org/2001/369/369_09_MythOfYouthCrime.shtml.

Roe v. Wade, 410 U.S. 113 (1973).

Rosen, Jeffrey. 2000a. The Book Club: The Unwanted Gaze. *Slate* (June 6, 2000) (Letter discussion of Rosen's book *The Unwanted Gaze*). http://slate.msn.com/toolbar.aspx?action=print&id=2000174 (cited July 15, 2004).

———. 2000b. *The Unwanted Gaze: The Destruction of Privacy in America*. New York: Vintage Books USA.

Ross, J. R. 2003. "Madison: Task Force on Wrongful Convictions Holds 1st Meeting." *St. Paul Pioneer Press*, Dec. 23.

Rottenberg, Marc. 2003. Statement to the National Commission on Terrorist Attacks on the United States. In National Commission on Terrorist Attacks upon the United States, Sixth Public Hearing. Dec. 8. http://www.9-11commission.gov/hearings/hearing6.htm.

Roylance, Frank D. 2004. "A Sort of Scientific Malpractice." *Baltimore Sun*, Oct. 11.

Russo, Ralph D., and Charles J. Mawdsley. 2004. "Locker Searches in Schools." *Today's School*, Jan./Feb. http://www.peterli.com/archive/ts/565.shtm.

Satcher, David, M.D. 2001. "Youth Violence: A Report of the Surgeon General." http://www.surgeongeneral.gov/library/youthviolence/toc.html.

Satel, Sally. 2002. "I Am a Racially Profiling Doctor." *New York Times Magazine*, May 5.

Scheeres, Julia. 2002. "Feds' Spying Plan Fades to Black." *Wired News*, Dec. 4. http://www.wired.com/news/politics/0,1283,56701,00.html.

Schneider, Mary Ellen. 2003. "Bush Signs Partial-Birth Abortion Ban: Legal Challenges Underway." *OB/GYN News*, Dec. 1, Vol. 38, no. 23.

Shapiro, Ian, ed. 2001. *Abortion: The Supreme Court Decisions, 1965–2000.* Indianapolis, IN: Hackett Publishing.

Slevin, Peter. 2004. "Arab Americans Report Abuse." *Washington Post*, July 29.

Solinger, Rickie. 1998. "Pregnancy and Power before *Roe v. Wade*, 1950–1970." In *Abortion Wars: A Half Century of Struggle, 1950–2000.* Berkeley and Los Angeles: University of California Press.

Solomon, Lois. 2004. "In-Class Camera Plan Billed as Teacher Aid Raises Privacy Fears." *South Florida Sun-Sentinel*, Jan. 10.

Spotts, Peter N. 2003. "Complete Genome Map Opens Road for Science." *Christian Science Monitor*, Apr. 15.

Stanley, Jay, and Barry Steinhardt. 2003. *Bigger Monster, Weaker Chains: The Growth of an American Surveillance Society.* New York: American Civil Liberties Union.

State of New Jersey. 1998. "New Jersey School Search Policy Manual and Companion Reference Guide." http://www.state.nj.us/lps/dcj/school/.

Steinhardt, Barry. 2000. Testimony of Barry Steinhardt, Associate Director of the American Civil Liberties Union, before the House Judiciary Committee Subcommittee on Crime, Mar. 23. http://www.aclu.org/About/About.cfm?ID=8976&c=191.

Stenberg v. Carhart, 530 U.S. 914 (2000).

Stetson, Dorothy McBride. 2001. "U.S. Abortion Debates, 1959–1998: The Women's Movement Holds On." In *Abortion Politics, Women's Movements, and the Democratic State: A Comparative Study of State Feminism.* New York: Oxford University Press.

Szekely, Peter. 2002. "Railroad to Pay $2.2 Million in DNA Test Case Illegally Testing Workers for Genetic Defects." *Reuters*, May 8.

United States v. Kincade, 379 F.3d 813 (9th Cir. 2004).

United States v. United States District Court for the Eastern District of Michigan (Plamondon et al., real parties in interest), 407 U.S. 297 (1972).

University of Michigan Institute for Social Research. 2003. "Student Drug Testing Not Effective in Reducing Drug Use." Press release, May 19.

U.S. Congress. 1976. Senate Select Committee to Study Governmental Operations with Respect to Intelligence Activities (Church Committee). Final Report—Book II. April 26, 1976. 94th Cong., 2d Sess. S. Rep. 94-755, Washington, DC: GPO.

———. 2002. House Permanent Select Committee on Intelligence and the Senate Select Committee on Intelligence (Joint Inquiry). Report of the Joint Inquiry into the Terrorist Attacks of September 11, 2001. 107th Cong., 2nd Sess., S. Rept. 107-351, H. Rept. 107-792. Washington, DC: GPO. http://news.findlaw.com/cnn/docs/911rpt/index.html.

Veronia School District 47J v. Acton, 515 U.S. 646 (1995).

Von Drehle, John. 2004. "Most Witnesses Blame Others." *Miami Herald*, Apr. 14. http://www.miami.com/mld/miamiherald/news/nation/8426586.htm.

Walker, Samuel. 2004. "Police DNA 'Sweeps' Extremely Unproductive." Sept. http://www.policeaccountability.org/dnareport.pdf.

Westin, Alan. 1967. *Privacy and Freedom*. New York: Atheneum.

Wilson, Glynn. 2003. "In Louisiana, Debate over a DNA Dragnet." *Christian Science Monitor*, Feb. 21.

Windy City Times. 2004. "Kansas Court to Hear Appeal Gay Teen's Case." *Windy City Times*, June 2.

Yamaguchi, Ryoko. 2003. "Relationship between Student Illicit Drug Use and School Drug-Testing Policies." *Journal of School Health*. Vol. 73, no. 4, April 1.

4

Chronology

Pre-   For most of history, privacy is not a single concept as
1600s   such, but exists in a variety of societal norms and laws
        as, variously, the confidentiality of information obtained
        in the doctor-patient relationship, protection of personal
        property (especially the home), respect for family rela-
        tions and the modesty of women, manners concerning
        what is to be kept out of public view, and religious criti-
        cism of data collection efforts such as the census.

1690   Philosopher John Locke publishes *The Two Treatises of
        Civil Government,* following the English revolution of
        1688, which establishes that the king is not above the
        laws of Parliament and leads to adoption of the English
        Bill of Rights. The *Treatises* argue that government is en-
        titled only to those powers that are granted to it by indi-
        viduals and that are necessary for it to protect those indi-
        viduals and their property. His philosophy helps spread
        the idea that individuals have the right to be free from
        unnecessary government intrusion.

1776   The thirteen American colonies adopt the Declaration of
        Independence, including a denunciation of the practice
        of quartering British troops in private houses.

1789   The French Revolution begins. The French issue the Dec-
        laration of the Rights of Man and of the Citizen, includ-
        ing a broad conception of liberty as freedom from un-
        warranted intrusion.

171

1791   Two years after adopting the Constitution, the United States adopts the Bill of Rights, including types of privacy protection in the First, Third, Fourth, Fifth, and Ninth Amendments.

1800s   Through much of this century, in both the United Kingdom and the United States, privacy rights develop as extensions of property rights. Although home invasions had long been punished as trespass to property, this idea is expanded, for example, to treat disclosure of a person's private records, artwork, or secrets as a violation of his or her property rights in those papers, works, or ideas. The concern in those cases of (what might now be called) "intellectual property" theft was not a loss of financial profits, but an invasion of privacy.

1826   In France, Joseph-Nicéphore Niepce takes the first recognizable photograph.

1837   Samuel Morse invents the telegraph.

1876   Alexander Graham Bell holds the first telephone conversation, saying, "Watson, come here. I want you."

1877   Thomas Edison files a patent for the first phonograph, which both records sound into rotating cylinders of tin foil and plays it back. The machine's first successful recording was the sentence "Mary had a little lamb."

1888   George Eastman invents the first portable camera and sells it with the slogan, "You press the button, we do the rest."

1890   Louis Brandeis and Samuel Warren publish "The Right to Privacy" in the *Harvard Law Review,* in which they describe the evolution of different legal claims into what could be described broadly as a "right to privacy."

1894   Mark Twain publishes *The Tragedy of Pudd'nhead Wilson,* thought to be the first popular account of the use of fingerprints to solve a crime (indeed, a case of identity theft) and a biting satire of racial discrimination and social sorting.

1895   In Italy, Guglielmo Marconi improves on earlier work with radio wave signals, sending and receiving his first radio message. Later, he will pioneer radio communication across the English Channel in 1899 and across the Atlantic Ocean in 1901.

In France, the brothers Lumière invent the first modern portable motion-picture camera and projector. They were also the first to present a movie to a paying audience.

1898   In Denmark, Valdemar Poulsen invents the telegraphone, the first device to magnetically record and play back speech and other sounds. In the first machine, the moment of magnetic recording occurred between the sending and receiving of a telephone or telegraph message. As such, the telegraphone can be considered the precursor not only to the tape recorder but also the telephone wiretap.

1928   In *Olmstead v. United States*, the U.S. Supreme Court issues its first decision dealing with wiretapping. The majority of the Court says the Fourth Amendment applies not to wiretapping, but only to physical invasions. Brandeis writes a now-famous dissenting opinion but will not be vindicated until nearly forty years later in *Katz v. United States*.

1933   Adolf Hitler becomes chancellor of Germany; persuades President Paul von Hindenburg to issue a decree suspending all civil liberties, including privacy of the mails and freedom from searches without a warrant; and begins his persecution of Jews and other minorities, including grave violations of their privacy and dignity.

1938   The National Socialist (Nazi) government of Germany requires all Jews living in Germany to apply for special identification cards.

1939 World War II begins.

1945 World War II ends. The United Nations is formed to promote peace and human dignity.

The Electronic Numerical Integrator and Calculator—a room-size computer—is completed in Philadelphia.

1948 The United Nations General Assembly adopts the Universal Declaration of Human Rights, which includes a right to privacy in Article 12.

1949 Author George Orwell publishes *1984*, which imagines an oppressive world regime controlled by constant surveillance and other invasions of privacy. The book features the regime's slogan, "Big Brother is watching you," which has since become shorthand for the dangers of government surveillance.

1950 European countries adopt the European Convention for the Protection of Human Rights and Fundamental Freedoms, which includes a right to privacy in Article 8, and create a court to enforce it. More commonly referred to as the European Convention on Human Rights, this treaty is now subscribed to by forty-five countries.

1965 In *Griswold v. Connecticut,* the U.S. Supreme Court announces the existence of a constitutional right to privacy and overturns a state law prohibiting the distribution of birth control pills.

1966 The UN adopts the International Covenant on Civil and Political Rights, which protects privacy in Article 17. The treaty is ratified by enough member states to enter into effect ten years later, in 1976.

1967 In *Katz v. United States,* the Supreme Court says the Fourth Amendment extends to electronic intrusions of a person's private space and a warrant is required to wiretap a public pay phone in which a person reasonably expects his conversations are private. The decision effectively overturns *Olmstead v. United States* (1928) and vindicates Brandeis's powerful dissent.

In *Berger v. New York*, the Supreme Court holds that the Fourth Amendment implies limitations on the duration and scope of surveillance as a "fundamental rule that has long been recognized as basic to the privacy of every home in America."

1969   The Organization of American States adopts the American Convention on Human Rights, which protects the right to privacy in Article 11.

1971   The U.S. Senate Committee on Constitutional Rights, chaired by Senator Sam Ervin, reveals extensive spying on U.S. citizens by the U.S. military. In 1974, the committee further reports that fifty-four federal agencies maintained more than 858 databases with more than 1 billion records on U.S. citizens.

1972   Burglars are caught breaking into the U.S. Democratic Party headquarters in the Watergate building in Washington, D.C., in order to tap the party's phones. The arrests lead to a chain of discoveries of White House abuse of power and ultimately to President Nixon's resignation.

1973   In *Roe v. Wade*, the U.S. Supreme Court holds that the right of privacy protects a woman's right to terminate her pregnancy in the first trimester, without government interference, with the medical judgment of the woman's doctor; in the second trimester subject to government restrictions related to maternal health; and in the third trimester subject to government prohibitions to protect the life of the fetus unless the abortion is necessary to preserve the life or health of the mother.

1974   Fueled in part by the privacy invasions by the Nixon administration, the U.S. Congress passes the Privacy Act, the Freedom of Information Act, and the Family Educational Rights and Privacy Act. The Privacy Act had been developed over many years, stemming from Congress's

1974,
cont.
research since the 1960s on how to address privacy concerns raised by new database technologies being employed by the federal government.

1975   U.S. Congress creates the Select Committee to Study Governmental Operations with Respect to Intelligence Activities, chaired by Senator Frank Church. In 1976, the committee reveals details of covert operations by the CIA, FBI, and NSA to spy on, disrupt, or discredit American groups and individuals in the opposing political party or deemed "radical," including Martin Luther King Jr., Joan Baez, and Democratic presidential candidate Senator Adlai Stevenson, as well as U.S. involvement in plots to assassinate or overthrow foreign heads of state.

1978   The U.S. Congress passes the Foreign Intelligence Surveillance Act to limit the types of spying U.S. agencies can do within the United States. The act creates a secret court (the FISA court) to issue secret warrants for surveillance of intelligence suspects in the United States. Of the thousands of requests submitted to it over the next thirty-five years, the FISA court rejects only one application for a warrant.

1981   The Council of Europe adopts the Convention for the Protection of Individuals with Regard to Automatic Processing of Personal Data, which requires signatory states to pass laws concerning the processing of personal data in their countries.

1986   The U.S. Congress passes the Electronic Communications Privacy Act, which attempts to update the privacy protections against surveillance to apply to electronic communications.

1988   In *California v. Greenwood*, the U.S. Supreme Court holds that police may search a person's curbside garbage without a warrant, because individuals do not have an expectation of privacy in the garbage they put outside for collection.

In response to a request under the Freedom of Information Act, the FBI admits to having wiretapped Supreme Court justices William Douglas, Earl Warren, Abe Fortas, and Potter Stewart years earlier.

1989   On April 19, the "Central Park jogger" is raped, robbed, and left for dead. "Wilding" bands of teens are falsely blamed, and five minority youths are wrongly convicted. Their convictions are overturned in 2002, but, in the intervening years, the image of savage youth fuels restrictive laws and practices targeting urban, mostly minority, youth.

1992   In *Planned Parenthood v. Casey,* the U.S. Supreme Court narrowly upholds *Roe v. Wade* but allows states to regulate abortions extensively, as long as they do not place an "undue burden" on the privacy right to an abortion.

1993   On February 26, foreign terrorists detonate a bomb in the garage of the World Trade Center in New York, killing 6 people, injuring 1,080 people, bursting a hole through four floors of heavy concrete, and disrupting phone service throughout New York City.

1995   The European Union issues "Directive 95/46/EC on the protection of individuals with regard to the processing of personal data and on the free movement of such data" (Data Protection Directive), which sets principles and rules for collecting and using data about individuals. The directive aims to harmonize data protection laws among the member states of the European Union. Privacy advocates view the directive as a necessary, strong framework for protecting privacy.

On April 19, American terrorists detonate a powerful bomb in front of the federal office building in Oklahoma City, Oklahoma, killing 168 people and wounding 850 more.

1996   U.S. Congress passes the Anti-Terrorism and Effective Death Penalty Enforcement Act, which gives federal law

1996,   enforcement increased powers of surveillance. Congress
cont.   also passes the Health Insurance Portability and Accountability Act, which gives additional privacy protections to a person's medical records.

1998   The Council of Europe replaces the old court with the new European Court of Human Rights to allow individuals in Europe direct appeal of violations of their rights under the European Convention on Human Rights. The new court rules eliminate the requirement of appealing to the European Commission of Human Rights, which gave states more control over what appeals would be heard.

1999   On April 20, two students terrorize Columbine High School in Littleton, Colorado, killing twelve children and one adult and wounding twenty-three others. The incident launches a wave of restrictive policies and monitoring of youth.

2000   Driving a small boat laden with explosives, terrorists blast a large hole in the U.S. destroyer USS *Cole* anchored in the port of Aden, Yemen, killing seventeen sailors and injuring thirty-nine.

The *Wall Street Journal* reveals that the FBI is using a high-powered program, dubbed Carnivore, that it installs on the computers of Internet service providers to monitor e-mail communications and Web traffic. Although the FBI insists that Carnivore reveals only information that fits its authorized search categories, it also admits that it sifts through every user's communications and Internet footprints first. Also in 2000, an internal FBI memo reveals that misprogramming resulted in the records of nonsuspects being disclosed. The FBI's use of Carnivore is not monitored by an independent agency, and the FBI will not disclose information about Carnivore.

2001   On September 11, nineteen foreign terrorists hijack four airplanes in the United States and drive one airplane into each of the two towers of New York's World Trade Center, one into the Pentagon, and another into the ground in rural Pennsylvania. The attacks kill more than 3,000 people.

On October 24, the House passes the USA PATRIOT Act, 357 votes for, 66 against; on October 25, the Senate passes the bill (Senator Russ Feingold voting against); and on October 26, President George Bush signs the bill into law.

2002   Among other antiterrorism initiatives bearing a large price for privacy, the White House proposes Operation TIPS (Terrorist Information and Prevention System) in January to recruit 1 million citizens, including people whose jobs permit them entry into others' homes, to report "suspicious" activities. In December, Congress passes a bill forbidding implementation of the project.

The Bush administration reveals the Total Information Awareness project, which merges information about millions of persons from government and commercial databases and matches the information against a terrorist profile to determine whether they are suspicious. Congress defunds the program, but the Pentagon outsources funding for the project to five states and changes the name to the Multistate Anti-Terrorism Information Exchange, known by its acronym, MATRIX.

2003   Details of the MATRIX program are revealed in a slide presentation by the program's manufacturer, Seisint, Inc. Seisint states it created a formula to predict who was likely to be a terrorist and assigned to each individual a high terrorist factor (HTF) score. Seisint asserts it provided the names of 120,000 people with the highest HTF scores to federal intelligence agencies.

In *Lawrence v. Texas*, the U.S. Supreme Court overrules its 1984 decision in *Bowers v. Hardwick* and finds that laws criminalizing private, consensual sodomy are a violation of the constitutional right to privacy.

2004   On April 26, approximately 1 million people demonstrate in the March for Women's Lives on the National

2004,   Mall in Washington, D.C. Six months prior to an election
cont.   expected to have a significant impact on the makeup of
         the U.S. Supreme Court and thus on many 5–4 decisions
         of the Court, the march sought to show broad political
         support for women's right to make private decisions
         about their reproductive health, including the right to
         have an abortion.

2005   Portions of the USA PATRIOT Act—including several,
         but not all, of the provisions that infringe on privacy—
         are set to expire on December 31 unless renewed by Con-
         gress and the president.

         On July 7, three bombs explode, nearly simultaneously,
         in the London Underground at the peak of the morning
         rush hour, and an hour later a fourth bomb explodes on
         a bus. The attacks kill at least 52 people and injure ap-
         proximately 700.

5

Biographical Sketches

John Ashcroft (1942–)

Prior to his appointment as U.S. attorney general in 2001 by President George W. Bush, John Ashcroft served two terms as governor of Missouri and one term as U.S. senator. Ashcroft is a political and religious conservative, whose appointment as head of the Department of Justice was lauded by social and religious conservatives in the Republican Party. There is evidence that Ashcroft was a moderate supporter of privacy rights prior to September 11, 2001. However, after the attacks, he led the Justice Department's efforts to combat terrorism, often using controversial initiatives and tactics that violated privacy rights. Critics argued these invasions were unconstitutional, unnecessary, and counterproductive. The Justice Department, which includes the Federal Bureau of Investigation (FBI), drafted and implemented the USA PATRIOT Act; conducted home and office visits to thousands of Middle Eastern men and Muslim and Arab Americans with no connection to terrorism; required men and boys from twenty-four Arab and Muslim countries who were living in the United States to register, interview, and reregister with the federal government; in the process (with the Department of Homeland Security) arrested and deported thousands of Arab and Muslim immigrants, often for minor technical violations of complicated immigration and registration requirements; and eliminated internal rules preventing the FBI from using international espionage tactics on U.S. citizens and other suspects in ordinary criminal investigations on U.S. soil. Ashcroft blamed such privacy protections rather than poor communication, information systems, and other agency failures for blinding the government, calling the privacy wall the "single greatest structural cause for the Sept. 11 problem." Ashcroft resigned as attorney general following the reelection of President George W. Bush in 2004.

William Baird (1933–)

Founder of the Pro-Choice League, Bill Baird was inspired to a life of activism and controversy when, in 1963, he saw a woman die from an abortion she had self-administered with a wire coat hanger. She left nine children behind. Baird was arrested eight times for speaking out about abortion and contraception and distributing contraceptives. He was the lead plaintiff in two important U.S. Supreme Court decisions on privacy: *Eisenstadt v. Baird* (1972), which extended the right to use contraceptives from married couples to unmarried persons, and *Bellotti v. Baird* (1979), which found unconstitutional a state law that severely restricted young people from having abortions without parental consent. The Court held that such age-based restrictions must allow case-by-case exceptions (decided by a judge) for young women based on their maturity or best interests.

Roger Baldwin (1884–1981)

Roger Baldwin cofounded the American Civil Liberties Union in 1920 and served as its director until 1950. Baldwin led the ACLU's efforts to bring the protections of civil liberties—including the right to privacy—embodied in the Constitution and Bill of Rights off the written page and into people's lives. He started his career as a social worker and juvenile probation officer in St. Louis, where he coauthored the influential *Juvenile Courts and Probation* in 1914. He was a pacifist and spent a year in prison for resisting the draft as a conscientious objector in 1918. During his tenure at the ACLU, he was intimately involved in efforts to protect people's freedom of association and freedom of expression regardless of political belief, the ACLU's defense of religious freedom in the Scopes "Monkey Trial," and the ACLU's challenges to the United States arbitrary arrest and internment of more than 100,000 Japanese Americans and Japanese immigrants in California in 1942. In 1947, General Douglas MacArthur arranged to have Baldwin brought to Japan to assist with the development of a constitutional system and culture of rights in that new postwar democracy. He provided similar assistance to South Korea, Germany, and Austria, as well as to Puerto Rico upon its becoming a commonwealth.

After his retirement from the ACLU, Baldwin served for fifteen years as chair of the International League for the Rights of Man (now the International League of Human Rights). He was awarded the Presidential Medal of Freedom in 1981. See Robert C. Cottrell, *Roger Baldwin and the American Civil Liberties Union* (New York: Columbia University Press, 2000); and Samuel Walker, *In Defense of American Liberties: A History of the ACLU*, 2d ed. (Carbondale: Southern Illinois University Press, 1999).

Robert Bork (1927–)

Robert Bork was a judge on the U.S. Circuit Court of Appeals for the District of Columbia from 1982 until his resignation in 1988 and an unsuccessful nominee to the U.S. Supreme Court in 1987. He was solicitor general from 1973 to 1974 under Presidents Nixon and Ford. He is an author, most recently of *Slouching toward Gomorrah*, in which he argues that liberals have distorted core American values and thereby contributed to America's decline. In a 1990 book, Bork argued that Justice William O. Douglas and the Supreme Court were guilty of inventing a right with no basis in the Constitution in *Griswold v. Connecticut*, the case that established the right to privacy.

During Judge Bork's Senate process to confirm his nomination to the Supreme Court, a Washington, D.C., newspaper published a list of his personal video rentals. Outrage over the privacy invasion led to passage of the Video Privacy Protection Act of 1988, which protects the privacy of video rentals. See Robert Bork, *The Tempting of America: The Political Seduction of the Law* (New York: Simon and Schuster, 1990).

Louis Brandeis (1856–1941)

Louis Brandeis was a justice of the U.S. Supreme Court from 1916 to 1939 and the first Jewish justice on the Court. As a lawyer in Boston, he represented working people in challenges to minimum age and wage laws, convincing the Supreme Court to hold in *Muller v. Oregon* (1908) that such laws were not unconstitutional. On the Court, Brandeis continued to encourage the Court to take positions that fostered social and economic reform, including President Franklin Roosevelt's New Deal policies. He also was a lifelong advocate of privacy rights. In 1890, he coauthored with Samuel Warren "The Right to Privacy," which was published in the *Harvard Law Review* and is cited as the first description of an integrated concept of the right to privacy. In 1928, Brandies wrote the dissenting opinion in the landmark decision *Olmstead v. United States*, in which he argued that the Court should recognize and protect a right to privacy against new technologies that threaten it. For his foresight, he is sometimes called the "father of privacy." Brandeis University in Massachusetts is named in his honor. See Philippa Strum, *Louis D. Brandeis: Justice for the People* (Cambridge, MA: Harvard University Press, 1984) and *Brandeis: Beyond Progressivism* (Lawrence: University Press of Kansas, 1993).

James Buckley (1923–)

A one-term U.S. senator from the state of New York from 1970 to 1976, James Buckley's name has become synonymous with the privacy of educational records. He sponsored with Senator Claiborne Pell the Family Educational Rights and Privacy Act of 1974, commonly referred to as FERPA or the Buckley amendment. The Buckley amendment restricts the release of a student's school records to only those school officials with a legitimate educational interest in the records and requires the school to give a student and her parents access to those records within forty-five days of a request. It applies to any school (public or private) that receives any federal funds. FERPA has been criticized by some as badly crafted and cumbersome, and it has been amended nine times since its adoption. However, it gives young people and their families substantial control over private information about themselves. Since his time in the Senate, Buckley has served as a federal district court judge and a judge on the U.S. Circuit Court of Appeals for the District of Columbia. See James L. Buckley, *If Men Were Angels: A View from the Senate* (New York: G. P. Putnam's Sons, 1975).

Morris L. Ernst (1888–1976)

A New York lawyer, Morris Ernst was an important leader in the protection and promotion of civil liberties and civil rights. Ernst was an important leader in the ACLU and NAACP. He successfully represented the publishers of *Ulysses*, the great James Joyce novel that was repeatedly banned and even publicly burned by government officials for supposed obscenity; Ernst helped win the case both at the trial level and on appeal to the federal circuit court. In the 1930s, he was among the first to litigate on behalf of individuals' right to use contraception. In 1962, he co-authored with Alan Schwartz one of the first popular books on the right to privacy, *Privacy: The Right to Be Let Alone* (New York: Macmillan 1962).

John Marshall Harlan (1899–1971)

John Marshall Harlan was a conservative member of the U.S. Supreme Court from 1955 until a few months before his death. His grandfather too had been a member of the Court, from 1877 to 1911. Although the younger Harlan did not agree with many of the positions or theories of the liberal Warren Court majority during his tenure, he is remembered for his dissent in *Poe v. Ullman* (1961), in which the majority upheld a law prohibiting married couples from using contraceptives (overturned by *Griswold* in 1965). Harlan dissented:

> I believe that a statute making it a criminal offense for married couples to use contraceptives is an intolerable and unjustifiable invasion of privacy in the conduct of the most intimate concerns of an individual's personal life . . . [T]he intimacy of husband and wife is necessarily an essential and accepted feature of the institution of marriage, an institution which the state not only must allow, but which always and in every age it has fostered and protected. It is one thing when the State exerts its power either to forbid extra-marital sexuality altogether, or to say who may marry, but it is quite another when, having acknowledged a marriage and the intimacies inherent in it, it undertakes to regulate by means of the criminal law the details of that intimacy. (*Poe v. Ulman,* 367 U.S. 497, 539, 1961).

See Morton J. Horwitz, *The Warren Court and the Pursuit of Justice* (New York: Hill and Wang, 1998); and Tinsley E. Yarborough, *John Marshall Harlan: Great Dissenter of the Warren Court* (New York: Oxford University Press, 1992).

J. Edgar Hoover (1895–1972)

John Edgar Hoover was director of the Federal Bureau of Investigation from 1924 to 1972, serving under eight presidents. He began his career in the Department of Justice in 1917, where, within two years, he was made special assistant to the director and given charge of investigating, arresting, and deporting suspected anarchists and communists, including the 10,000 people arrested in what have become known as the Palmer Raids. Hoover was inspired to catalog detailed information on "dangerous" people by the Library of Congress's massive cataloging of books, which he observed while working at the library when he was attending law school. Over the course of Hoover's tenure, the FBI collected files on hundreds of thousands of persons he deemed suspicious or radical, including conservative John Birch, civil rights activist Martin Luther King Jr. and rock star John Lennon. Hoover kept his own secret stash of files and information on politicians, presidents, and others in Washington over whom he wished to keep power. He transformed an office of investigations at the Justice Department into the FBI, securing broad powers of investigation and enforcement for the bureau. He expanded the bureau's use of surveillance to include widespread use of wiretapping and infiltration. See Richard Hack, *Puppetmaster: The Secret Life of J. Edgar Hoover* (Beverly Hills, CA: New Millennium Press, 2004).

John Locke (1632–1704)

John Locke's parents died when he was young. He was sent to be a student and religious scholar at Christ Church, Oxford, but he also dabbled in medicine. When he successfully operated on the prominent Earl of Shaftesbury, he was catapulted into high society and politics. His controversial views—that science and reason were superior to unexamined tradition or faith and that the king did not inherit a divine right to govern—kept him in the political minority until the revolution of 1688. Soon after, Locke published a masterpiece of political philosophy that he had been working on for several years, *Two Treatises on Civil Government*. In his *Treatises*, Locke argues that legitimate government rests on the consent of those being governed; that rebellion is permissible when government betrays its responsibility to protect life, liberty, and property; and that the public welfare is the measure for what governments can ask of their people. Locke's work laid the philosophical foundation for individual rights and popular government and greatly influenced the American and French Revolutions. See Peter Laslett, ed., *John Locke: Two Treatises of Government*, 3d student ed. (Cambridge: Cambridge University Press, 1988).

Catharine MacKinnon (1946–)

Catharine MacKinnon is a law professor at the University of Michigan and a world-renowned expert on sex equality and discrimination. MacKinnon pioneered the argument that sexual harassment is a form of sexual discrimination and won recognition of this legal claim in the U.S. Supreme Court in 1986. She pioneered other important legal claims before the Supreme Court of Canada. Concerning privacy, MacKinnon has forcefully pointed out how the social and legal construction of privacy can be detrimental to those without power, particularly women. Whereas privacy can be a refuge for some, it can also be a sphere of isolation and impunity for egregious wrongdoing. Within the private sphere—take, for instance, the home or bedroom, which often includes a man and woman—the benefits of privacy go to the more powerful. Given the legal, social, and historical preferences accorded men, the woman in the private sphere must either consent or run the risk of irredressable coercion. Therefore, even though the law purports to protect a woman's right to privacy when it comes to contraception, abortion, and family life, in fact the law and society abandon her to the control of more powerful men who come within her private sphere. "For women the measure of the intimacy has been the measure of the oppression. This is why feminism has had to explode the private. This is why feminism has seen the personal as the political. The private is public for those for whom the personal is political. In this sense, for women there is no private . . . Feminism confronts the fact that women have no privacy to lose or to guarantee" (*Feminism Unmodified: Discourses on Life and Law* [Cambridge, MA: Harvard University Press, 1987], 100–102; see also MacKinnon, "Reflections on Sex Equality under Law," *Yale Law Journal* 100, 1281 [Mar. 1991]).

George Orwell (1903–1950)

In 1949, George Orwell, the pseudonym of Englishman Eric Arthur Blair, published *1984*. The novel vividly depicts a government that uses war to justify infringement of personal liberties.

Among the government tactics Orwell imagines are speech codes and the use of technology to monitor political opposition and thought crimes. Orwell describes the government's intrusive role in the now familiar term *Big Brother*.

Orwell lived a colorful and challenging life. From being beaten by his schoolmasters in boarding school for wetting his bed to growing up in British colonized India and volunteering in the Spanish civil war, Orwell experienced the complexities and dangers of power. He received acclaim for *1984* and his satire *Animal Farm* (1945). See William J. Boerst, *Generous Anger: The Story of George Orwell* (Greensboro, NC: Morgan Reynolds, 2001).

Anthony Romero (1966–)

In 2001, at age thirty-five, Anthony Romero became the executive director of the American Civil Liberties Union and the organization's first Latino and first openly gay director. The ACLU is the leading defender of privacy and other civil liberties in the United States. Whether lobbying or bringing legal action, the organization appeals to the U.S. Constitution to protect a woman's right to abortion and contraception, to limit government surveillance and databasing, and to give ordinary people control over their own personal information.

Romero was raised by Puerto Rican immigrants in the Bronx and was the first in his family to graduate high school, college, or graduate school. After law school, he quickly rose through the ranks of the Ford Foundation, gaining responsibility for more than $90 million in grant distributions for civil rights and social justice causes. Weeks after he started as director of the ACLU, terrorists flew airplanes into the World Trade Center, a half mile from the ACLU's headquarters in New York. Romero was cast into the ensuing fight between those who wanted to restrict liberties and infringe privacy in the name of homeland defense and the ACLU, which had nurtured and protected those rights since its formation in 1920. Romero chose to emphasize that the United States could promote homeland security without eviscerating rights and discriminating against Arab and Muslim minorities and that smarter policies, better policing, better internal communication, and cooperation with Arab and Muslim Americans would allow the United States to be both "safe and free."

Romero has presided over an unprecedented effort to mobilize Americans, and the ACLU ranks grew substantially in re-

sponse to fears of government abuse of privacy and other freedoms under President George W. Bush. In 2003, Romero said, "If
you believe in openness in government and the right to privacy
for individuals . . . , if you believe that racial and ethnic profiling
has no place in law enforcement . . . , and if you refuse to choose
between a free America and a safe America—because we can't
have one without the other—stand with us." Romero, Anthony.
"Redoubling Our Efforts," Speech, June 11, 2003, http://www.
aclu.org/Conference/Conference.cfm?ID=12882&c=256.

Eleanor Roosevelt (1884–1962)

Eleanor Roosevelt was the wife of Franklin D. Roosevelt and first
lady of the United States from 1933 to 1945. In 1945, after her husband's death, Roosevelt was asked by President Truman to represent the United States on the United Nations Commission on Human Rights. She joined notable jurists, thinkers, and leaders from
around the world, including René-Samuel Cassin of France, Peng
Chun Chang of China, Charles Malik of Lebanon, Hansa Mehta
of India, and Carlos Romulo of the Philippines. This distinguished commission elected Roosevelt chair. Under her direction,
and with staff assistance from Canada's John Humphrey and others, they drafted the Universal Declaration of Human Rights. Pre-
senting the declaration to the UN General Assembly, Roosevelt
said, "We stand today at the threshold of a great event both in the
life of the United Nations and in the life of mankind. This declaration may well become the international Magna Carta for all
men everywhere." After 1,400 rounds of voting on nearly every
phrase, the declaration was adopted without dissent on December 10, 1948. Two decades before the U.S. Supreme Court officially recognized an implicit right to privacy in the U.S. Constitution, the declaration enshrined an explicit principle forbidding
"arbitrary interference with [a person's] privacy, family, home or
correspondence" (Art. 12). See Mary Ann Glendon, *A World Made
New: Eleanor Roosevelt and the Universal Declaration of Human
Rights* (New York: Random House, 2002); and Eleanor Roosevelt,
The Autobiography of Eleanor Roosevelt (New York: Harper, 1961).

Jeffrey Rosen (1964–)

Author of the book *The Unwanted Gaze: The Destruction of Privacy
in America* (2000), Jeffrey Rosen is the legal affairs editor of the

New Republic and a professor at George Washington University School of Law. In *The Unwanted Gaze,* which was praised for its original insight and persuasive inquiry into the subject of privacy, Rosen argues that, in a high-tech age of information overload and short attention spans, revealing private information about people subjects them to gross misjudgments and simplifications of who they are. He argues that judges, newspaper editors, and others should exercise discretion that balances the need for disclosure of private information against the harm it is likely to cause in the information age. He is also author of *The Naked Crowd: Reclaiming Security and Freedom in an Anxious Age* (2004), which examines issues of privacy and security after the attacks of September 11, 2001. In *The Naked Crowd,* he argues that Western society's growing aversion to risk is leading people to accept intrusions that make them feel safer but do not in fact make them safer.

Marc Rottenberg (1963–)

Marc Rottenberg has been executive director of the Electronic Privacy Information Center (EPIC), which seeks to protect personal privacy in the digital realm from government and industry intrusion, since its founding in 1994. Through comprehensive reports, freedom of information requests to the government, and collaboration with projects and activists across the globe, Rottenberg and the staff at EPIC have quietly built the organization into one of the most respected, influential watchdogs for privacy in the world. In an industry flowing with consulting money and side deals, Rottenberg takes his work and his independence seriously. He does not accept corporate speaking fees or own stock in technology industries. As EPIC's Web site says, "We have no clients, no customers, and no shareholders." Their independence earns them credibility and gives them cover, for example, to go after Internet advertising behemoth DoubleClick when it announced plans to merge offline customer data with Internet surfers' electronic surfing trail.

Margaret Sanger (1879–1966)

In 1916, Margaret Sanger opened the first birth control clinic in the United States. From her Brooklyn clinic, Sanger defied the Comstock Act of 1872, which forbade distribution of birth control devices and information. Her advocacy for reproductive rights eventually led to the founding of the American Birth Control League, which became the Planned Parenthood Federation of America in 1942. Central to Sanger's work was to advocate for women's right to make private decisions about their own reproductive health. See Margaret Sanger, *An Autobiography* (New York: W. W. Norton, 1938; New York: Dover Publications, 2004); and Gloria Moore and Ronald Moore, *Margaret Sanger and the Birth Control Movement* (New York: Rowman and Littlefield, 1995).

Barry Steinhardt (1953–)

Barry Steinhardt is director of the American Civil Liberties Union's Technology and Liberty Program. He is a cofounder of the Global Internet Liberty Campaign (GILC), the first international coalition to fight for online free expression and privacy. He served as president of the Electronic Frontier Foundation and as chair of the 2003 Computer Freedom and Privacy conference. Steinhardt coauthored the ACLU's 2003 report titled *Bigger Monster, Weaker Chains* decrying the growth of the U.S. surveillance-industry complex and the diminishment of laws to protect people's privacy. Steinhardt has written, "It is not too late to tame the surveillance monster. Privacy is not dead, as some have suggested, but it is on life support" (Steinhardt 2003).

Alan Westin (1929–)

Author of one of the most important books on privacy, *Privacy and Freedom* (1967), Alan Westin is an academic who has sought a balance between the interests of businesses and governments and the privacy protections desired by consumers and citizens. In *Privacy and Freedom,* he coined the term *data shadow,* which refers to the facts or fiction that are implied by the recorded data of people's transactions (for example, large alcohol purchases could imply either a drinking problem or hosting a party). He wrote two other texts on the topic of privacy, which are still widely viewed as seminal: *Information Technology in a Democracy* (1971) and *Databanks in a Free Society* (1972).

Westin is a professor emeritus of government at Columbia University; founder of the nonprofit think tank the Center for Social and Legal Research (CSLR); and, as president of CSLR, publisher of the Web site PrivacyExchange.org and the newsletter *Privacy and American Business*, which advise the business community on "managing the privacy revolution." Westin's pragmatic "middle way" has been criticized by privacy advocates for giving too much weight to business and government interests. He has advised numerous government agencies and hundreds of large companies on their privacy policies and procedures.

Byron White (1917–2002)

Byron White served as a justice on the U.S. Supreme Court from 1962 to 1993. He was considered a "swing" justice—he typically voted with liberals on civil-rights cases and with conservatives on personal liberty and criminal justice issues. Although White recognized a right to privacy in *Griswold v. Connecticut*, he wrote a dissenting opinion to the landmark case *Roe v. Wade* that guaranteed a woman's right to an abortion. In 1986, White wrote the lead opinion in *Bowers v. Hardwick* upholding a Georgia law criminalizing sodomy and holding that constitutional protections of privacy do not extend to homosexual conduct. That decision was overturned in 2003 in *Lawrence v. Texas*. In 1990, another justice who voted with White's majority in *Bowers*, Lewis Powell Jr., told New York University law students, "I think I probably made a mistake in that one" (Biskupic and Barbash 1998).

John Wilkes (1725–1797)

John Wilkes was an outspoken member of the British Parliament and a newspaper editor who curried the wrath of the Crown. After denouncing one of King George III's speeches in his newspaper, Wilkes was arrested and sent to the Tower of London to await trial. His arrest raised issues about the rights of Englishmen and members of Parliament against the king's agents, and his case gained widespread popular sympathy both in England and in the American colonies. Could members of the press be arrested for criticizing the king? Could members of Parliament be arrested for what they expressed before Parliament? Could the king's sheriffs storm an Englishman's home and search his papers? Wilkes's friends secured a writ of habeas corpus to appear before a neutral magistrate to review his arrest and detention, and Wilkes was released. He then sued the sheriffs for trespass and won a monetary award. Wilkes's success ultimately inspired further enlargement of the right to free speech, freedom of the press, and privacy.

References

Biskupic, Joan, and Barbash, Fred. 1998. "Retired Justice Lewis Powell Dies at 90." *Washington Post.* August 26. A1.

Steinhardt, Barry. 2003. "Taming the Surveillance Monster." *CIO Magazine,* Fall/Winter. http://www.cio.com/archive/092203/steinhardt.html.

6

Important Privacy Documents

Circa 400 BCE Hippocratic Oath (excerpt of original version)

What I may see or hear in the course of the treatment or even outside of the treatment in regard to the life of men, which on no account one must spread abroad, I will keep to myself, holding such things shameful to be spoken about.

Circa 50 to 220 The Mishnah

Hezzekh Reah ("The injury caused by seeing")

The Mishnah is a collection of ancient Jewish laws based on teachings handed down through the Jewish oral tradition and the rulings and disputes of different rabbis. It covers, for example, the rules of prayer, marriage, and sacrificial worship, as well as the structure of judicial authority.

No one may place an entrance . . . opposite the entrance [of another] . . . nor a window opposite [another's] window . . . No one shall open up windows facing a jointly owned courtyard . . .

Even the smallest intrusion into private space by the unwanted gaze causes damage, because the damage caused by the gaze has no measure.

Circa 610 The Qur'an

Chapter 24, verses 27–28

O you who believe! enter not houses other than your own, until you have asked permission and saluted those in them: that is best for you, in order that you may heed [what is seemly].

Circa 800 The Bible, Second Book of Samuel (New Revised Standard Version)

In the Bible, God orders a counting of people or fighting-age men on several occasions (Exod. 38:26; Num. 1, 3:14–43, 26). But in the second book of Samuel, when King David of Israel orders a census, God is upset. David usurped God's role by conducting the census without divine instruction and by making every household in the kingdom look to him, rather than God, as a focal point of authority and importance.

2 Samuel 24:1–15

1 Again the anger of the Lord was kindled against Israel, and he incited David against them, saying, "Go, count the people of Israel and Judah." **2** So the king said to Joab and the commanders of the army, who were with him, "Go through all the tribes of Israel, from Dan to Beer-sheba, and take a census of the people, so that I may know how many there are." **3** But Joab said to the king, "May the Lord your God increase the number of the people a hundredfold, while the eyes of my lord the king can still see it! But why does my lord the king want to do this?" **4** But the king's word prevailed against Joab and the commanders of the army. So Joab and the commanders of the army went out from the presence of the king to take a census of the people of Israel . . . **8** So when they had gone through all the land, they came back to Jerusalem at the end of nine months and twenty days. **9** Joab reported to the king the number of those who had been recorded: in Israel there were eight hundred thousand soldiers able to draw the sword, and those of Judah were five hundred thousand. **10** But afterward, David was stricken to the heart because he had numbered the people. David said to the Lord, "I have sinned greatly in what I have done. But now, O Lord, I pray you, take away the guilt of your servant; for I have done very foolishly." . . . **13** So Gad came to David and told him; he asked him, "Shall three years of famine come to you on your land? Or will you flee three months before your foes while they pursue you? Or shall there be three days' pestilence in your land? Now consider, and decide what answer I shall return to the one who sent me." . . . **15** So the Lord sent a pestilence on Israel from that morning until the appointed time; and seventy thousand of the people died, from Dan to Beer-sheba.

Circa 1500 Constitution of the Iroquois Nations

For background on the Iroquois Constitution, see Gerald Murphy, "About the Constitution of the Iroquois Nations," at the From Revolution to Reconstruction hypertext project of the University of Groningen, the Netherlands, http://odur.let.rug.nl/~usa/D/1776-1800/constitution/iroq_const_i.htm.

Protection of the House
A certain sign shall be known to all the people of the Five Nations which shall denote that the owner or occupant of a house is absent. A stick or pole in a slanting or leaning position shall indicate this and be the sign. Every person not entitled to enter the house by right of living within it upon seeing such a sign shall not approach the house either by day or by night but shall keep as far away as his business will permit.

1604 Semayne's Case (England)

The house of everyone is to him his castle and fortress, as well as his defense against injury and violence, as for his repose; and although the life of a man is a thing precious and favoured in the law so that, although a man kills another in his defense, or kills one per infortunium without any intent, yet it is a felony, and in such case he shall forfeit his goods and chattels for the great regard the law has to a man's life, but if thieves come to a man's house to rob him, or murder, and the owner or his servants kill any of the thieves in defense of himself and his house it is not a felony, and he shall lose nothing.

1767 Blackstone's Commentaries on the Laws of England

Book 4, Chapter 16, "Burglary"

And the law of England has so particular and tender a regard to the immunity of a man's house, that it stiles it his castle, and will never suffer it to be violated with impunity; agreeing herein with the sentiments of ancient Rome, as expressed in the words of Tully (Marcus Tullius Cicero): *"quid enim sanctius, quid omne religione munitius, quam domus uniuscujusque civium?"* (For what is more sacred, what is more protected from any religious observance, than the home of each citizen?)

1789 Declaration of the Rights of Man and of the Citizen (France)

Article 4

Liberty consists in the freedom to do everything that injures no one else; hence the exercise of the natural rights of each man has no limits except those which assure to the other members of the society the enjoyment of the same rights. These limits can only be determined by law.

1791 Bill of Rights (United States)

First Amendment

Congress shall make no law respecting an establishment of religion, or prohibiting the free exercise thereof; or abridging the freedom of speech, or of the press; or the right of the people peaceably to assemble, and to petition the Government for a redress of grievances.

Third Amendment

No Soldier shall, in time of peace be quartered in any house, without the consent of the Owner, nor in time of war, but in a manner to be prescribed by law.

Fourth Amendment

The right of the people to be secure in their persons, houses, papers, and effects, against unreasonable searches and seizures, shall not be violated, and no Warrants shall issue, but upon probable cause, supported by Oath or affirmation, and particularly describing the place to be searched, and the persons or things to be seized.

Fifth Amendment

No person shall be held to answer for a capital, or otherwise infamous crime, unless on a presentment or indictment of a Grand Jury, except in cases arising in the land or naval forces, or in the Militia, when in actual service in time of War or public danger; nor shall any person be subject for the same offense to be twice put in jeopardy of life or limb, nor shall be compelled in any criminal case to be a witness against himself, nor be deprived of life, liberty, or property, without due process of law; nor shall private property be taken for public use, without just compensation.

Ninth Amendment

The enumeration in the Constitution, of certain rights, shall not be construed to deny or disparage others retained by the people.

1890 "The Right to Privacy" by Samuel Warren and Louis Brandeis in the *Harvard Law Review*

Recent inventions and business methods call attention to the next step which must be taken for the protection of the person, and for securing to the individual what Judge Cooley calls the right "to be let alone." Instantaneous photographs and newspaper enterprise have invaded the sacred precincts of private and domestic life; and numerous mechanical devices threaten to make good the prediction that "what is whispered in the closet shall be proclaimed from the house-tops." For years there has been a feeling that the law must afford some remedy for the unauthorized circulation of portraits of private persons; and the evil of invasion of privacy by the newspapers, long keenly felt, has been but recently discussed by an able writer. The alleged facts of a somewhat notorious case brought before an inferior tribunal in New York a few months ago, directly involved the consideration of the right of circulating portraits; and the question whether our law will recognize and protect the right to privacy in this and in other respects must soon come before our courts for consideration.

Of the desirability—indeed of the necessity—of some such protection, there can, it is believed, be no doubt. The press is overstepping in every direction the obvious bounds of propriety and of decency. Gossip is no longer the resource of the idle and of the vicious, but has become a trade, which is pursued with industry as well as effrontery. To satisfy a prurient taste the details of sexual relations are spread broadcast in the columns of the daily papers. To occupy the indolent, column upon column is filled with idle gossip, which can only be procured by intrusion upon the domestic circle. The intensity and complexity of life, attendant upon advancing civilization, have rendered necessary some retreat from the world, and man, under the refining influence of culture, has become more sensitive to publicity, so that solitude and privacy have become more essential to the individual; but modern enterprise and invention have, through invasions upon his privacy, subjected him to mental pain and distress, far greater than could be inflicted by mere bodily injury. Nor is the harm wrought by such invasions confined to the suffering of those who may be the subjects of journalistic or other enterprise. In this, as in other branches of commerce, the supply creates the demand. Each crop of unseemly gossip, thus harvested, becomes the seed of more, and, in direct proportion to its circulation, results in the lowering of social standards and of morality. Even gossip apparently harmless, when widely and persistently circulated, is potent for evil. It both belittles and perverts. It belittles by inverting the relative importance of things, thus dwarfing the thoughts and aspirations of a people. When personal gossip attains the dignity of print, and crowds the space available for matters of real interest to the community, what wonder that the ignorant and thoughtless mistake its relative importance. Easy of comprehension, appealing to that weak side of human nature which is never wholly cast down by the misfortunes and frailties of our neighbors, no one can be surprised that it usurps the place of interest in brains capable of other things. Triviality destroys at once robustness of thought and delicacy of feeling. No enthusiasm can flourish, no generous impulse can survive under its blighting influence.

1919 Constitution of the Weimar Republic (Germany)

Articles 114, 115, and 117

114. The rights of the individual are inviolable. Limitation or deprivation of individual liberty is admissible only if based on the laws. Persons deprived of their liberty have to be notified, at the next day on the latest, by which authority and based on which reasons the deprivation of their liberty has been ordered; immediately they have to be given the opportunity to protest against the deprivation of liberty.

115. Every German home is an asylum and inviolable. Exceptions are admissible only if based on law.

117. Privacy of correspondence, of mail, telegraphs and telephone are inviolable. Exceptions are admissible only if based on a Reich law.

1928 *Olmstead v. United States* (U.S. Supreme Court)

Privacy did not win the day in 1928 when the Supreme Court ruled that police wiretapping without a warrant was constitutionally per-

missible. A 5–4 majority held that there was no unreasonable search of the defendant Olmstead's property, because the police did not enter the property but rather tapped "wires reaching into the whole world from the defendant's house or office." But Justice Louis Brandeis's dissenting opinion would be vindicated when the Court effectively overturned Olmstead *in the 1967 case* Katz v. United States. *Brandeis wrote:*

> Discovery and invention have made it possible for the government, by means far more effective than stretching upon the rack, to obtain disclosure in court of what is whispered in the closet. Moreover, "in the application of a Constitution, our contemplation cannot be only of what has been, but of what may be." The progress of science in furnishing the government with means of espionage is not likely to stop with wire tapping. Ways may some day be developed by which the government, without removing papers from secret drawers, can reproduce them in court, and by which it will be enabled to expose to a jury the most intimate occurrences of the home. Advances in the psychic and related sciences may bring means of exploring unexpressed beliefs, thoughts and emotions . . .
>
> The makers of our Constitution undertook to secure conditions favorable to the pursuit of happiness. They recognized the significance of man's spiritual nature, of his feelings and of his intellect. They knew that only a part of the pain, pleasure and satisfactions of life are to be found in material things. They sought to protect Americans in their beliefs, their thoughts, their emotions and their sensations. They conferred, as against the government, the right to be let alone—the most comprehensive of rights and the right most valued by civilized men. To protect that right, every unjustifiable intrusion by the government upon the privacy of the individual, whatever the means employed, must be deemed a violation of the Fourth Amendment. And the use, as evidence in a criminal proceeding, of facts ascertained by such intrusion must be deemed a violation of the Fifth.

1933 Reichstag Fire Decree Suspending Civil Liberties in Germany

On February 27, 1933—soon after Adolf Hitler was appointed chancellor of Germany—someone set fire to the Reichstag, the ornate landmark building of the German national legislature and a symbol of parliamentary democracy. Hitler and the other leaders of the National Socialist Party accused communists of committing the arson and launching an effort to take over Germany by revolution. Hitler persuaded the aged German president, Paul von Hindenburg, to issue a decree the next day suspending the articles of the Weimar Constitution that guaranteed civil liberties, including provisions guaranteeing habeas corpus (Article 114), inviolability of the home (Article 115), and the secrecy of letters and communications (Article 117). The "Decree of the Reich President for the Protection of the People and State" (commonly referred to as the Reichstag Fire Decree) contained no safeguards, such as the right to a judicial hearing, leaving Hitler the power to invade homes, arrest people in secret, detain them indefinitely without evidence, and subject them to inhumane treatment. Articles 2 through 6 of the decree gave the Hitler regime the ability to seize power from the German states, introduced the death penalty for a long list of offenses, and made the decree effective immediately.

Article 1

Sections 114, 115, 117, 118, 123, 124, and 153 of the Constitution of the German Reich are suspended until further notice. Thus, restrictions on personal liberty [meaning, essentially, habeas corpus], on the right of free expression of opinion, including freedom of the press, on the right of assembly and the right of association, and violations of the privacy of postal, telegraphic, and telephonic communications, and warrants for house-searches, orders for confiscation as well as restrictions on property, are also permissible beyond the legal limits otherwise prescribed.

1939 The Warsaw Diary of Chaim A. Kaplan

Chaim Kaplan was a journalist and teacher in Warsaw, Poland, when the Nazis invaded in 1939. He was also Jewish and detailed in his diary the systematic way in which the Nazis terrorized the Jews, starting with collecting details about them, as in the following entry from October 28, 1939.

> Today, notices informed the Jewish population of Warsaw that next Saturday there will be a census of the Jewish inhabitants . . . Our hearts tell us of evil—some catastrophe for the Jews of Warsaw lies in this census . . . The order for a census stated that it is being held to gather data for administrative purposes. That's a neat phrase, but it contains catastrophe . . . We are certain that this census is being taken for the purpose of expelling "nonproductive elements." And there are a great many of us now . . . We are all caught in a net, doomed to destruction.

Source: Katsch, Abraham, ed. *The Warsaw Diary of Chaim A. Kaplan* (New York: Collier Books, 1965).

1948 Universal Declaration of Human Rights (United Nations)

Article 12
No one shall be subjected to arbitrary interference with his privacy, family, home or correspondence, nor attacks upon his honour and reputation. Everyone has the right to the protection of the law against such interference or attacks.

1949 Publication of George Orwell's *1984*

When invasions of privacy, particularly surveillance, are discussed, Orwell's 1984 is invariably mentioned. The book begins as follows:

> It was a bright cold day in April, and the clocks were striking thirteen. Winston Smith, his chin nuzzled into his breast in an effort to escape the vile wind, slipped quickly through the glass doors of Victory Mansions, though not quickly enough to prevent a swirl of gritty dust from entering along with him.
>
> The flat was seven flights up, and Winston, who was thirty-nine, and had a varicose ulcer above his right an-

kle, went slowly, resting several times on the way. On each landing, opposite the lift shaft, the poster with the enormous face gazed from the wall. It was one of those pictures which are so contrived that the eyes follow you about when you move. BIG BROTHER IS WATCHING YOU, the caption beneath it ran . . .

Behind Winston's back the voice from the telescreen was still babbling away about pig iron and the overful-fillment of the Ninth Three Year Plan. The telescreen received and transmitted simultaneously. Any sound that Winston made, above the level of a very low whisper, would be picked up by it; moreover, so long as he remained within the field of vision which the metal plaque commanded, he could be seen as well as heard. There was of course no way of knowing whether you were being watched at any given moment. How often, or on what system, the Thought Police plugged in on any individual wire was guesswork. It was even conceivable that they watched everybody all the time. But at any rate they could plug in your wire whenever they wanted to. You had to live—did live, from habit that became instinct—in the assumption that every sound you made was overheard, and, except in darkness, every movement scrutinized.

Source: Orwell, George. *1984* (New York: Signet Books, 1980).

1950 European Convention for the Protection of Human Rights and Fundamental Freedoms (Council of Europe)

Article 8

1. Everyone has the right to respect for his private and family life, his home and his correspondence.

2. There shall be no interference by a public authority with the exercise of this right except such as in accordance with the law and is necessary in a democratic society in the interests of national security, public safety or the economic well-being of the country, for the prevention of disorder or crime, for the protection of health or morals, or for the protection of the rights and freedoms of others.

1965 *Griswold v. Connecticut* (U.S. Supreme Court)

*"Penumbras" are shadows; here, Justice William O. Douglas is refer-
ring to rights that are not mentioned in the Bill of Rights but that are
naturally a part of those rights specifically mentioned.*

Specific guarantees in the Bill of Rights have penumbras, formed by emanations from those guarantees that
help give them life and substance . . . Various guarantees create zones of privacy. The right of association
contained in the penumbra of the First Amendment is
one, as we have seen [that protects the privacy of an organization's membership records in order to safeguard
the members' rights to free expression]. The Third
Amendment in its prohibition against the quartering of
soldiers "in any house" in time of peace without the
consent of the owner is another facet of that privacy.
The Fourth Amendment explicitly affirms the "right of
the people to be secure in their persons, houses, papers,
and effects, against unreasonable searches and
seizures." The Fifth Amendment in its Self-Incrimina-
tion Clause enables the citizen to create a zone of privacy which government may not force him to surrender
to his detriment. The Ninth Amendment provides: "The
enumeration in the Constitution, of certain rights, shall
not be construed to deny or disparage others retained
by the people." . . .

The present case, then, concerns a relationship lying
within the zone of privacy created by several fundamental constitutional guarantees. And it concerns a law
which, in forbidding the use of contraceptives rather
than regulating their manufacture or sale, seeks to
achieve its goals by means having a maximum destructive impact upon that relationship. Such a law cannot
stand in light of the familiar principle, so often applied
by this Court, that a "governmental purpose to control
or prevent activities constitutionally subject to state regulation may not be achieved by means which sweep unnecessarily broadly and thereby invade the area of protected freedoms." Would we allow the police to search
the sacred precincts of marital bedrooms for telltale
signs of the use of contraceptives? The very idea is re-

pulsive to the notions of privacy surrounding the marriage relationship.

1969 American Convention on Human Rights (Organization of American States)

Article 11

1. Everyone has the right to have his honour respected and his dignity recognised.

2. No one may be the object of arbitrary or abusive interference with his private life, his family, his home, or his correspondence, or of unlawful attacks on his honour or reputation.

3. Everyone has the right to the protection of the law against such interference of attacks.

1976 International Covenant on the Protection of Civil and Political Rights (United Nations)

Article 17

1. No one shall be subjected to arbitrary or unlawful interference with his privacy, family, home or correspondence, nor to unlawful attacks on his honour and reputation.

2. Everyone has the right to the protection of the law against such interference or attacks.

1980 Organisation for Economic Cooperation and Development Guidelines on the Protection of Privacy and Transborder Flows of Personal Data

The guidelines include important principles on how, when, and what types of data should be collected on individuals.

Part 2

Collection Limitation Principle

7. There should be limits to the collection of personal data and any such data should be obtained by lawful

and fair means and, where appropriate, with the knowledge or consent of the data subject.

Data Quality Principle

8. Personal data should be relevant to the purposes for which they are to be used, and, to the extent necessary for those purposes, should be accurate, complete and kept up-to-date.

Purpose Specification Principle

9. The purposes for which personal data are collected should be specified not later than at the time of data collection and the subsequent use limited to the fulfilment of those purposes or such others as are not incompatible with those purposes and as are specified on each occasion of change of purpose.

Use Limitation Principle

10. Personal data should not be disclosed, made available or otherwise used for purposes other than those specified in accordance with Paragraph 9 except:

(a) with the consent of the data subject; or

(b) by the authority of law.

Security Safeguards Principle

11. Personal data should be protected by reasonable security safeguards against such risks as loss or unauthorised access, destruction, use, modification or disclosure of data.

Openness Principle

12. There should be a general policy of openness about developments, practices and policies with respect to personal data. Means should be readily available of establishing the existence and nature of personal data, and the main purposes of their use, as well as the identity and usual residence of the data controller.

Individual Participation Principle

13. An individual should have the right:

(a) to obtain from a data controller, or otherwise, confirmation of whether or not the data controller has data relating to him;

(b) to have communicated to him, data relating to him

(i) within a reasonable time;

(ii) at a charge, if any, that is not excessive;

(iii) in a reasonable manner; and

(iv) in a form that is readily intelligible to him;

(c) to be given reasons if a request made under subparagraphs (a) and (b) is denied, and to be able to challenge such denial; and

(d) to challenge data relating to him and, if the challenge is successful, to have the data erased, rectified, completed or amended.

Accountability Principle

14. A data controller should be accountable for complying with measures which give effect to the principles stated above.

1986 African Charter on Human and Peoples' Rights (Organization of African Unity)

Article 5

Every individual shall have the right to the respect of dignity inherent in a human being and to the recognition of his legal status. All forms of exploitation and degradation of man particularly slavery, slave trade, torture, cruel, inhuman or degrading punishment and treatment shall be prohibited.

2001 USA PATRIOT Act — Brochure from the Center for Democracy and Technology

WHAT'S WRONG WITH THE PATRIOT ACT AND HOW TO FIX IT

There has been a lot of confusing publicity about the PATRIOT Act. Here we try to cut through the hype, describe plainly the biggest problems with the PATRIOT Act, and offer a roadmap for restoring the balance.

No Accountability—The PATRIOT Act weakened key oversight and accountability checks on the powers of the Executive Branch, reducing judges to mere "rubber stamps" and leaving many decisions about investigative techniques to the discretion of FBI agents.

Restoring the Balance: Although the FBI should have the power it needs to investigate terrorism, the courts and Congress should have the authority to ensure that the FBI does not overreach.

Sneak & Peek Searches—The PATRIOT Act broadened the government's power to search an individual's home without telling her until weeks or months later, and to do so in any criminal case.

Restoring the Balance: Secret searches should be allowed only in special circumstances, such as if someone's life is at stake or evidence will be destroyed. Otherwise, FBI agents should have to knock on a person's door and announce that they have a search warrant, as intended by the Fourth Amendment.

Access to Sensitive Business Records—The PATRIOT Act gave the FBI nearly unlimited power to obtain business records, including sensitive files like medical, library and bookstore records, with a secret court order issued with no factual showing of need.

Restoring the Balance: The FBI should only be able to obtain files about people suspected of being terrorists or spies. It should not be able to get entire databases of information about innocent people.

Broad Definition of Terrorism—The PATRIOT Act contains a definition of "domestic terrorism" so broad that someone committing a misdemeanor could end up being dubbed a terrorist, thereby facing asset forfeiture and other serious consequences.

Restoring the Balance: Only the most serious crimes should be considered terrorism.

Monitoring Computer "Trespassers" Without a Court Order—The PATRIOT Act allows ISPs, universities and network administrators to authorize government surveillance of anyone they deem a "computer trespasser" without a court order, and with no notice to the person being monitored.

Restoring the Balance: Surveillance of computer users should occur with proper judicial review, not secretly with no judicial involvement.

Secret Investigations—The FBI's domestic intelligence investigations under the Foreign Intelligence Surveillance Act (FISA), a statute that was expanded by the PATRIOT Act, occur in total secrecy, with almost no information released to the public.

Restoring the Balance: The FBI should do more public reporting, on a statistical basis, about the use of secret FISA investigative techniques so the public knows how much information is gathered about U.S citizens and using what methods.

Monitoring of Email and Web Surfing—The PATRIOT Act extended to the Internet the already broad authority to monitor transactional (non-content) information about communications with very little justification. A record of every call you make and every email you receive offers a full picture of your life, even without the contents.

Restoring the Balance: Approval to monitor who is calling whom should be granted only when a judge finds there is reason to believe that a crime is being committed. And in the Internet context, there should be a bright-line distinction between monitoring transactional data and intercepting content.

Expansive "Roving" Wiretap Authority—The PATRIOT Act permitted the FBI to use "roving" wiretaps in intelligence investigations, but it did not include safeguards long used in criminal investigations to avoid recording the conversations of innocent people.

Restoring the Balance: The FBI should be granted wiretap orders only where it specifies either the name of the target or the telephone or computer to be tapped. And in carrying out a roving tap, an FBI agent should have to verify that the person named in the order is about to use a particular phone before the tap is turned on.

End-Run Around Standard Criminal Procedures—The PATRIOT Act authorized the FBI to use special intelligence investigative techniques under FISA, which has lower standards than regular criminal law, even where the primary purpose of the investigation is to obtain information for a criminal trial. This essentially permits the FBI to collect evidence for criminal cases under lower standards.

Restoring the Balance: The special intelligence standards should be used only where intelligence gathering is the primary purpose for the investigation.

Source: http://www.cdt.org/security/usapatriot/brochure.pdf. Used with permission of the Center for Democracy and Technology.

2004 ACLU Bust Card: Pocket Guidelines on Encounters with the Police

1. What you say to the police is always important. What you say can be used against you, and it can give the police an excuse to arrest you, especially if you bad-mouth a police officer.

2. You must show your driver's license and registration when stopped in a car. Otherwise, you don't have to answer any questions if you are detained or arrested, with one important exception. The police may ask for your name if you have been properly detained, and you can be arrested in some states for refusing to give it. If you reasonably fear that your name is incriminating, you can claim the right to remain silent, which may be a defense in case you are arrested anyway.

3. You don't have to consent to any search of yourself, your car or your house. If you **DO** consent to a search, it can affect your rights later in court. If the police say they have a search warrant, **ASK TO SEE IT**.

4. Do not interfere with, or obstruct the police – you can be arrested for it.

IF YOU ARE STOPPED FOR QUESTIONING

1. It's not a crime to refuse to answer questions, but refusing to answer might make the police suspicious about you. If you are asked to identify yourself, see paragraph 2 above.

2. Police may "pat-down" your clothing if they suspect a concealed weapon. Don't physically resist, but make it clear that you don't consent to any further search.

3. Ask if you are under arrest. If you are, you have a right to know why.

4. Don't bad-mouth the police officer or run away, even if you believe what is happening is unreasonable. That could lead to your arrest.

IF YOU'RE STOPPED IN YOUR CAR

1. Upon request, show them your driver's license, registration, and proof of insurance. In certain cases, your car can be searched without a warrant as long as the police have probable cause. To protect yourself later, you should make it clear that you do not consent to a search. It is not lawful for police to arrest you simply for refusing to consent to a search.

2. If you're given a ticket, you should sign it; otherwise you can be arrested. You can always fight the case in court later.

3. If you're suspected of drunk driving (DWI) and refuse to take a blood, urine or breath test, your driver's license may be suspended.

IF YOU'RE ARRESTED OR TAKEN TO A POLICE STATION

1. You have the right to remain silent and to talk to a lawyer before you talk to the police. Tell the police nothing except your name and address. Don't give any explanations, excuses or stories. You can make your defense later, in court, based on what you and your lawyer decide is best.

2. Ask to see a lawyer immediately. If you can't pay for a lawyer, you have a right to a free one, and should ask the police how the lawyer can be contacted. **Don't say anything without a lawyer.**

3. Within a reasonable time after your arrest, or booking, you have the right to make a local phone call: to a lawyer, bail bondsman, a relative or any other person. The police may not listen to the call to the lawyer.

4. Sometimes you can be released without bail, or have bail lowered. Have your lawyer ask the judge about this possibility. You must be taken before the judge on the next court day after arrest.

5. Do not make any decisions in your case until you have talked with a lawyer.

IN YOUR HOME

1. If the police knock and ask to enter your home, you don't have to admit them unless they have a warrant signed by a judge.

2. However, in some emergency situations (like when a person is screaming for help inside, or when the police are chasing someone) officers are allowed to enter and search your home without a warrant.

3. If you are arrested, the police can search you and the area close by. If you are in a building, "close by" usually means just the room you are in.

We all recognize the need for effective law enforcement, but we should also understand our own rights and responsibilities – especially in our relationships with the police. Everyone, including minors, has the right to courteous and respectful police treatment. If your rights are violated, don't try to deal with the situation at the scene. You can talk to a lawyer afterwards, or file a complaint with the Internal Affairs or Civilian Complaint Board.

Produced by the American Civil Liberties Union.
ARREST THE RACISM. Tell us about your race- or ethnic-based traffic or pedestrian stop. **Call 1-877-6-PROFILE or go to aclu.org/profiling**

What To Do If You're Stopped By The Police

Think carefully about your words, movement, body language, and emotions.

Don't get into an argument with the police. Remember, **anything you say or do** can be used against you.

Keep your hands where the police can see them.

Don't run. Don't touch any police officer.

Don't resist even if you believe you are innocent.

Don't complain on the scene or tell the police they're wrong or that you're going to file a complaint.

Do not make any statements regarding the incident.

Ask for a lawyer immediately upon your arrest.

Remember **officers' badge & patrol car** numbers.

Write down everything you remember ASAP.

Try to find **witnesses** & their names & phone numbers.

If you are injured, **take photographs of the injuries** as soon as possible, but make sure you **seek medical attention** first.

If you feel your rights have been violated, **file a written complaint** with police department's internal affairs division or civilian complaint board, or call the ACLU hotline, **1-877-6-PROFILE**.

7

Directory of Organizations and Government Agencies

Organizations

American Civil Liberties Union (ACLU)
125 Broad Street
New York, NY 10004
Phone: 212-549-2500
Web site: http://www.aclu.org

The ACLU is the premier defender of rights in the United States. Founded in 1920, the ACLU staffs offices in every state, the District of Columbia, and Puerto Rico. The ACLU protects civil liberties, principles enshrined in the Bill of Rights that safeguard individuals from the abuse of government power, including rights to privacy, free expression, press freedom, religious freedom, separation of church and state, equal protection of the law, and due process. Positions taken by the ACLU, which are often viewed as controversial when first asserted, have often become the law of the land and part of fundamental American values in subsequent years. The ACLU uses litigation (representing individuals free of charge), lobbying, public education, and organizing to achieve its mission. Young people may form ACLU campus groups at their colleges or high schools.

Center for Democracy and Technology (CDT)
1634 I Street Northwest, Suite 1100
Washington, DC 20006
Phone: 202-637-9800
Web site: http://www.cdt.org

With an emphasis on practical solutions and consensus building, CDT promotes free expression, privacy, and democracy in global communications and digital media.

Coalition against Unsolicited Commercial Email (CAUCE)
Web site: http://www.cauce.org

Some people are so upset about their e-mail boxes being full of unsolicited commercial e-mail ("spam") that they have dedicated time and resources to creating an all-volunteer online organization to fight it. With the motto "Take back your mailboxes," CAUCE is mobilizing e-mail users in Australia, Europe, India, and the United States to fight for legislative restrictions on spam.

Computer Professionals for Social Responsibility (CPSR)
P.O. Box 717
Palo Alto, CA 94302
Phone: 650-322-3778
Web site: http://www.cpsr.org

CPSR believes that the decisions made by policy makers and computer scientists concerning the uses and development of computer technologies have a far-reaching impact on society. Through its Web site and local events, CPSR's members, who are themselves computer experts, advise the public and policy makers about the good and bad effects of existing policies and policy choices.

Consumer Privacy Guide
Web site: http://www.consumerprivacy.org

Sponsored by CDT, Common Cause, and other organizations, this site aims to help consumers concerned about their online privacy. It includes a "how to" guide to online privacy and a top-ten list of ways to protect your privacy.

Consumers against Supermarket Privacy Invasion and Numbering (CASPIAN)
Web site: http://www.nocards.org
Web site: http://www.spychips.com

Some of the most subtle yet pervasive invasions of privacy are occurring at the supermarket register and through the labeling of products we purchase. CASPIAN opposes these invasions of privacy, focusing both on the discount cards issued by supermarkets and on new RFID labeling of products.

Council for Responsible Genetics
5 Upland Road, Suite 3
Cambridge, MA 02144
Phone: 617-868-0870
Web site: http://www.gene-watch.org

A Web site and magazine that monitor the social, ethical, and environmental consequences of developments in biotechnology. It includes links to articles and position papers on privacy and genetics, as well as a "Genetic Bill of Rights."

Cousin Couples
Web site: http://www.cousincouples.com

An information source and support network for romantic couples who are cousins. Based on long-standing legend, there remains a widespread bias, particularly in the United States, against first-cousin marriages and relationships. Twenty-four U.S. states have laws forbidding cousins to marry even though study after study show that cousin couples have only a slightly higher risk of birth defects than noncousins. This organization supports repeal of these laws, which discriminate and invade the privacy of the marital relationship.

Electronic Frontier Foundation (EFF)
454 Shotwell Street
San Francisco, CA 94110
Phone: 415-436-9333
Web site: http://www.eff.org

EFF was one of the first organizations dedicated to addressing government abuse of rights in the digital age. Formed in 1990, it brought a case in the United States that established that e-mail was entitled to the same privacy protection from government intrusion as telephone calls. EFF inspired the creation of chapters and imitators (now independent) all over the world, including Electronic Frontier organizations in Australia, Canada, Finland, and Italy.

Electronic Privacy Information Center (EPIC)
1718 Connecticut Avenue Northwest, Suite 200
Washington, DC 20009
Phone: 202-483-1140
Web site: http://www.epic.org

EPIC is the leading advocacy think tank on privacy and liberty in the digital age. It publishes an online newsletter, reports, and books, including the most comprehensive account of privacy in countries around the world, *Privacy and Human Rights: An International Survey of Privacy Laws and Developments.*

Global Internet Liberty Campaign (GILC)
Web site: http://www.gilc.org

A coalition of more than sixty-five organizations around the world, GILC was formed to respond to the problem that privacy invasions no longer respect national borders. Many rules and structures that affect privacy are being established by international entities such as the Group of 8 (G-8) and the Organization for Economic Cooperation and Development. GILC also maintains a list of official government privacy commissioners around the world.

Intersex Society of North America (ISNA)
979 Golf Course Drive, #282
Rohnert Park, CA 94928
Web site: http://www.isna.org

ISNA seeks to reduce the shame and stigma surrounding "intersex" people, those who were born with some mix of male and female chromosomes, internal organs, or genitalia. It also urges the end to early surgeries to change the physical appearance of an intersex newborn.

National Workrights Institute
166 Wall Street
Princeton, NJ 08540
Phone: 609-683-0313
Web site: http://www.workrights.org

Does it bother you that your employer monitors your personal e-mail, restricts what you can do after hours, and puts surveillance cameras in the office bathrooms? Private employees in the United States have almost no privacy rights, but the National Workrights Institute is working to change that by exposing the most egregious employer practices and seeking legal reform.

Police Assessment Resource Center (PARC)
Biltmore Court
520 South Grand Avenue, Suite 1070
Los Angeles, CA 90071
Phone: 213-623-5757
Web site: http://www.parc.info

PARC helps police departments to improve their practices, including those respecting the right to be free from unreasonable searches and seizures and other privacy rights. PARC works with all parties implicated in police reform—members of the public, civic groups, politicians, and the police departments themselves. It also publishes *Police Practices Review,* which provides news on the latest developments in police reform.

Privacy International (PI)
6-8 Amwell Street
London EC1R 1UQ
United Kingdom
Phone: +44-7947 778247
Web site: http://www.privacyinternational.org

An international human rights organization based in London and Washington, PI is coauthor with EPIC of *Privacy and Human*

Rights. It hosts conferences, organizes campaigns, works with national human rights organizations around the world, and maintains an extensive archive of documents concerning privacy.

Privacy Rights Clearinghouse
3100 Fifth Avenue, Suite B
San Diego, CA 92103
Phone: 619-298-3396
Web site: http://www.privacyrights.org

The name says it all. The Web site includes fact sheets on topics such as "How private is my credit report?" and "Are you being stalked? Tips for protection." The organization also maintains a telephone and Web site hotline to report abuses and ask questions. Its director, Beth Givens, is an able spokesperson for the cause of privacy protection and provides some of the best sound bites about privacy issues.

Government Agencies

African Commission on Human and Peoples' Rights
Kairaba Avenue
P.O. Box 673
Banjul, The Gambia
Phone: 220-392-962
Web site: http://www.achpr.org

Creation of the commission was called for in the African Charter on Human and Peoples' Rights, which charged the entity with promoting and protecting the rights in the charter. It was inaugurated in 1987 and took its headquarters in The Gambia in 1989. The commission is to be complemented by the Court on Human and Peoples' Rights, which the African Union is in the process of creating.

Australian Privacy Commissioner
GPO Box 5218
Sydney NSW 2001
Australia

Phone: 1300-363-992
Web site: http://www.privacy.gov.au

The Office of the Federal Privacy Commissioner oversees the implementation of Australia's privacy laws and seeks to promote a culture that respects privacy. The commissioner's office answers questions about Australia's privacy laws, investigates complaints of abuse, audits companies' adherence to the laws, and reviews privacy laws and practices for potential improvements.

Canadian Privacy Commissioner
112 Kent Street
Ottawa, Ontario K1A 1H3
Canada
Phone: 613-995-8210
Web site: http://www.privcom.gc.ca

The commissioner advocates for Canadians' privacy rights. The office investigates complaints, conducts audits, publishes reports, conducts research, and educates the public.

European Court of Human Rights (ECHR)
Council of Europe
F-67075 Strasbourg-Cedex
France
Phone: 33-0-3-88-41-20-18
Web site: http://www.echr.coe.int

This court hears complaints against member states of the Council of Europe based on alleged violations of the European Convention on Human Rights. Search the press releases for the words *private* or *Article 8*, which is the section of the convention that guarantees protection of "private and family life."

Hong Kong Privacy Commissioner
Unit 2401, 24/F, Office Tower, Convention Plaza
1 Harbour Road
Wanchai, Hong Kong
Phone: 2827-2827
Web site: http://www.pco.org.hk

Transferred from British to Chinese control in 1997, Hong Kong retains a tenuous semiautonomy from its communist motherland. The privacy commissioner enforces the Personal Data (Privacy) Ordinance, which was passed just prior to the transfer of power. The commissioner also maintains a great Web site in both Chinese and English, which has an entertaining Privacy Zone for Youngsters.

Inter-American Court of Human Rights
Partado Postal 6906-1000
San José, Costa Rica
Phone: 506-234-058
Web site: http://www.corteidh.or.cr/index_ing.html

This court, which was established as part of the American Convention on Human Rights (Part 2, Chapter 7), has both the power to judge particular cases and, when asked, to advise countries on how the convention applies to a law or matter being considered by the member state. The court has seven members and sits in San José, Costa Rica.

Kidz Privacy
Web site: http://www.ftc.gov/bcp/conline/edcams/kidzprivacy

A Web site created by the U.S. Federal Trade Commission to explain the rules in the Children's Online Privacy Protection Act, which was passed in 1998 to prevent companies from collecting information from children twelve and younger without their parents' permission.

United Nations Commission on Human Rights
Web site: http://www.unhchr.ch/html/menu2/2/chr.htm

The commission is the UN's high-level committee on human rights. It comes together once a year for six weeks starting in March to discuss human rights abuses around the world, consider individual cases, and pass resolutions. Although the commission cannot itself force a nation to change its ways, its opinions can affect a nation's (or a government's) reputation, lead to more serious action by the UN Security Council, or affect a nation's chances of serving in leadership roles within the UN.

United Nations High Commissioner for Human Rights
8-14 Avenue de la Paix
1211 Geneva 10
Switzerland
Phone: 41-22-917-9000
Web site: http://www.unhchr.org/english

This UN body is charged with alerting governments and the public to abuses of human rights, promoting proactive efforts to create conditions that support respect for human rights (such as a rule-of-law system and economic development), and, when asked, consulting a nation on its human rights policies and performance. The commissioner's office also provides staff assistance for the UN Commission on Human Rights and other bodies.

8

Movies, Books, and Internet News Sources

Movies

Minority Report
Director: Steven Spielberg
Stars: Tom Cruise and Colin Farrell
Genre: Action, Suspense, Crime, Sci-Fi
Studio: Universal Studios
Date: 2002

This action thriller takes place in Washington, D.C., in the year 2054, when the current trend toward "preventive policing" and increased surveillance has reached its zenith. Police no longer wait for murders to occur; through the use of psychic technology, they have harnessed the power to foresee crimes and intervene just prior to their occurring. The system is not 100 percent accurate, and mayhem ensues when one of the top precrime cops (Cruise) is wrongly preidentified as an imminent killer. The plot is less interesting than the world created by the movie. In 1999, Spielberg and production designer Alex McDowell convened a three-day meeting of futurists to brainstorm the future on which the movie is based.

In its big themes and little details, the movie convincingly portrays a future in which today's threats to privacy have become tomorrow's realities. Notably, the premise embodies our increasing departure from the legal tradition, particularly deep in Anglo-American law, that government is not permitted to predict who will commit crimes or convict persons for evil thoughts alone. In 2054, inhibiting people's actions through total surveillance and the threat of police officers dropping from the skies has replaced the libertarian tradition of holding people to account for their actions.

In one scene, the police release extraordinarily deft, high-tech, and creepy mechanical spiders to race through people's apartments, scan eyes, and search an entire apartment building. The scene, like several others in the movie, is even more compelling because it is based on technology that is not so far out of reach and tactics already coming into fashion: compare the use of unmanned drones for surveillance by the U.S. military and border patrol. Of course, what Spielberg casts in such frightening form (creepy spiders) would more likely enter society in much friendlier form, such as surveillance bunny rabbits or smiley-face blimps. As a blimp manufacturer recently remarked in a story about the growth of surveillance blimps: "Universally, blimps give people a big warm fuzzy. People just like blimps." Spielberg also gives the viewer a taste of the friendlier, convenience-oriented side of a privacy-free future. As Tom Cruise's character walks the shopping mall, futuristic billboards identify him by name and tailor advertisements to his personal preferences.

Enemy of the State
Director: Tony Scott
Stars: Gene Hackman, Will Smith, and John Voight
Genre: Action, Drama, Suspense
Studio: Touchstone Video
Date: 1998

This thriller derives its suspense from the government's extraordinary power to track individuals whenever they interact with anything networked: pay phones, computers, credit cards, security cameras, or almost anything electronic. The U.S. government can then zap you through its satellites in your identified location "on the grid." Although exaggerated, the movie plausibly anticipates advancements in existing technology from Echelon and Carnivore to GPS locators. The action begins when Robert Dean (Smith) comes across proof of an assassination orchestrated by the head of the National Security Agency (Voight). The NSA freezes Dean's bank accounts, falsely discredits him with his family and employer, ransacks his house, and tries its best to blow him up. Dean seeks the assistance of Brill (Hackman) a retired NSA agent who conducts surveillance operations for lawyers and others willing to pay his high fees.

The movie graciously acknowledges the privacy classic *The Conversation* by resurrecting Harry Caul, "the best bugger on the West Coast," in the character of Brill—both played by Hackman. The consistency of Hackman's characters contrasts with the extraordinary change in surveillance technology in the intervening twenty-four years.

The Truman Show
Director: Peter Weir
Star: Jim Carrey
Genre: Drama, Comedy
Studio: Paramount Studios
Date: 1998

The Truman Show must be understood in its popular-culture context. In 1992, MTV aired the first season of *The Real World*, in which television cameras followed the real lives of seven young, diverse strangers made to live together in New York City. *The Real World* had important precedents, including the 1973 Public Broadcasting System docudrama *The American Family*, which detailed the real-life fights, adultery, and coming out of members of the Loud family of Santa Barbara, and such shows as *Candid Camera* and *Real People* in the 1970s and *Cops* and *America's Most Wanted* in the 1980s. But it was *The Real World* that launched pure voyeurism as entertainment in the United States. Followed by such television hits—many of them imports from other countries—as *Road Rules, Big Brother, The Bachelor, Survivor, Who Wants to Marry a Millionaire, American Idol,* and *The Apprentice,* MTV's *The Real World* catalyzed the phenomenon now known as reality television and brought cameras into ever more intimate and sacred parts of people's lives.

While this phenomena was brewing (that is, after *Road Rules* but before *Survivor* and *Big Brother*), *The Truman Show* imagined an extreme scenario: While still a baby, Truman Burbank (Carrey) was given up for adoption to a nonstop television show of his life. Unbeknownst to him, Truman is filmed by 5,000 cameras in a world that is make-believe to everyone but him. Viewers around the world watch Truman's life unfold and his spontaneous reactions to scenes orchestrated by the show's producer. In fact, some events are so orchestrated that Truman starts to take notice. After a mistaken encounter with the father he believed dead, Truman seeks to break through the barriers of his small world—smaller than even he realizes until his sailboat rips through the edge of the TV studio.

Through Truman's torment, the movie warns us of the damage that can result from indulging the insatiable temptation to spy on the lives of others. The latest reality television shows, including shows that tempt couples to cheat on one another and that provide plastic surgery to unattractive women so they can compete in beauty pageants, indicate that the warning has not been heeded.

Eleven years before *The Truman Show,* another movie also anticipated the darker side of reality television voyeurism. *The Running Man,* based on a Stephen King story and starring Arnold Schwarzenegger, imagines a nationally televised game show in which convicts can win their freedom by evading murderous stalkers. It is a less compelling movie than *The Truman Show* but also enjoyable.

Gattaca
Director: Andrew Niccol
Stars: Ethan Hawke, Jude Law, and Uma Thurman
Genre: Drama, Suspense, Sci-Fi
Studio: Columbia/TriStar Studios
Date: 1997

The movie takes place sometime in the future when humans have established thriving space colonies and space travel is as common as subway riding. Thanks to genetic science and a bit of fascism, the social order is stratified between perfectly engineered humans (the valids) and the rest of us (the invalids). The valids enjoy all the privileges and opportunities; the invalids, like Vincent (Hawke), work as janitors. However, in order to fulfill his dream of becoming an elite space explorer, Vincent purchases the identity (as well as the skin cells, hair, blood, urine samples, and heartbeat recording) of a valid Jerome (Law). Jerome, despite his perfect genes, was paralyzed in an accident and is therefore an outcast of a similar kind. Vincent carefully scrubs off every loose skin cell, applies false fingertips, and takes other extreme measures to avoid detection of his true identity by the ubiquitous high-tech sensors. Things at the Gattaca Corporation space center are going according to Vincent's plan until gene-identifying vacuums suck up an eyelash belonging to Vincent at the scene of a crime and he becomes a suspect in a murder.

Like *Minority Report*, this movie depicts a disturbing future in which there is little privacy. However, in *Gattaca*, privacy is eclipsed more through genetic engineering and identification than through electronic surveillance. If *Minority Report* is a descendant of George Orwell's *1984*, then *Gattaca* is in the line of Aldous Huxley's *Brave New World*.

The Conversation

Director: Francis Ford Coppola
Stars: Gene Hackman, Frederic Forest, Cindy Williams, Harrison Ford, and Robert Duval
Genre: Drama, Mystery
Studio: Paramount Studios
Date: 1974

The recipient of the Cannes Film Festival's Palme d'Or and three Academy Award nominations, *The Conversation* is a classic 1970s film, even more so because it was released while the Watergate wiretapping scandal was playing out in each day's headlines.

Harry Caul (Hackman) is hired by a corporate CEO to bug two employees. Harry, a preeminent surveillance specialist, grows worried that his work may lead to the employees' murder. The allure, danger, and monotony of snooping on the private lives of others are the meat of this psychological mystery. The movie opens with the garbled dialogue of the two targets, heard through the various eavesdropping devices of the surveillance team tracking them. When Harry gets home, he is annoyed to find his landlord invaded his privacy by leaving him a birthday present in his apartment—despite his locks, alarm system, and, so he thought, private age and birth date. Reflecting on the movie, Coppola wrote, "I realize [now] that I wasn't making a film about privacy, as I had set out to do, but rather, once again, a film about responsibility" (Aubry 2000). Privacy, its value and invasion, nonetheless permeates every scene.

Rear Window

Director: Alfred Hitchcock

Stars: James Stewart, Grace Kelly, Thelma Ritter, and
Raymond Burr
Genre: Mystery, Suspense
Studio: Paramount Studios
Date: 1954

In *Rear Window,* Hitchcock plays with human behavior and pro-
clivities, including the irresistible temptation to snoop. The
drama unfolds—at various visual depths—in the Greenwich Village apartment of professional action photographer Jeff Jeffries
(Stewart). Recovering from a broken leg, Jeffries takes to observing, then spying, on his neighbors in the apartments facing his
rear window. Through his binoculars, he sees in each neighbor
the mix of ordinary and peculiar behaviors that make every human suspicious, boringly unique, or both: the otherwise respectable, regular couple who forego their bed to sleep on the fire
escape; the unsustainably yet understandably ravenous newly-
weds; and the lonely woman who pretends to share meals with
her absent or imaginary partner. Most suspicious of all, there is a
salesman who tends to his physically disabled, bitter wife, until
she disappears and he starts keeping odd hours, cleaning saws,
and shipping a large, mysterious package. While Jeffries obsesses
about his neighbors and the woman's disappearance, his private
drama proves equally suspicious-dull—dismissing the affections
of his stunningly beautiful suitor Lisa Freemont (Kelly).

Hitchcock spares his audience any indictment of human
character. *Rear Window*'s satire is, depending on whom you ask,
either lighthearted or profoundly subtle. In the end, Jeffries's ad-
diction to snooping comes off as the most condemnable of natural human eccentricities.

Books

Alderman, Ellen, and Caroline Kennedy. *The Right to Privacy.*
New York: Alfred A. Knopf, 1995.

Unlike books that obsess over the definition of privacy and the
coherence of different types of privacy rights, this book avoids
those rich, but exhausted, debates. Instead, it gets to work
quickly and simply by telling real-life stories of people whose
rights to privacy have been infringed, what that meant to them,
and how the law treats their claims. It is an excellent, accessible

introduction to privacy rights in U.S. law on a range of specific issues, such as the balance between freedom of the press and privacy, monitoring in the workplace, police searches, and the right to die. Each issue is addressed through a prominent Supreme Court case, but the authors go behind the law to explore the stories of the real people and conflicts in the cases.

Brin, David. *The Transparent Society: Will Technology Force Us to Choose between Privacy and Freedom?* New York: Bantam, 1999.

Brin attempts to reconcile a seeming hypocrisy: privacy advocates call for a reduction of government surveillance of the public but an increase in public surveillance of the government. Surveillance is surveillance, argues Brin, and it is here to stay. The key to preserving democratic society in the surveillance era is to grant everyone access to society's surveillance apparatuses. Members of the public could watch out for abuses of rights, whether by thieves and rapists or by police and public officials. However, Brin's transparent society stops at the front door to our homes, which he believes must be protected from the onslaught of surveillance technology. Brin is better known for his fiction, such as the environmental sci-fi thriller *Earth* (1990), which is also concerned with privacy, surveillance, databases, total information, and technology.

Huxley, Aldous. *Brave New World.* New York: Perennial, 1998.

Originally published in 1932, Huxley's novel takes place sometime in the future (AF 632) in the one World State. Social control is maintained through science and ostensibly voluntary incentives. For example, gradated castes of superior and inferior humans are created through bioengineering and made to long for their place in life through careful environmental conditioning at the youngest ages, but all of this begins with individuals voluntarily submitting their eggs and sperm for a six-month salary bonus. In contrast to *1984*'s political control through deprivation, the World State maintains social control through consumption, promiscuity, the elimination of pain and suffering, and indulgence manufactured and channeled through Feelies (emotionally cathartic movies) and the hallucinogen Soma. The plot is less remarkable than the premise that constitutes Huxley's social critique. (Huxley himself regretted the story's shortcomings but chose not to rewrite it.) This book is usually cited in the same breath as *1984* due to their mutual fixation with totalitarianism and futuristic "dystopian" story lines, as well as the interesting contrast in how each author imagines totalitarianism might be achieved—consumerism in *Brave New World* versus surveillance in *1984*. *Brave New World* is not typically referenced as a book about privacy. Yet, in many respects, it is: First, in the state's interference in reproduction and, ever more poignantly today, its involvement in genetic manipulation. Second, in the state's destruction of intimate relationships of couples and family, and, more complicatedly, in the protagonist's retreat from society into an unsatisfying solitude.

Lyon, David. *Surveillance after September 11.* Cambridge: Polity Press, 2003.

This short, readable book describes the new trends in surveillance since the terrorist attacks of September 11, 2001. Lyon argues that the new surveillance is not just more of the same; rather, old technologies are being networked and used in new ways, such as social sorting and racial profiling, that represent a pernicious change in democratic society. Further, these new approaches, incubated mostly in the United States, are emerging globally. Even with new technologies layered on top, Lyon argues, these new surveillance systems cannot be justified by their likely effectiveness in stopping terrorist attacks. Yet surveillance societies are emerging so as to touch every person's everyday life with grave implications not only for democracy but also for relationships, community, and mutual trust.

National Commission on Terrorist Attacks. *The 9/11 Commission Report: Final Report of the National Commission on Terrorist Attacks upon the United States.* New York: W. W. Norton, 2004.

The 9/11 Commission Report is not only important, thorough, and historic but also well written, earning a National Book Award nomination. It is a story of one of the most tragic days in U.S. history, the terrorists and terrorist networks that planned it, the intelligence failures that allowed it to transpire undetected, and the commission's recommendations for better detection and prevention of future attacks. From a privacy perspective, the report is valuable for its comprehensive treatment of the September 11 attacks in all their complexity. That is, although the report does not absolve from blame the so-called privacy wall between intelligence operations and criminal investigations, it puts this problem in its proper perspective among the many missed opportunities and intelligence failures that had nothing to do with privacy rights or restrictions. Another book worthy of reading on the same subject is Richard A. Clarke's *Against All Enemies* (2004).

Newton, David E. *Gay and Lesbian Rights: A Reference Handbook.* Denver: ABC-CLIO, 1994.

Like other volumes in the Contemporary World Issues series, this book gives an overview of issues related to the rights of gay men and lesbians, including their right to privacy. It describes the history of the movement for gay rights and the discrimination that still exists in housing, employment, criminal law, legal recognition of the relationships of gay couples, HIV treatment, and public attitudes. It also includes biographical sketches of notable activists in the movement for gay rights, key documents on gay rights issues, and organizations, books, and other resources on gay rights. You may wish to supplement this overview with the more recent book *The Rights of Gay Men, Lesbians, Bisexuals, and Transgendered People* (2004) by Nan D. Hunter, Courtney G. Joslin, and Sharon M. McGowan.

Orwell, George. *1984.* New York: Signet Book, 1990.

The paradigmatic story of privacy invasion as a tool of totalitarianism, Orwell's classic gave us expressions so common today that we forget they came from this one book: Thought Police, Big Brother, Memory Hole, newspeak, doublethink, thoughtcrime. Originally published in 1949, the story takes place in 1984 in London, a city in the state of Oceania. The world is made up of three totalitarian states in perpetual war, or so the authorities would have you believe. Having independent thoughts is a crime; keeping a journal is a crime, punishable by death. Telescreens in each apartment both provide propaganda and monitor behavior. The main character, Winston Smith, is a midlevel bureaucrat whose job is to alter historical documents to comport with the Ministry of Truth's latest version of events. His job gives him insight into the blatant lies of the government and helps him realize that freedom is the right to say that two plus two equals four. To the extent love and sex are true, they too are freedom and subversion. Smith buys a journal, finds love and sex, and evades the telescreens for a time. He even connects with the revolutionary underground, which helps him to understand the regime's need for perpetual war, the reduction and manipulation of language, and the eradication of independent thought. But, in a dark twist, these discoveries ultimately serve as kindling for the destruction of his independence and freedom.

The richness of the world Orwell creates and especially its convincing political analysis cannot be overstated. That he was able to weave this commentary into a relatively tight, captivating story of suspense and love is what earns the book a place in the pantheon.

Rosen, Jeffrey. *The Unwanted Gaze: The Destruction of Privacy in America.* New York: Random House, 2000.

This book was inspired by Kenneth Starr's investigation into the prurient details of President Bill Clinton's affair with Monica Lewinsky. In it, Rosen sets out to understand the present legal reality that allowed Lewinsky's library selections, unsent love letters, and consensual sexual activities to be examined with seemingly no regard for her privacy. The Starr investigation is merely one lens for the author's detailed, thoughtful, and eminently readable account of the "destruction of privacy in America," as well as his thoughts on how to reconstruct it. Rosen also echoes privacy's earliest proponents, including Brandeis, Warren, and their little-discussed predecessor James Fitzjames Stephen. His thesis is that revealing personal, private information about people (without their permission) subjects them to unfair, inaccurate judgments and simplifications. Rosen places this problem in its disturbing, modern context of information overload and consequently short attention spans. In a society that reloads its Internet news pages every ten minutes, there is no time for the full story, perspective and empathy, or meaningful retractions. What is needed, and what is so far missing, is human discretion that appropriately weighs the value of personal privacy in its decisions. Without this discretion, the courts, news media, and other purveyors of information will further the descent of creativity, sense of identity, and trust that are essential for human relations and civic interaction.

Schoeman, Ferdinand David, ed. *Philosophical Dimensions of Privacy: An Anthology*. New York: Cambridge University Press, 1984.

This collection of articles is much more than "philosophical." It includes many of the foundational articles on privacy, such as Warren and Brandeis's 1890 *Harvard Law Review* article, William Prosser's 1960 elaboration of privacy torts, Charles Fried's 1968 compelling defense of the moral value of privacy, Robert Murphy's "Social Distance and the Veil" (1967), Alan Westin's opening chapter to *Privacy and Freedom* (1967), and Richard Posner's "Economic Theory of Privacy" (1978). If philosophical dimensions are what you seek, then the editor's introduction provides a helpful breakdown and overview of ways of thinking and arguing about privacy. Several of the articles delve further into the meaning of privacy for human identity, being, and relations. You may wish to supplement this book with the more recent collections *The Right to Privacy* (2000), edited by Ellen Frankel Paul, Fred D. Miller Jr. and Jeffrey Paul, and *Privacies: Philosophical Evaluations* (2004), edited by Beatte Rössler.

Stetson, Dorothy McBride, ed. *Abortion Politics, Women's Movements, and the Democratic State.* New York: Oxford University Press, 2001.

In the United States, the issue of abortion rights remains a fiercely contested battlefield in the political-cultural war despite 60 percent of Americans believing women should have that right. Although the debate may be more pitched in the United States, it is nonetheless a challenging, controversial topic throughout Western society. This compilation of articles looks at the recent history of abortion debates in the United States, Canada, and Europe, including Austria, Belgium, France, Germany, Ireland, Italy, the Netherlands, Spain, and the United Kingdom. Although the editor aspires to provide a political and social system analysis to understand commonalities among prochoice movements, the book's primary value is historical. It is a good book for gaining perspective on national debates on abortion and the role of privacy in those debates, and it is one of few to put international examples side by side.

Walker, Samuel. *In Defense of American Liberties: A History of the ACLU*, 2d ed. Carbondale: Southern Illinois University Press, 1999.

Across the spectrum of privacy issues—police searches, intelligence surveillance, databasing, abortion and contraception, gay and lesbian rights, youth rights, freedom of conscience and association—the ACLU has been the leading advocacy organization in the United States since its establishment in 1920. This comprehensive history recounts the ACLU's biggest battles, from the Scopes Monkey Trial to the Japanese internment, as well as the organization's protection of privacy in cases such as *Loving v. Virginia*, which overturned Virginia's law prohibiting couples of different races to marry. For a more recent overview of the range of civil liberties issues, you will enjoy Walker's *Civil Liberties: A Reference Handbook* (2004).

Westin, Alan. *Privacy and Freedom.* New York: Atheneum, 1967.

Westin's classic text begins with "Privacy in the Animal World," in which we learn that the robin's song and the monkey's shriek are not songs of joy but a "defiant cry for privacy, given within the borders of the animal's private territory to warn off possible intruders." But Westin is not concerned with animals' rights to privacy. Rather, he seeks to document the many ways in which humans are obsessed with examining, observing, testing, tracking, and archiving one another in areas that are deeply personal and private; the innate need for privacy; and this conflict's implications for democratic freedom. Given its age, the book is at points a time capsule of surveillance "technology," focusing on the problems of peepholes, polygraphs, and dossiers. But Westin is prescient in his description of the lightning-quick advancement of technology in surveillance and databasing, as well as in his understanding of the threat they pose. Indeed, genius director Francis Ford Coppola's 1974 movie *The Conversation* seems quaint and outdated in comparison to the problems and technologies described in Westin's book of seven years earlier.

Westin remains a prominent scholar on the issue of privacy and technology, and his subsequent books, including *Data Banks in a Free Society* (1972), are also classics. Today, he is a moderate middle-of-the-roader on protecting privacy. But in *Privacy and Freedom*'s depiction of the "crisis of surveillance technology," one sees a more critical view.

Internet News Sources

http://www.compseconline.com

Compsec Online provides information on computer security intelligence, including *smart cards*, data sharing, digital surveillance, digital forensics, and biometrics. The site's audience is business users of technology, and several of its publications require a paid subscription. But some resources are provided free of charge and comprehensively address privacy concerns.

http://www.dnaresource.com

DNA Resource provides information on the latest developments in forensic DNA policy. The site is a project of a for-profit firm, based in the United States and United Kingdom, that provides lobbying services and legal representation. The site includes useful media reports on national and international data on forensic DNA, an extensive listing of U.S. state statutes and proposed bills on DNA database laws, and other types of forensic DNA bills. Site visitors can sign up for a free weekly newsletter, *DNA Report*.

http://www.news.com.com

A leading provider of technology news, C | Net News necessarily covers many stories relating to privacy. Visit the site and type *privacy* into the search box to find out the latest developments and controversies related to privacy and cutting-edge technology.

http://www.politechbot.com

Maintained by a technology journalist, Politechbot allows anyone to sign up for a moderated mailing list with news and commentary on politics and technology topics, such as privacy, free speech, corporate monopolies, and corporate and government actions related to technology.

http://www.privacilla.org

From a "free market liberal (or libertarian) stance," Privacilla provides issue papers on a range of privacy topics. The authors' libertarian philosophy holds that "limited government allows entrepreneurs in competition with one another to innovate and produce goods and services that best satisfy the wants and needs of the most consumers at the lowest cost." It considers privacy an important value, not a fundamental right. It opposes some privacy regulations that, in its view, overly restrict businesses without sufficient benefit to consumers' true desire for privacy.

http://www.privacy.org

A "site for news, information, and action," Privacy.org is a joint project of EPIC and Privacy International. It provides daily news clips of developments in privacy.

http://www.privacyexchange.org

Privacy Exchange is a source for information, laws, and news on privacy around the world from a for-profit business perspective. It focuses on consumer privacy, commerce, and data protection. Its funders include many corporations, and it is intended as a means for businesses to keep track of developments in privacy requirements in markets around the world, as well as to share model policies. (Other business-perspective privacy organizations include the Online Privacy Alliance and Privacy and American Business.)

http://www.privacytimes.com

Privacy Times is an expensive subscription newsletter for professionals and attorneys who need to track legal and commercial developments related to information privacy. Evan Hendricks, the author and publisher of the newsletter, also consults, speaks, and serves as an expert witness for a fee. Although his services may be too expensive for the average reader, this site is an example of how privacy has become big business and how a person can make a living as an expert on privacy. (Another such site and service is *Privacy Journal*, published by Robert Ellis Smith the author of *Ben Franklin's Web Site: Privacy and Curiosity from Plymouth Rock to the Internet*.)

http://www.queensu.ca/sociology/surveillance/intro.htm

An academic project of the Queen's University in Kingston, Canada, the Surveillance Project studies all aspects of surveillance. It lists papers written by scholars and runs a project on the globalization of personal data.

http://www.surveillance-and-society.org

A "fully peer-reviewed transdisciplinary online surveillance studies journal," *Surveillance and Society* publishes its scholarly articles online. The journal treats themes as diverse as "Foucault and Panopticism Revisited" and "CCTV and Politics in Europe."

http://www.wirednews.com

Wired Magazine is one of the first (and still best) news sources on technology developments, including a frequent focus on the privacy implications of new technologies. Type *privacy* into the search box or select the "Politics" page for the latest news on privacy controversies and issues.

Reference

Aubry, Kim. 2000. "Production Notes." *The Conversation: 2000 Restoration for DVD*, http://www.lifestyle.com/article/item.phtml?ID=792&Page=0.

Index

About the Author

Kevin Keenan is an attorney and Executive Director of the ACLU of San Diego and Imperial Counties. He graduated from Swarthmore College and Yale Law School.